931916

WRITING WOMEN AND SPACE

MAPPINGS: Society / Theory / Space
A Guilford Series

Editors

MICHAEL DEAR
University of
Southern California

DEREK GREGORY
University of
British Columbia

NIGEL THRIFT
University of Bristol

WRITING WOMEN AND SPACE
Colonial and Postcolonial Geographies
Alison Blunt and Gillian Rose, Editors

TRAVEL, GENDER, AND IMPERIALISM
Mary Kingsley and West Africa
Alison Blunt

POSTMODERN CONTENTIONS
Epochs, Politics, Space
John Paul Jones III, Wolfgang Natter,
and Theodore R. Schatzki, Editors

THE POWER OF MAPS
Denis Wood (with John Fels)

APPROACHING HUMAN GEOGRAPHY
An Introduction to Contemporary Theoretical Debates
Paul Cloke, Chris Philo, and David Sadler

Forthcoming
LAW, SPACE, AND THE GEOGRAPHIES OF POWER
Nicholas K. Blomley

WRITING WOMEN AND SPACE

Colonial and Postcolonial Geographies

Edited by
ALISON BLUNT
GILLIAN ROSE

THE GUILFORD PRESS
New York London

©1994 The Guilford Press
A Division of Guilford Publications, Inc.
72 Spring Street, New York, NY 10012
Marketed and distributed outside North America
by Longman Group Limited.

Printed in the United States of America

This book is printed on acid-free paper.

Last digit is print number: 9 8 7 6 5 4 3 2 1

Library of Congress Cataloging-in-Publication Data

Writing women and space : colonial and postcolonial geographies /
edited by Alison Blunt, Gillian Rose.
    p. cm. – Mappings
  Includes bibliographical references and index.
  ISBN 0-89862-497-5. – ISBN 0-89862-498-3 (pbk.)
  1. Feminism. 2. Space perception – Social aspects. 3. Personal
space. I. Blunt, Alison. II. Rose, Gillian. III. Series.
HQ1233.W75 1994
305.42 – dc20   94-11691
                                                              CIP

Contributors

Alison Blunt is a doctoral student in the Department of Geography at the University of British Columbia, Vancouver, Canada

Jane M. Jacobs is a Lecturer in the Department of Geography at the University of Parkville, Victoria, Australia

Louise Johnson is a Lecturer in the School of Australian and International Studies at Deakin University, Geelong, Victoria, Australia

Judy Barrett Litoff is a Professor of History at Bryant College, Smithfield, Rhode Island

Cheryl McEwan is a post-doctoral research tutor in the Department of Geography at the University College of Swansea, Swansea, West Glamorgan, Wales

Sara Mills is a Senior Lecturer in the Department of English and Drama at Loughborough University, Loughborough, Leicestershire, England

Catherine Nash is a Lecturer in the Department of Geography at St. David's University College, Lampeter, Wales

Jennifer Robinson is a Lecturer in the Department of Geographical and Environmental Sciences at the University of Natal, Durban, South Africa

Gillian Rose is a Lecturer in the Department of Geography at the University of Edinburgh, Edinburgh, Scotland

Kay Schaffer is an Associate Professor in the Department of Women's Studies at the University of Adelaide, Adelaide, South Australia, Australia

David C. Smith is the A. and A. Bird Professor of History at the University of Maine, Orono, Maine

Contents

PART II: RETHINKING MAPPING

WRITING WOMEN AND SPACE

1

Introduction:
Women's Colonial
and Postcolonial Geographies

ALISON BLUNT
GILLIAN ROSE

Western feminisms have always been concerned with the spatial politics of difference. In order to introduce the discussions of space, power, and difference in the contributions brought together here, this chapter explores some of the diverse ways in which feminists have seen space as central both to masculinist power and to feminist resistance. In particular, we explore certain arguments from feminists of color and from poststructuralism that have influenced current discussions about maps and power in historical and contemporary contexts.

One of the earliest explicit discussions of the spaces of patriarchy, and thus of the need for feminists to consider geography, was the collection of essays brought together by anthropologist Shirley Ardener in 1981.[1] Ardener focused on difference between the genders. She argued that the "social map" of patriarchy created "ground rules" for the behavior of men and women, and that the gender roles and relations of patriarchy constructed some spaces as "feminine" and others as "masculine" and thus allocated certain kinds of (gendered) activities to certain (gendered) places. Gender difference was thus seen as inscribing spatial difference. Marilyn Frye offers an example of this geography of gender in her discussion of a woman exploring the restrictions placed upon her articulacy by the encoding of certain spaces as more "hers" than "his":

No two women live, in a daily and detailed way, in identical spaces created by identical ranges of the concept of Woman. . . . For better or for worse, though, in each of our lives, others' concepts of us are revealed by the limits of the intelligibility of our anger. Anger can be an instrument of cartography. By determining where, with whom, about what and in what circumstances one can get angry and get uptake, one can map others' concepts of who and what one is.

One woman took this thought home with her and tried it out. She walked about the apartment she shares, not unhappily, with her young husband, testing in imagination for the viability of her anger – in what situations would it "work," would get uptake. She discovered that the pattern was very simple and clear. It went with the floor plan. She could get angry quite freely in the kitchen and somewhat less freely and about a more limited range of things in the living room. She could not get angry in the bedroom.

Anger. Domain. Respect.[2]

Frye suggests that the possibilities for behaving in particular ways depend on the meaning given to femininity – to Woman – in patriarchal discourses, and that those meanings are grounded in physical spaces – in this example, the rooms of an apartment. In that apartment, a woman can speak with authority and be heard more easily in the kitchen because under the patriarchal division of labor this is the space in which she has the greatest authority; but in the bedroom she is not to be eloquent with her mind but only with her body, for there she exists for her husband's pleasure.

Feminist analyses of the power relations embedded in such geographies for a long while focused almost exclusively on the distinction between public and private space. For Michelle Rosaldo, for example, another anthropologist, that distinction was fundamental to the universal oppression of women.[3] In her 1974 essay, Rosaldo attempted to explain why "men are the locus of cultural value" by examining the hierarchy between the gendered public and private. Rosaldo defined the private – or, as she termed it, the domestic – thus: " 'domestic,' as used here, refers to those minimal institutions and modes of activity that are organized immediately around one or more mothers and their children; 'public' refers to activities, institutions, and forms of association that link, rank, organize, or subsume particular mother-child groups."[4] She argued that in patriarchal societies the domestic was the place of women, while the public realm of culture, politics, and the economy was seen as the sphere of men. Following the work of Nancy Chodorow,[5] Rosaldo argued that these two arenas were defined by two kinds of sociality. The domestic sociality of women is interpersonal and particularistic; because women are daughters and mothers, women relate to other people as individuals, seeing each as different and unique. In contrast, men's public sociality is concerned not with the particular but with the maintenance of the economic, cultural, and political system as a whole. Thus Rosaldo concluded that women's domestic sociality is necessarily subsumed by the public sociality of men, and men's control of the public world means that women become devalued outsiders.

More recent anthropological work exploring the relationship between gendered identity and space has suggested that gendered spaces should be understood less as a geography imposed by patriarchal structures, and more as a social process of symbolic encoding and decoding that produces "a series of homologies between the spatial, symbolic and social orders."[6] The social construction of gender difference establishes some spaces as women's and others as men's; those meanings then serve to reconstitute the power relations of gendered identity. However, since the outcome of the decoding process can never be guaranteed, contestation and renegotiation of the meaning of spaces is also always possible. Certainly, many of the struggles of Western feminism can be seen as a diverse array of challenges to the distinction between the public and the private and to the comparative value accorded them. There have been efforts to build domestic spaces that do not rely on the privatized domestic labor of women; there have been many struggles to reconstitute the public so that women have a right to occupy its spaces and participate in its activities; there have been attempts to nurture the qualities of the domestic and valorize them over and above the sociality of the public; and feminists have also struggled to erase the distinction entirely.[7] Indeed, Carole Pateman has gone so far as to suggest that "the dichotomy between the private and the public is central to almost two centuries of feminist struggle; it is, ultimately, what the feminist movement is about."[8]

Pateman's claim may be exaggerated, however, for much recent feminist work suggests that the distinction between public and the private space is more important in some women's lives than in others, and thus that struggles over the public and the private are typical not of all feminisms but rather of particular kinds of feminism. Feminist historians, for example, have described the emergence of the division between public and private spaces from the early 19th century onward in Europe and North America as part of the cultural project of an emerging middle class.[9] The elaboration of the private as a domestic haven of feminine grace and charm, and of the public as the arena of aggressive masculine competition, is increasingly seen as a development that enabled the bourgeoisie to distinguish themselves from other social groups. This project of distinction was as much material as symbolic; the suburban villa was intended to be the site of private domesticity triumphant, inscribing in bricks and mortar the values of middle-class familial order. And if the distinction between the public and the private must be seen as specific in terms of class, so too it must be understood as specific in terms of race. Several black feminist historians have also pointed out that the valorization of the difference between the public and the private must be seen as central to the constitution of the 19th-century middle class as white. Although neither the distinction between the public and the private nor that between the middle class and its others was ever quite stabilized even among the bourgeoisie, it was quite impossible for hegemonic discourses to acknowledge a black woman as a "lady" in the post-Emancipation United States, as Evelyn Brooks Higginbotham has remarked.[10] Moreover, the definition of the private as a domestic space separate from the public world of commerce was rarely meaningful in black communities; to the extent that it did resonate, the private was understood as a place, often a neighborhood, beyond everyday encounters with white racism. For many black communities, however, that privacy itself was and continues to be far more fragile than the privacy of the bourgeois home; as Aida Hurtado notes, the state intervenes far more often and with greater violence in black homes and neighborhoods than in white ones.[11] For all these reasons, then, the geography of the public/private division should be seen as mostly relevant to white, middle-class feminism. Attempts to universalize its neat distinction between two spaces and two genders erase its implicit race and class specificities.[12] This development is clearly one consequence of the much wider critique made by black feminisms during the 1980s of the universalizing tendencies of white feminisms.

Accompanying this critique of the universality accorded to the public and the private in the white feminist imaginary has been the elaboration of other geographies that resonate with the forms of oppression faced by women who are not middle class and white. Of particular relevance to the concerns of this volume, many feminists of color, while articulating their resistance to racism and imperialism, have developed a range of spaces structured by their particular experiences of exploitation and the specificities of their resistances. Chandra Tolpade Mohanty, for example, writes of a "third world" no longer located only in the South but also to be found in New York, Los Angeles, Paris, London, and Berlin, and of its collective political protest against the continuing exploitation of its diverse peoples. She has used the image of the diaspora to articulate its resistance to contemporary racism and neoimperialism. This protest is what imagines the geography of the diaspora: "imagined communities of women with divergent histories and social locations, woven together by the *political* threads of opposition to forms of domination that are not only pervasive but also systemic."[13] Gloria Anzaldúa uses a different spatial image in her discussion of the need to overcome the divisions and dualisms that legitimate racism and imperialism. She has written about the "borderlands" between Mexico and the United States and about the "mestiza consciousness" that straddles both cultures, drawing on each but belonging to neither. In her work, this specific borderland becomes an image for thinking about healing the racist divisions and enmities which so many borders evoke, with their hostile definitions of "us" and "them" and their violent visions of "insiders" and "outsiders." She says that "at some point, on our way to a new consciousness, we will have to leave the opposite bank, the split between the two mortal combatants somewhat healed so that we are on both shores at once, and at once see through the serpent and the eagle eyes."[14] The spatial configurations through which feminisms analyze both their enemies and their own resistance have become much more varied over the last decade, then, as the geopolitical imaginary of feminist discourse has been shifted by the analytical work of feminists of color among others. The significances of particular physical locations for feminists resonate with politicized imagined geographies.

If these imagined geographies are understood in terms of the discursive construction of spaces, then parallels with certain developments in poststructuralist theory become evident. We might say that spaces are constituted through struggles over power/knowledge; we certainly think it is important to consider the ways in which different epistemological claims about women's identity produce different interpretations of space itself. For example, feminist arguments that evoke essentialist or universalist accounts of femininity produce and depend upon what we will call, following Lefebvre, an "illusion of transparency," so that "within the spatial realm the known and the transparent are one and the same thing."[15] Transparent space assumes that the world can be seen as it really is and that there can be unmediated access to the truth of objects it sees; it is a space of mimetic representation. Trinh Minh-ha argues that "vision as knowledge is the ideology . . . which postulates the existence of a central unshakable certitude."[16] That certitude is the self-confidence of what Donna Haraway terms "the master subject": white, middle-class, masculine, and heterosexual.[17] Yet such confidence entails costs. The claim of the master subject to be "an autonomous subject who observes social conflicts from a privileged and unconflicted place . . . can be converted from fantasy into reality only by denying the relational character of subjectivity and by relegating other viewpoints – different subjectivities – to invisible, subordinate, or competing positions."[18] Lefebvre too suggests that transparent space tends toward homogeneity, toward a denial of difference. These are criticisms that must also be leveled at the feminisms that invoke transparency. Essentialist feminism, in its claim to know for absolute certain the true nature of all women, depends on and produces a space in which the essence of femininity is immediately accessible and transparently obvious. All women need to do, according to writers such as Mary Daly and Susan Griffin, is to be as we really are and we will enter a new, pure space free of the distorting mediations of power. Griffin remarks:

> We are no longer pleading for the right to speak: we have spoken; space has changed; we are living in a matrix of our own sounds; our words resonate, by our echoes we chart a new geography; we recognize this new landscape as our birthplace, where we invented names for ourselves; here language does not contradict what we know; by what we hear we are moved again and again to speak.[19]

In this new, transparent space we will know ourselves and each other completely, suggests Griffin; there will be no opacities of alterity, only the transparency of total knowledge. Although essentialist feminisms often imply a space of the "impure" beyond their own utopian boundaries, within those boundaries no difference is possible. Universalist feminisms also claim a transparent space of knowledge, but through a rather different strategy with different consequences. Their claim to know what women are assumes that women are the same everywhere and always. Arguments like Robin Morgan's that "sisterhood is global" depend on a confident claim to understand the fundamental oppressions of all women's lives, and this in turn produces a global vision of solidarity between all women everywhere. An assumption that all women can be known denies all boundaries. Once again, however, as Mohanty has remarked, radical difference is refused.[20] The confidence with which those who imagine transparent space assert that to see is to know has been criticized, therefore, for its exclusions and repressions, just as the public/private distinction has been criticized for its erasures and absences; in this volume both Jane Jacobs and Catherine Nash elaborate this critique in their discussions of ecofeminisms. Both universalist and essentialist claims to really know what women are depend on a transparent space in which to be visible is also to be vulnerable to claims of mimetic representation.

The central task for many feminists today is to articulate the extraordinarily complex and simultaneous interaction of gender, class, race, and sexuality (to name just four of the most frequently mentioned axes of identity, oppression, and resistance) that create differences between women;

the politics of difference with which many feminists are now concerned is not only the politics of difference *between* two genders, but also the politics of diversity *among* women. Adrienne Rich coined the term "politics of location" to refer to the interpretation of the specificity of a particular woman. This elaboration of a subject position marked by the histories and geographies of power relations denies the erasure of self enacted by the master subject. In this volume, for example, Jenny Robinson explores some of the specificities of feminisms in South Africa. Such an emphasis on specificity also refuses access to the vantage point from which transparent space is seen, insisting instead on the situatedness of knowledge. We would like to suggest, then, that the space through which the notion of a "politics of location" is mapped is one that rejects the transparency so often used to delete difference. Instead, feminists plotting the politics of location imagine "an insistent, simultaneous, nonsynchronous process characterized by multiple locations"[21]: a space that is fragmented, multidimensional, contradictory, and provisional. We are not suggesting that this vision of space is inherently more emancipatory than another; rather, we assert that certain political projects construct spaces according to their strategic context and needs. The chapters in this collection written by Judy Barrett Litoff and David Smith and by Catherine Nash are both concerned with detailing the specific contexts of two rather different challenges to transparent space. The multidimensionality of the space of a politics of location arises from what Haraway describes as "geometrics of difference and contradiction"[22]: an interpretation of the diverse axes of identity that constitute any and every subject position and that never neatly align into a stable and coherent sense of self. Instead of accepting a transparent space that marginalizes difference, feminists like Haraway imagine a plurilocated, fluid space that tries to acknowledge difference. The fluidity of such geometries is insisted upon partly because the dynamics of power are always shifting and, as Chela Sandoval argues, this mobility requires a mobile response.[23] But provisionality is also required because the politics of resistance demand a certain accountability from a feminist writer toward her audience. No feminist today can innocently represent all women, and so the position from which any feminist speaks must be continually interrogated and relocated as circumstances change. The need for accountability is especially acute since, as Teresa de Lauretis points out, this particular feminist formulation of identity implies a much less "pure" subject position than that offered in feminist discourses that simply oppose masculinity to femininity; as de Lauretis says, the feminist subject it assumes "is most likely ideologically complicit with 'the oppressor' whose position it may occupy in certain sociosexual relations (if not in others)."[24]

Feminists, especially those occupying more privileged positions, must continually consider this question of complicity.

As two white feminists working in a discipline that is only just beginning to consider critically its own involvement in imperialism, which has hardly begun to trace the legacy of that involvement in its contemporary forms of knowledge, and in which feminism is still rendered peripheral, we feel that it is vital to begin thinking about the intersection of race, gender, sexuality, and class in the representation of other places and people. We feel that this critical interrogation of modes of representation is necessary before other, more emancipatory, forms of representation can be formulated. For the question of complicity is not self-evident; exploring its implications is a central theme of this volume. We are especially interested in the image of mapping. Maps are central to colonial and postcolonial projects. Mapping operates in hegemonic discourses as a form of mimetic representation – it textually represents the gaze through transparent space – but this form of mapping is contested in discourses of resistance.[25] Mapping thus appears to be a spatial image that directly addresses the politics of representation as they are bound into the politics of location. The next two sections elaborate this claim.

DRAWING THE MAP

Hegemonic claims for the mimetic representation of transparent space underpin both imperial mapping and many subsequent mappings of imperialism. Recent feminist critiques have disrupted this imposed coherence of space and subject in both the production of imperial maps and the writing of imperialist history.[26] In Chapter 2 of this volume Sara Mills provides an overview of these critiques by focusing on late-19th-century British imperialism. Spatial imagery has been influential both in feminist theory and in critiques of imperialist history, and these perspectives can inform each other in attempts to make women visible as both colonizers and colonized. To overlook the roles played by colonizing women helps to perpetuate imperial notions of transparent space and its unproblematic mimetic representation not only of an "other" but also of itself. Instead, a focus on white, colonizing women raises questions of complicity with and resistance to hegemonic strategies of domination.

The earliest stages of "women's history" and the study of women in geography were marked by essentialist, often positivist, accounts intended to add "women's experience" to historical and geographical inquiry.[27] At first, "women's history . . . sought to challenge traditional, masculinist, 'objective' 'history' by making women visible, by writing women into 'history.' That 'history,' however, was in most other respects informed by traditional, thus masculinist, categories and historical periods and reflected masculinist values."[28] In this way, it furthered rather than challenged structural inequalities. Women and gender relations should not only become visible in historical study, they should "remake the very categories through which the past is discursively constituted."[29] Rather than merely add a gendered subject, the construction of subjectivity itself should become a central point of inquiry. Interest in white women colonizers is particularly pertinent to historiographies of geography. Mona Domosh cites imperial women travelers in her outline of a feminist historiography of geography. Her work begins to question the masculinist foundations of geography as an academic discipline and focuses attention on women who have been long neglected. However, her statement that "geography's roots in the exploratory tradition are . . . quite inspiring and should act as sources of pride" not only reproduces but also celebrates the imperialist foundations of the study of geography.[30] It is crucial to locate women within a historiography of geography, but this act should question the very basis of that historiography rather than reproduce it, albeit in a revised form.

Recent overviews have revealed the many, diverse roles played by white women in imperialism that have been traditionally ignored or downplayed.[31] Since the 1980s interest in colonial women has found outlets in literature, television, and film, and has often taken the form of romantic, nostalgic imagery.[32] Such interest has been supported by historiographical foundations whereby "the fields of women's history and imperial history have intersected."[33] This interest often celebrates individual "heroic" women rather than questions constructions of gender both in the metaphorically colonial context of patriarchal inequality and the literal places and spaces of colonization.[34] By neglecting the construction of gendered subjectivity, such approaches also continue to silence the experiences of colonized women.[35]

A more complex and shifting notion of both space and subject positionality undermines claims to mimetic representation. Colonial maps often codified mimetic representation and today should be deconstructed to destabilize the power and authority of claims for such representation. Maps were graphic tools of colonization, themselves colonizing spaces perceived as empty and uninscribed.[36] If, as argued by Brian Harley, "maps are preeminently a language of power, not of protest,"[37] their starkest expression relates to imperial conquest. The supposedly scientific "space discipline" imposed by mapping legitimized colonization, enhanced the possibilities for surveillance, and facilitated imperial rule by helping to distance those exercising power from its consequences.[38] The rhetorical strategies of mapping reveal the far reaching implications of colonial maps and include "the reinscription, enclosure and hierarchization of space, which provide an analogue for the acquisition, management and reinforcement of colonial power."[39] Claims for mimetic representation have been reproduced by certain mappings of colonialism. Imperialist history, like colonial mapping, emphasized visibility in its legitimation of conquest. Both the colonial mapmaker and the imperial historian perceived an external reality to be mimetically represented. Carter develops a theatrical metaphor to call attention to the practices whereby history is played out on an apparently fixed stage occupied by historical individuals who are actors directed by forces of destiny.[40] The double meaning of "stage" as spatially bounded and visible but also part of a linear temporal progression is particularly significant. Both senses, and their reconciliation within the writings of imperialist historians, depend on Enlightenment appeals to universalizing reason only accessible to a masculine gaze.[41]

Mapping is a distinctive form of spatial representation because it can be interpreted as visual and/or textual. To read maps as texts highlights their social construction and their potential for multiple interpretations by both producers and consumers,[42] and the landscapes that maps represent are themselves, for some, written and read as texts.[43] Landscapes can also be interpreted as visual. It is important to distinguish between landscapes and texts: the spatial imagery of mapping can expose tensions between the dynamics of the visual and the written.

The feminization of colonized landscapes can illustrate the positionality inherent in viewing/reading landscapes – and maps purporting to represent them – as both visual and written. The association of indigenous women with colonized land legitimated perceptions of both women and land as objects of colonization.[44] Imperialist literature often incorporated sexual imagery to create and sustain the heroic stature of male colonizers who conquered and penetrated dangerous, unknown continents, often characterized by the fertility of both indigenous vegetation and women.[45] The construction of a "sexual space" paralleled the construction of space to be colonized,[46] and the desire for colonial control was often expressed in terms of sexual control.[47] The motif of, for example, "the veiled woman" embodied masculine desire whereby "the process of exposing the female Other, of literally denuding her . . . [came] to allegorize the Western masculinist power of possession, that she, as a metaphor for her land, becomes available for Western penetration and knowledge."[48] Representations of women and landscapes as sites of colonization were often codified through mapping because "the map operates . . . as a dual paradigm for the phallocentric discourse which inscribes woman, and the rationalistic discourse which inscribes the land, as 'Other.' "[49] Theoretical parallels can be drawn between the disciplinary power and surveillance imposed on landscapes by mapping and imposed on the body by, for example, discourses of medicine and sexuality.[50] Such parallels seem materially explicit in the context of colonial domination and are inseparable from constructions of race, gender, and sexuality.

According to Jane Haggis, the study of colonizing women is inherently contradictory. To isolate gender from its interactions with, for example, race and class, seems essentialist. Studying gender differences between colonizing men and women often leaves unproblematized the constructions of racial difference that legitimized imperialism. In this way, essentialist constructions of racial inferiority have been perpetuated rather than challenged.[51] This contradiction means that white women can potentially become visible at the expense of colonized women, reproducing an exclusionary, ethnocentric discourse.[52] In an attempt to overcome this contradiction, Cheryl McEwan in Chapter 4 addresses textual representations of colonized women in West Africa by white colonizing women. She argues that the dichotomization between colonizing men and women should be deconstructed and constructions of gender difference should not be isolated from constructions of racial difference. Overall, this should be informed by the deconstruction of the binary opposition between colonizer and colonized that "inhibits examination of what Spivak calls the heterogeneity of 'Colonial Power' at the same time that it masks the roles women play, whether [and both] as colonizers or as colonized."[53] Studying white, colonizing women can disrupt imperial claims of transparent space and mimetic representation by revealing the fluidity rather than fixity of space. Alison Blunt illustrates this point in Chapter 3 through a discussion of the landscape descriptions of Mary Kingsley, who was a white woman traveling in Africa at a time of imperial rule. Recognizing this possibility of disruption helps to destabilize the binary oppositions between both male/female and colonizer/colonized because "the intersection of colonial and gender discourses involves a shifting, contradictory subject positioning, whereby Western women can simultaneously constitute 'centre' and 'periphery,' identity and alterity."[54]

A critique of the mimetic representation that legitimized colonial maps and that is perpetuated by "imperial history" involves a critique of representation itself.[55] Bhabha's work on subject positionality is crucial here. Highlighting the ambivalence of colonial discourse provides greater potential for the study of colonial constructions of gender differences. Colonial discourse depends upon fixity in its construction of "otherness," which is, however, an ambivalent form of representation, reproducing "rigidity and an unchanging order as well as disorder, degeneracy and daemonic repetition."[56] Colonial stereotyping reflects this ambivalence because it "is a form of knowledge and identification that vacillates between what is always already 'in place,' already known, and something that must be anxiously repeated."[57] Critics who do not take account of a sense of ambivalence reify transparency and perpetuate the hegemonic metanarrative of "otherness" legitimating colonial discourses. Colonial dialectics of seeing/knowing depend on visibility, and colonial mapping illustrates the status of the visual. For example, visibility is maintained through surveillance, which depends on distance for "its strategies of objectification, normalisation and discipline."[58] However, the exercise of colonial power is inherently contradictory because "to be authoritative, its rules of recognition must reflect consensual knowledge or opinion; to be powerful, these rules of recognition must be breached in order to represent the exorbitant objects of discrimination that lie beyond its purview."[59] Discrimination relates to the splitting that gives rise to a "colonial hybrid,"[60] whereby constructions of otherness and the visibility of colonial authority are destabilized by the recognition of differentiation: "If the unitary (and essentialist) reference to race, nation, or cultural tradition is essential to preserve the presence of authority as an immediate mimetic effect, such essentialism must be exceeded in the articulation of 'differentiatory,' discriminatory identities."[61] Representations of colonizing women reflect many of the debates concerning representation itself. Drawing on Bhabha, we find that the notion of *complex* ambivalence can facilitate the study of multiple identities differentiated by, most significantly in this context, constructions of race and gender.

In contrast to Domosh's attempts to map women onto histories of geography, spatially sensitive feminist critiques can undermine the status of both colonial maps and traditional mappings of colonialism by viewing space as more fluid than fixed. Carter has proposed "spatial history" as an alternative to "imperial history." This proposal is grounded in the claim that "space itself was a text that had to be written before it could be interpreted."[62] Louise Johnson's chapter in this collection emphasizes the continual and shifting processes of that writing. Space itself could thus be interpreted in multiple ways but only after its construction in the minds of those perceiving it. Carter focuses on naming as a strategy to bring the imperial landscape into existence. Just as Bhabha stresses the active repetition of stereotypes, Carter's method also emphasizes the active rather than the passive construction of space because "the map was an instrument of interrogation, a form of spatial interview which made nature answer the invader's need for information."[63] Colonial mapping illustrates the imposition of colonial forms of knowledge so that "the spatiality of historical experience evaporates before the imperial gaze."[64] The attempt to reclaim the spatiality of historical experience thus serves to critique both colonial mapping and the mappings of colonialism associated with imperialist history. To emphasize "the imperial gaze" highlights the visual and/or textual politics of representation and location. Describing colonized space as constructed clearly undermines claims for mimetic representation by colonial mapping and imperialist history. To relate naming to language reflects the formalized production of colonial knowledge and the relations of domination on which it is based. As well as revealing the constructions of racial differentiation legitimizing colonial conquest, such articulations of domination also illuminate constructions of gender difference among both colonizers and colonized.

"Spatial history" seems particularly pertinent to the study of colonizing women when it is supplemented by the spatial imagery widely employed within much work by feminists of color and those espousing poststructuralist feminist theory.[65] In this context, "women have a history of reading and writing in the interstices of masculine culture, moving between use of the dominant language or form of expression and specific versions of experience based on their marginality."[66] Such marginality was, however, relative for white colonizing women who were positioned both inside and outside colonial discourses. According to Sara Mills, patriarchal and colonial "discourses of difference" were spatially distinct.[67] In this way, white, colonizing women were marginalized within patriarchal contexts when they were perceived primarily in terms of gender inferiority. However, within colonial contexts, constructions of racial superiority could overcome those of gender inferiority, and thus colonizing women could share in colonial discourses of power and authority. In her focus on women travel writers, Mills adopts an explicitly Foucauldian perspective, locates women as producers of signification as well as signifiers within colonial discourses, and views travel writing as one channel for the production of knowledge that is clearly differentiated by gender.[68] The subject positions of such women, informed by patriarchal and colonial discourses of difference, were unstable and decentered over space and time.

The positioning of colonizing women within discourses of difference can be seen in conjunction with the spatial imagery of partial and situated knowledges and the politics of location. Such imagery also serves as a critique of both colonial mapping and imperialist history because it highlights the production of knowledge and its inseparability from broader networks of power and constructions of "truth." In her discussion of Australian captivity narratives about Eliza Fraser, Kay Schaffer in Chapter 5 reveals the different stories told to different audiences over space and time. Situated knowledges represent sites of potential resistance to totalizing metanarratives because "they are re-markings, reorientatings, of the great maps that globalized the heterogeneous body of the world in the history of masculinist capitalism and colonialism."[69]

Spatial histories of colonizing women should by definition involve remappings of colonialism. Claims for mimetic representation advanced by both colonial maps and imperialist history can be challenged by deconstructing both representation and notions of transparent space. In the former case, complex ambivalence undermines the dichotomization of a colonial self and a colonized "other" and raises possibilities for the discussion of gender differentiation among both colonizers and colonized. In the latter case, "spatial history" and feminist uses of spatial imagery can reconcile critiques of both colonial maps and the mapping of colonialism associated with imperialist history. Such critiques illustrate the need to ground the subject positionality of women in historical and geographical research. Constructions of subjectivity should be recognized as both spatially and temporally specific if feminism is to ground itself in a "self-conscious politics of location."[70] As a site for this, the claim that "a place on the map . . . is . . . also a locatable place in history"[71] should involve deconstructions of and resistance to not only "the map" and "history," but also "place" itself.

RETHINKING MAPPING

Feminist historians, then, have argued that the deconstructive imperatives of resistance must be brought to bear on the spatial strategies of imperialism, whether textual or visual. Similar arguments have been made in contemporary feminist work. This introduction has already suggested that the effort made through a politics of location to locate an author(ity) in terms of her position in a complex and shifting matrix of power relations involves a fluid and fragmented sense of both identity and space. We now want to explore this complex notion of space further. It is central to the efforts of many feminists to rethink the hegemonic maps of representation in order to move toward the postcolonial moment. It has been articulated both textually and visually; and it must be understood, we think, in terms of a particular critique of transparent space and its false claim to mimetic representation.

Fabian has argued that European modernity and European imperialism share a law of identical temporality, which positions all places on a hierarchy of progress toward "civilization" as represented by Europe.[72] As we have argued, they also share a similar notion of space. Through transparent space, all places can be mapped in terms of their relationship to Europe. Imperialist maps not only describe colonies: they also discipline them through the discursive grids of Western power/knowledge. Much feminist work strips these maps of their ideological transparency by describing transparent space as *territory*. The term "territory" renders the power implicit in such mapping explicit because territory is an image of land claimed and conquered. Trinh Minh-ha describes claims to truly know a place as "territorialized knowledge" that

> secures for the speaker a position of mastery: I am in the midst of a knowing, acquiring, deploying world – I appropriate, own and demarcate my sovereign territory as I advance – while the "other" remains in the sphere of acquisition. Truth is the instrument of a mastery which I exert over areas of the unknown as I gather them within the fold of the known.[73]

Trinh is referring to transparent space, but through an image of territory that emphasizes the complicity of transparent space with the epistemic and physical violence of imperialism. By naming it as territory, Trinh insists that transparent space is about power, knowledge, and control. It is something that has to be constituted, imposed on spaces and places not imagined through itself. And, as several writers insist, that imposition is never guaranteed: there is always a space of some kind for resistance. The notion of territory enables several possible ways of arguing this position.

One is to insist that the imagined geographies that the imposition of transparent space attempts to subdue may simply never be conquered; they may remain as an imaginative resource with which to challenge territorialization. Another mode of critique, often inspired by deconstructionist tactics, argues that transparency has within it "a kind of self-alienating limit"[74]: its internal need for something outside itself against which it can define itself is a contradiction that always subverts the ability of transparent space to become completely hegemonic. Just as imperialist history depends on those outside its assumption of progress to render itself meaningful,[75] so imperialist geography requires something beyond transparent space to render its territorial conquests important. The center needs its margin; the inside requires an outside; and, as Lefebvre argued, the homogenizing tendency of transparent space is always threatened by the persistent presence of difference. There is always "an elsewhere that does not merely lie outside the center but radically striates it."[76] Hence the paradox that the "others" of the master subject are marginalized and ignored in its gaze at space, but are also given their own places: the slum, the ghetto, the harem, the colony, the closet, the inner city, the Third World, the private. These places haunt the imagination of the master subject, and are both desired and feared for their difference. Thus a strategy to subvert what we can now describe as the *apparent* erasures of transparent space/territory is to emphasize these internal disruptions. Contradictions are nurtured; the margin is not simply valorized but its fundamental relationship to the center is emphasized.

This is one of the strategies adopted by Minnie Bruce Pratt in her influential essay "Identity: Skin Blood Heart," which has been widely cited in the context of multiple, fragmented identities and spaces of power.[77] Pratt grew up in the U.S. South, a white Christian girl, and her project in that essay is to situate herself in relation to her political commitment to "the longed-for but unrealized world, where we each are able to live, but not by trying to make someone less than us, not by someone else's blood or pain."[78] She contrasts this effort with the position of her father whose identity, she feels, depended very much on excluding and marginalizing others. His sense of who he was depended on rigid boundaries that separated him from his others. In white southern culture, Pratt remarks, "We have gotten our jobs, bought our houses, borne and educated our children by the negatives: no niggers, no kikes, no wops, no dagos, no spics, no A-rabs, no gooks, no queers."[79] At several points in her essay, Pratt suggests that this form of identity is territorialized. For example, she mentions "the narrow circle I was raised in,"[80] "the terror of [white] people who have set themselves apart,"[81] "the narrow circle of the self,"[82] the "coffined heart and body" of her father,[83] "what a limited, narrow space" her dream of freedom would be "if only my imagination and knowledge and abilities were to go into the making of it."[84] Gradually and continually, Pratt begins to see not a geography defined by the exclusions of a racist, capitalist, patriarchal center, but by complexity. Her sense of space also shifts. Her father wanted her to see the panorama of her hometown from its courthouse tower: a view replete with social hierarchies and erasures. Instead, Pratt begins to imagine a different space:

> I learn a way of looking at the world that is more accurate, complex, multi-layered, multi-dimensional, more truthful: to see the world of overlapping circles, like movement on a millpond after a fish has jumped.[85]

The ripples on a millpond structure a complicated space for Pratt, a space that is multidimensional and fluid. This spatial complexity is echoed in the narrative confusion of her text. Although her essay is autobiographical, Pratt refuses to construct her changing interpretations of herself as a narrative of her progress toward enlightenment. Instead, she moves backword and forward in time and to and fro across space in her essay, in order to emphasize that her childhood, especially the racist fears of her father, continue to shape her: "Each of us carries around those growing-up places, the institutions, a sort of back-drop, a stage-set."[86] More subversively, however, there is also a sense in her essay that, rejected as she has been by the society in which she grew up, she refuses to go away. She persists in thinking about links between herself and her "home," about how her politics were in some ways enabled by the extremism of the center. Her text continually links her own politics to those of her family: her lesbianism was radicalized by her husband refusing to let her see her children, her antiracism initiated by the atrocities of the Ku Klux Klan. Pratt thus begins to displace the boundary between the center and the margin so important to her father and to suggest its fragility. In her search in this volume for a research methodology sensitive to issues of power and representation, Jenny Robinson advocates a similar notion of hybridity as a further strategy for displacing the power-ridden relation between margin and center.

Pratt engages textually with the exclusions of transparent space. Other spaces imagined by feminists engaged, like Pratt, in thinking through the structures of power that underpin identity also try to displace the distinction between center and margin so necessary to the master subject, but do so visually. They try to challenge the gaze that constructs transparent space. Many of the performances and installations of artist Mona Hatoum, for example, display the imbrication of transparent space with what it marginalizes. In her performance *Roadworks,* Hatoum paced barefoot through the streets of Brixton, London; tied to each of her feet by its laces was a massive black boot.[87] Where she walked, leading, the boot of the police followed. Hatoum seems to be implying that the power of the state depends on what it sees as so much more vulnerable than itself. In more recent work, Hatoum's effort to articulate internal contradictions has focused more on the domestic and on personal relationships. In a video called *Changing Parts,* the camera gazes at the everyday objects in an ordinary bathroom: tiles, taps.[88] It lingers over them so long that they begin to appear strange; the specificity of the quotidian begins to appear. This steady gaze is then disrupted by glimpses of a naked figure, smeared in mud, caught behind a transparent, plastic screen, dragging herself across the screen (Hatoum herself). As Philippi remarks in her commentary on this piece, the effect is to suggest that the stable, transparent, self-evident space of the everyday is premised on the absence of such visceral scenes but also on the possibility of their violation of its normality.[89] A stable sense of time or space is made impossible. The very transparency of transparent space has ruptured.

The image of transparent space as a territory also allows for dreams of something beyond its boundaries; it permits efforts to imagine its dismembering from without as well as from within. Homi Bhabha, for example, has argued that efforts to displace the discursive structures of the master subject must depend on a sense of possibilities beyond the territory defined by the dominant. He has described this as a search for a third space beyond the discursive limits of the master subject.[90] Teresa de Lauretis also articulates this desire for something completely different in terms of a space beyond the field of the Same and its "others:"

> It is the elsewhere of discourse here and now, the blind spots, or the space-off, of its representations. I think of it as spaces in the margins of hegemonic discourses, social spaces carved in the interstices of institutions and in the chinks and cracks of the power-knowledge apparati.[91]

This notion of a space-off is similar to the "zone of indiscernability" that Gilane Tawadros has argued is found in the work of many black feminist artists. One of the central strategies of artists such as Sonia Boyce, Sutapa Biswas, and Lubaina Himid is to produce images that imply a space beyond the dualisms that form the territory of the Same and its "others."[92] Tawadros spends some time discussing Lubaina Himid's *Freedom and Change*. The disruptions enacted by this painting are several. First, the large central canvas pinned to the wall barely contains the figures of two black women running wonderfully along a beach. Tawadros comments that this is an ironic appropriation by a black woman of a canvas by Picasso of two women on a beach, ironic because Picasso himself appropriated so much African art for his own work. But "whereas Picasso's women race across a space which aspires to the status of the universal and transcendental and which paradoxically remains confined within the perimeters of the frame, Himid's women significantly tread a borderline which marks the threshold between real and imagined space, and between lived experiences and expressions of that experience."[93] They also occupy a space between a past and a possible future, and between the master subject and emancipated subjects; on the left of the canvas, stuck to the wall at ground level, are the heads of two white men buried up to their necks in sand, and on the right are a group of black dogs leading the exhilerating women somewhere new. The central canvas thus is a kind of pivot between several aspects of the territory of the master subject and the journey to a different kind of place, where difference can be acknowledged and not disavowed.

The remaking of spaces is central, then, to much feminist and post-colonial work, as shown by Catherine Nash in Chapter 10 in the context of mapping the body and land in Ireland. The argument that the representation of the "other" depends on a transparent space that both erases yet depends upon marginal spaces and differences within itself has meant that many strategies of epistemological critique also reimagine spaces and the mapping process in different ways. Some writers and artists focus on those necessary margins; others try to imagine somewhere beyond both margin and center. The chapters in the second section of this volume address this task of displacing the hegemonic cartography of transparent space with something more disruptive.

CONCLUDING REMARKS

Western feminisms have been concerned with the spatial politics of difference in a variety of ways. The initial importance of a distinction between public and private spheres has been criticized for its exclusivity and neglect of difference. Essentialist and universalist perceptions of both space and subjectivity are underpinned by a sense of transparency which in turn is supported by claims for mimetic representation. To critique essentialism, universalism, and transparency necessarily involves critiquing such claims for mimetic representation. Through such critique, more fragmented, complex, and often contradictory notions of both space and subjectivity can emerge. Rather than map apparently unproblematic and transparent space, its construction and contestation are then revealed. In this way, transparent space is disrupted by subject positionality, the politics of location, and the situatedness of knowledge that reflect partial and multiple mapping strategies.

The two parts of this chapter correspond to the two parts of the volume as a whole. "Drawing the Map" raises questions about white women's historical complicity with and resistance to hegemonic and, specifically, imperialist mapping strategies. The chapters in Part I discuss a number of historically, geographically, and socially specific contexts in which white women traveled to different places either because of colonization or war. All of these chapters cite written representations of spatial differentiation, with texts including travel accounts, captivity narratives, and letters. In contrast, "Rethinking Mapping" addresses the postcolonial imperatives for resisting maps of supposedly transparent space in contemporary contexts. The chapters in Part II trace representations of space and difference through a wider variety of media than written texts alone, and the reconstruction of power through new maps of meaning and more emancipatory mapping strategies are discussed.

The chapters in both parts of this volume examine questions of mapping space and difference, the intersection of, most notably, race with class and gender, complicity and/or resistance, and strategies of critique and disruption. Moving beyond an essentialist notion of space as transparent which can and should be mimetically represented, the fragmentary, ambivalent, and shifting ways in which subjects construct and contest more fluid spaces can be discerned. In this way, a critical study of women's colonial and postcolonial geographies should address not only the multiple and complex construction of subjectivity but also of space itself.

ACKNOWLEDGMENTS

We would like to thank the contributors to this collection for their help in formulating the ideas we explore in this introduction, and Derek Gregory for his encouragement.

NOTES

1. Shirley Ardener, "Ground Rules and Social Maps for Women: An Introduction," in *Women and Space: Ground Rules and Social Maps,* Shirley Ardener, ed. (London: Croom Helm, 1981).

2. Marilyn Frye, *The Politics of Reality: Essays in Feminist Theory* (Trumansburg, NY: Crossing Press, 1983), 93.94.

3. Michelle Zimbalist Rosaldo, "Woman, Culture and Society: A Theoretical Overview," in *Women, Culture and Society,* Michelle Zimbalist Rosaldo and Louise Lamphere, eds. (Stanford, CA: Stanford University Press, 1974), 17.42. The public and the private is discussed at some length in Eva Gamarnikow, David H. J. Morgan, June Purvis, and Daphne Taylerson, eds., *The Public and the Private* (London: Heinemann, 1983); and in Janet Siltanen and Michelle Stanworth, *Women and the Public Sphere: A Critique of Sociology and Politics* (London: Hutchinson, 1984).

4. Rosaldo, "Women, Culture, and Society," 23.

5. Nancy Chodorow, *The Reproduction of Mothering: Psychoanalysis and the Sociology of Gender* (Berkeley: University of California Press, 1978).

6. Henrietta L. Moore, *Space Text Gender: An Anthropological Study of the Marakwet of Kenya* (Cambridge, U.K.: Cambridge University Press, 1988), 1.

7. For a few examples of such struggles, see Dolores Hayden, *The Grand Domestic Revolution* (Cambridge, MA: MIT Press, 1980); Kathleen B. Jones, "Citizenship in a Woman-Friendly Polity," *Signs 15,* no. 4 (Summer 1990): 781.812; Mary

P. Ryan, *Women in Public: Between Banners and Ballots, 1825–1880* (Baltimore: Johns Hopkins University Press, 1990); Jane Rendall, ed., *Equal or Different: Women's Politics 1800–1914* (Oxford: Basil Blackwell, 1987); G. Rose, "The Struggle for Political Democracy: Emancipation, Gender and Geography," *Environment and Planning D: Society and Space 8,* no. 4 (1990): 395–408; Martha Vicinus, *Independent Women: Work and Community for Single Women 1850–1920* (London: Virago Press, 1985).

8. Carole Pateman, *The Disorder of Women: Democracy, Feminism and Political Theory* (Cambridge, U.K.: Polity Press, 1989), 118.

9. See especially Leonore Davidoff and Catherine Hall, *Family Fortunes: Men and Women of the English Middle Class, 1780–1850* (London: Hutchinson, 1987).

10. Evelyn Brooks Higginbotham, "African-American Women's History and the Metalanguage of Race," *Signs 17,* no. 2 (Winter 1992): 251–274, esp. 258–262.

11. Aida Hurtado, "Relating to Privilege: Seduction and Rejection in the Subordination of White Women and Women of Color," *Signs 14,* no. 4 (Summer1989): 833–855. See also Patricia Hills Collins, *Black Feminist Thought: Knowledge, Consciousness and the Politics of Empowerment* (London: HarperCollins, 1990).

12. For recent discussions of such erasures, see Jos Boys, "Women and the Designed Environment: Dealing with Difference," *Built Environment 16,* no. 4 (1990): 249–256; and Rickie Sanders, "Integrating Race and Ethnicity into Geographic Gender Studies," *Professional Geographer 42,* no. 2 (1990): 228–231.

13. Chandra Talpade Mohanty, "Introduction: Cartographies of Struggle: Third World Women and the Politics of Feminism," in *Third World Women and the Politics of Feminism,* Chandra Talpade Mohanty, Ann Russo, and Lourdes Torres, eds. (Bloomington: Indiana University Press, 1991), 1–47, quote from p. 4.

14. Gloria Anzaldúa, *Borderlands/La Frontera* (San Francisco: Spinsters/Aunt Lute Books, 1987), 78.

15. Henri Lefebvre, *The Production of Space,* Donald Nicholson-Smith, trans. (Oxford: Basil Blackwell, 1991), 28. The distinction made here between essentialist and universalist feminisms depends on Elizabeth Grosz, "Conclusion: A Note on Essentialism and Difference," in *Feminist Knowledge: Critique and Construct,* Sneja Gunew, ed. (London: Routledge, 1990), 332–344.

16. Trinh Minh-ha, "Cotton and Iron," in *Out There: Marginalization and Contemporary Cultures,* Russell Ferguson, Martha Gever, Trinh-Minh-ha, and Cornel West, eds. (New York: New Museum of Contemporary Art and Massachusetts Institute of Technology, 1990), 327–336, quote from p. 334.

17. Donna Haraway, *Simians, Cyborgs, and Women: The Reinvention of Nature* (London: Free Association Books, 1991).

18. R. Deutsche, "Boys Town," *Environment and Planning D: Society and Space 9,* no. 1 (1991): 5–30, quote from p. 7.

19. Susan Griffin, *Woman and Nature: The Roaring Inside Her* (New York: Harper Colophon, 1978), 195.

20. Chandra Talpade Mohanty, "Feminist Encounters: Locating the Politics of Experience," *Copyright 1* (Fall 1987): 30–44.

21. Mohanty, "Feminist Encounters," 41.

22. Haraway, *Simians, Cyborgs, and Women,* 170.

23. Chela Sandoval, "U.S. Third World Feminism: The Theory and Method of Oppositional Consciousness in the Postmodern World," *Genders 10* (1991): 1–24.

24. Teresa de Lauretis, "Feminist Studies/Critical Studies: Issues, Terms, Contexts," in *Feminist Studies/Critical Studies,* Teresa de Lauretis, ed. (London: Macmillan, 1986), 137.

25. J. B. Harley, "Deconstructing the Map," in *Writing Worlds: Discourse, Text and Metaphor in the Representation of Landscape,* Trevor J. Barnes and James S. Duncan, eds. (London: Routledge, 1992), 231–247; Graham Huggan, "Decolonizing the Map: Post-Colonialism, Post-Structuralism and the Cartographic Connection," *Ariel 20,* no. 4 (1989): 115–131.

26. We are referring to imperialist history in the same sense as Paul Carter's discussion of "imperial history" in *The Road to Botany Bay: An Exploration of Landscape and History* (New York: Alfred A. Knopf, 1988). We will discuss this term and his alternative–"spatial history"–in greater detail below.

27. Mariana Valverde, "Poststructuralist Gender Historians: Are We Those Names?" *Labour/Le Travail 25* (Spring 1990): 227–236. Also see Sophie Bowlby, Jane Lewis, Linda McDowell, and Jo Foord, "The Geography of Gender," in *New Models in Geography,* vol. 2, Richard Peet and Nigel Thrift, eds. (Boston: Unwin Hyman, 1989), 157–175.

28. Judith Newton, "History as Usual?: Feminism and the 'New Historicism,' " *Cultural Critique 9* (Spring 1988): 87–121.

29. Jean E. Howard, "Feminism and the Question of History: Resituating the Debate," *Women's Studies 19* (1991): 149–157.

30. Mona Domosh, "Toward a Feminist Historiography of Geography," *Transactions of the Institute of British Geographers,* n.s., *16* (1991): 95–104.

31. See, for example, the special edition of *Women's Studies International Forum 13,* no. 4 (1990). Many of these essays were reprinted, together with others, in Nupur Chaudhuri and Margaret Strobel, eds., *Western Women and Imperialism: Complicity and Resistance* (Bloomington: Indiana University Press, 1992). For a concise, yet wide-ranging, overview, see Margaret Strobel, *European Women and the Second British Empire* (Bloomington: Indiana University Press, 1991). Also see Vron Ware, *Beyond the Pale: White Women, Racism and History* (London: Verso, 1991).

32. Nupur Chaudhuri and Margaret Strobel, "Western Women and Imperialism," *Women's Studies International Forum 13,* no. 4 (1990): 289–293.

33. Ibid., 290.

34. This is well illustrated by an account of feminist historical biography writing, when "unpalatable facts" are often unavoidable. See, for example, Dea Birkett and Julie Wheelwright, " 'How Could She?' Unpalatable Facts and Feminists' Heroines," *Gender and History 2,* no. 1 (Spring 1990): 49–57.

35. Gayatri Chakravorty Spivak, "Three Women's Texts and a Critique of Imperialism," *Critical Inquiry 12* (Autumn 1985): 243–261.

36. Michel de Certeau, *The Practice of Everyday Life,* Steven Randall, trans. (Berkeley: University of California Press, 1984).

37. J. B. Harley, "Maps, Knowledge, and Power," in *The Iconography of Landscape: Essays on the Symbolic Representation, Design and Use of Past Environments,* Denis

Cosgrove and Stephen Daniels, eds. (Cambridge, U.K.: Cambridge University Press, 1988), 277–312.

38. Ibid.

39. Huggan, "Decolonizing the Map."

40. Carter, *Road to Botany Bay.*

41. Ibid.

42. Harley, "Maps, Knowledge, and Power," and John Pickles, "Texts, Hermeneutics and Propoganda Maps," in *Writing Worlds: Discourse, Text and Metaphor in the Representation of Landscape,* Trevor J. Barnes and James S. Duncan, eds. (London: Routledge, 1992), 193–230.

43. It is also possible to attempt to read cultures as texts. See, for example, Clifford Geertz, *The Interpretation of Cultures: Selected Essays* (New York: Basic Books, 1973), in which he advocates "thick description" to illuminate the semiotic web of signification that is culture. The work of Geertz has been influential in shaping the "new cultural geography" which includes the Duncans' work on reading landscapes as texts, as in James Duncan and Nancy Duncan, "(Re)reading the Landscape," *Environment and Planning D: Society and Space 6* (1988): 177–126; and James Duncan, *The City as Text: The Politics of Landscape Interpretation in the Kandyan Kingdom* (Cambridge, U.K.: Cambridge University Press, 1990).

44. A. P. A. Busia, "Miscegenation as Metonymy: Sexuality and Power in the Colonial Novel," *Ethnic and Racial Studies 9 (1986): 360–372.*

45. Busia Said and Edward Said, *Orientalism* (New York: Pantheon, 1978).

46. Rana Kabbani, *Europe's Myths of Orient: Devise and Rule* (London: Macmillan, 1986). Also see Kay Schaffer, *Women and the Bush: Forces of Desire in the Australian Cultural Tradition* (Cambridge, U.K.: Cambridge University Press, 1990).

47. Sander L. Gilman, "Black Bodies, White Bodies: Toward an Iconography of Female Sexuality in Late Nineteenth Century Art, Medicine, and Literature," *Critical Inquiry 12* (Autumn 1985): 204–242.

48. Ella Shohat, "Gender and Culture of Empire: Toward a Feminist Ethnography of the Cinema," *Quarterly Review of Film and Video 13* (1991): 45–84.

49. Graham Huggan, "Maps and Mapping Strategies in Contemporary Canadian and Australian Fiction" (Ph.D. diss., University of British Columbia, 1989), 16.

50. Benjamin S. Orlove, "Mapping Reeds and Reading Maps: The Politics of Representation in Lake Titicaca," *American Ethnologist 18* (1991): 3–38. Orlove draws on the work of Michel Foucault.

51. Jane Haggis, "Gendering Colonialism or Colonising Gender?: Recent Women's Studies Approaches to White Women and the History of British Colonialism," *Women's Studies International Forum 13,* nos. 1–2 (1990): 105–115.

52. Ibid.

53. Christine Anne Holmlund, "Displacing Limits of Difference: Gender, Race and Colonialism in Edward Said and Homi Bhabha's Theoretical Models and Marguerite Dura's Experimental Films," *Quarterly Review of Film and Video 13* (1991): 1–22.

54. Shohat, "Gender and Culture of Empire," 63.

55. Harley, "Deconstructing the Map."

56. Homi K. Bhabha, "The Other Question . . . ," *Screen 24,* no. 6 (1983): 18–36, quote from p. 8.

57. Ibid., 18.

58. Ibid., 35.

59. Homi K. Bhabha, "Signs Taken for Wonders: Questions of Ambivalence and Authority under a Tree outside Delhi, May 1817," *Critical Inquiry 12* (Autumn 1985): 144–165.

60. Ibid.

61. Ibid., 154.

62. Carter, *Road to Botany Bay,* 41.

63. Ibid., 113.

64. Ibid., xxii.

65. See, for example, bell hooks *Yearning: Race, Gender and Cultural Politics* (Boston: South End Press, 1990).

66. Caren Kaplan, "Deterritorializations: The Rewriting of Home and Exile in Western Feminist Discourse," *Cultural Critique 6* (Spring 1987): 187–198.

67. Sara Mills, "Discourse of Difference," *Cultural Studies 4,* no. 2 (1990): 128–140, and Sara Mills, *Discourses of Difference: An Analysis of Women's Travel Writing and Colonialism* (London: Routledge, 1991).

68. Mills, *Discourses of Difference.*

69. Haraway, *Simians, Cyborgs, and Women.*

70. Mohanty, "Introduction," 31.

71. Ibid., 34.

72. Johannes Fabian, *Time and Other: How Anthropology Makes Its Object* (New York: Columbia University Press, 1983).

73. Trinh, "Cotton and Iron," 327.

74. Homi Bhabha, "Interview with Homi Bhabha: The Third Space," in *Identity: Community, Culture, Difference,* Jonathan Rutherford, ed. (London: Lawrence and Whishart, 1990), 207–221, quote from p. 210.

75. Christina Crosby, *The Ends of History: Victorians and "The Woman Question"* (London: Routledge, 1991).

76. Trinh, "Cotton and Iron," 328.

77, Minnie Bruce Pratt, "Identity: Skin Blood Heart," in *Yours in Struggle: Three Feminist Perspectives on Anti-Semitism and Racism,* E. Bulkin, M. Bruce Pratt, and B. Smith, eds. (New York: Long Haul Press, 1984), 9–63. For a very helpful commentary on Pratt's work, see Biddie Martin and Chandra Tolpade Mohanty, "Feminist Politics: What's Home Got to Do with It?," *Feminist Studies/Critical Studies,* Teresa de Lauretis, ed. (London: Macmillan, 1986), 191–212.

78. Ibid., 13.

79. Ibid., 39.

80. Ibid., 17.

81. Ibid.

82. Ibid., 18.

83. Ibid., 39.

84. Ibid., 30.

85. Ibid., 17.

86. Ibid.

87. Mona Hatoum, "Body and Text," *Third Text 1* (Autumn 1987): 26–33.

88. Mona Hatoum, *Changing Parts,* 24 minutes, black and white video (Vancouver, B.C.: Western Front Video, 1984).

89. Desa Philippi, "The Witness Beside Herself," *Third Text 12* (Autumn 1990): 71–80, esp. 74–76.

90. Homi Bhabha, "The Other Question: Difference, Discrimination and the Discourse of Colonialism," in *Out There: Marginalization and Contemporary Cultures,* Russell Ferguson, Martha Gever, Trinh Minh-ha, and Cornel West, eds. (New York: New Museum of Contemporay Art and Massachusetts Institute of Technology, 1990), 71–88.

91. Teresa de Lauretis, *Technologies of Gender: Essays, Film and Fiction* (London: Macmillan, 1987), 25.

92. Gilane Tawadros, "Beyond the Boundary: The Work of Three Black Women Artists in Britain," *Third Text 8/9* (Autumn–Winter 1989): 121–150.

93. Ibid., 123.

I

DRAWING THE MAP

2

Knowledge, Gender, and Empire

SARA MILLS

The aim of this chapter is to explore the relationship between the production of knowledge and gender in the period of late-19th-century high British imperialism. This study forms part of a wider study that aims to formulate more productive models for the analysis of imperial expansion.[1] Early analyses of writing within the imperial context, such as Edward Said's *Orientalism* and work that subsequently emanated from his ideas, were extremely important because they stressed the role of the production of knowledge in the maintenance of imperial rule and in mapping out territories in preparation for imperial expansion.[2] However, this work tended to characterize imperial knowledge as a fairly homogeneous form of information that was relatively "transparent" to the reader and therefore simple to analyze. These analyses focused on textual elements, and for this reason little account was taken of the possibilities of multiple interpretations; similarly, because of a focus on fairly well-known writers, questions of gender were skirted and little attention was paid to accounts that could not be fitted into a conventional case of "othering." Subsequent researchers have taken pains to try to examine the complexities of the production of knowledge, even if that has meant that the model of imperial activity or, for that matter, the interpretation, has not been a straightforward one; thanks to them, it has become possible to allow for the differences within the ways in which knowledges are produced and treated.[3] This chapter will focus primarily on the way that the knowledges produced within an imperial context are profoundly gendered, not only in terms of the way that they were written but also in the way that they were judged.[4] This does not mean that I am asserting that women's and men's writing are always fundamentally and necessarily different; on the contrary, I am asserting that gender always makes a difference, particularly within the imperial context that is produced as a profoundly gendered environment. This may seem like a fine distinction, but, as I hope to show, gender has an impact that is not simply a question of the sexes writing in different ways.

Later in the chapter, I will analyze the work of a female travel writer in India, Fanny Parkes, since travel writing is one of the many genres within which imperialist knowledges are produced. This analysis does not aim to prove that Parkes was anti-imperialist, or to prove that she was a protofeminist, or to evaluate her work in relation to male writing. Rather, I will analyze the way within the imperial context in which knowledge produced by women and men is affected by gender norms – that is, I will argue that gender shapes the parameters of the possible textual structures within which writers construct their work. "Gender" is a term I will be using in a relational way, that is to say, the very fact of discussing "women's" travel writing only makes sense in relation to the body of work labeled "men's" travel writing, and those elements that are codified as stereotypically "feminine" and "masculine" within those works. These gendered terms are, of course, intersected by other factors such as race, class, and sexual orientation, as the Introduction to this volume has shown. As Parker et al. state, " 'man' and 'woman' define themselves reciprocally (though never symmetrically)."[5] Thus, I aim to analyze the importance of the factor of gender in the production of knowledge.

DIFFERENT MODELS OF EMPIRE
AND COLONIAL DISCOURSE

Recently, in theorizing colonial discourse, there has been a move away from governmental and institutional-centered views of imperialism. As a result of increasing interest in gender and imperialism, it has become apparent that conventional models of imperialism cannot accommodate the variety of activity that took place within the imperial context. Although the stereotype of imperial activity has often been epitomized either by the figure of the adventuring hero or by the administrator as the symbol of state relations, when gender issues are foregrounded, it is clear that empire is a much more complex entity than a simple relation between two states at a governmental level.[6] Recent work, such as Mary Louise Pratt's *Imperial Eyes,* drawing on a Foucauldian relational model of power, has pointed to the fact that an empire is maintained by a nexus of relations between colonizer and colonized.[7] She asserts that instead of viewing the imperial relation in simplistic terms as an imposition of power upon another nation, it is more accurate to see it more complexly, as a collision of cultures in what she calls "the contact zone," "social spaces where disparate cultures meet, clash and grapple with each other, often in highly assymetrical relations of domination and subordination."[8] She stresses the idea it is inadequate simply to describe the colonizer's view of this contact zone, as has been the case with much early work on imperialism; to provide an adequate account the activity of both countries must be scrutinized for complicity, affirmation, and resistance. Pratt does not describe European travel writing as simply an affirmation of colonial norms because she is interested in the way that knowledge is infiltrated; although imperial writers try to maintain the notion of difference and distance, part of the lived experience of colonialism is the infiltration of one nation by the other: "While the imperial metropolis tends to understand itself as determining the periphery . . . it habitually blinds itself to the ways in which the periphery determines the metropolis – beginning, perhaps, with the latter's obsessive need to present its peripheries and its other continually to itself."[9]

It is important also to bear in mind Peter Hulme's work, which has significantly influenced other work on colonial discourse, in that in opposition to Said's rather monolithic and continuous view of imperial intervention, Hulme stresses the fact that when examining colonial discourse "no smooth history emerges, but rather a series of fragments, which read speculatively, hint at a story that can never be fully recovered."[10] This move toward a certain suspicion of our own acts of interpretation is important, especially since work such as Said's seemed to take it for granted that certain texts have a clear and unequivocal meaning. Instead, Hulme sees texts less as displaying their meaning in their surface structure, than as constituting palimpsests made up of a variety of conflicting and contradictory discursive frameworks. If that is the case, reading them in a monologic way is to be avoided.

Hulme's work also allows us to examine the variety of discourses that are produced within different colonial settings and periods. Just as Pratt in her early work was intent on revealing the differences within the narrative voices in travel writing, identifying not a single unified adventuring hero voice but many different styles and effects, Hulme is also keen to assert the differences within the process of "othering."[11] He examines the types of discourse generated within the Caribbean during the first colonial encounters and he identifies two very different discursive frameworks for describing the "natives," what he terms "the discourse of Oriental civilisation and the discourse of savagery."[12] This stress on the differences within colonial discourse is important in that it enables him to emphasize the specificity of each imperial relation. Porter's work similarly tries to stress the different discourses available to travel writers; he shows that both male and female travel writers had a range of discursive frameworks to draw on and were not constrained simply to produce representations of "otherness."[13] Writing in stark opposition to Said's globalizing theories, he identifies elements within male travel writing that could be said to undermine the "othering" which these texts also contain. Thus a more complex view of both textuality and interpretation is now called for.

There has also been a realization that it is not enough to examine the representations of the colonized country itself when examining imperial relations, since the imposition of rule is also maintained and contested within the colonizing nation. Particularly when women's activities are considered, it is clear that a wide range of activities that have been glossed by dominant discourses as fairly trivial serve as the supports for the imperial enterprise. As Chaudhuri has shown, even relatively minor activities such as the British fashion and food industries and the move toward using Indian products were a part of the maintenance of imperial rule. In much the same way as Pratt, she states: "Diffusion of a subordinate, not to imply inferior, culture into a dominant one is a major effect of colonial rule. The exportation of aspects of Indian cultures by memsahibs was one significant dimension of such diffusion."[14] The financing of imperial activities was often something in which women in Britain were very much involved, because of the stress at this time on philanthropic activities by middle-class women in Britain.[15] Chaudhuri further shows that it is not enough simply to analyze the activities of British women in the colonial setting; for example, within India many of these women refused to buy Indian products, but once they returned home they presented themselves as experts on Indian cookery, customs, and clothing. As Strobel states, "The apparent triviality of the lives of some European women in the colonies masks their important functions within the male centred colonial system of domination."[16] Even the writing of cookbooks and travel accounts was an important element in maintaining and affirming colonial relations. Thus, rather than viewing imperial activity as the imposition of rule by an army or the "discovery" of a country by an explorer, imperialism can instead be seen to consist of a myriad number of activities that took place in both the public and the private sphere, and that played a role in producing knowledges that affirmed and naturalized the imperial presence.

It is clear that a great deal of this rewriting of colonial history is due to feminist intervention into debates on colonial discourse; as Chaudhuri and Strobel have noted, "The study of Western women in colonial settings is but the most recent construction of now fast-changing imperial history, one that rejects the notion of empire solely as male space . . . or even of imperial history as solely constituted by what policymakers in London or in other Western capitals attempted to achieve."[17] But for most feminist critics, feminist analyses of imperialism cannot be content simply to analyze women's activities or the effects of imperialism on women; instead, what is demanded is a fundamental rethinking of colonial categories. As Sangari and Vaid state when they describe feminist historiography, "A feminist historiography rethinks historiography as a whole and discards the idea of women as something to be framed by a context, in order to be able to think of gender differences as both structuring and structured by a wide set of social relations." They go on to state that a wholesale rethinking of imperial analysis is called for.[18] Drawing on their work, Radhakrishnan states, "The articulation and the politicisation of gender as an analytic category belongs initially with feminism narrowly conceived as exclusively women's categories, but does not and cannot merely stop with that. If indeed gender is a necessary category in the context of cultural and historical and political analysis, how can its operations be circumscribed within the narrow confines of its origins? . . . Gender has a particular placement that is local and specific to women's questions but it is by no means merely a regional concern."[19] Thus, Radhakrishnan is concerned that the analysis of gender infiltrates all aspects of colonial analysis, rather than being hived off into a concern with "women's issues."

Other elements that have begun to be analyzed within colonial discourse include factors apart from or intersecting with race and gender. Early analysts of colonial discourse focused exclusively on the representation of racial differences, while feminist theorists have insisted on the necessity for an analysis of gender, but now many researchers are insisting that an analysis of class difference is also essential. For example, Blake in her analysis of Mary Hall's writing in Africa, contrasting it with several male writers, shows that Hall "rejects racial superiority as a source of power because it is inseparable from gender superiority . . . [but she] replaces the authority of race with that of class."[20] Thus, Hall represents her treatment of the Africans she meets as if they were from different class backgrounds to herself, and although this means that she describes them in terms that are hierarchical it does at least allow her "to acknowledge the social distinctions Africans themselves make."[21] Blake points out that this perspective on Africans does not mean that Hall is not racist, but she suggests that because of women's divided and fragmented sense of self in the imperial setting, they are more likely to be able to view the colonized subjects in less homogeneous ways. These concerns with different and more complex visions of imperialism certainly have an effect on the way that we can conceptualize the production of knowledge within the imperial context.

KNOWLEDGE AND POWER

Much of the work on colonial discourse is deeply indebted to Michel Foucault's work on the interrelation of knowledge and power.[22] Travel writing within the imperial context clearly produces knowledge about the colonized country, and much of the critical writing concerned with this genre has extensively discussed the production of "manners and customs" information, that is, knowledge that describes the inhabitants of the colonized country in terms that reify them and construct them as an "other." However, travel texts also produce a great deal of other "commonsense" knowledge, for example, knowledge about the home country, and knowledge about the relations between males and females both within the imperial context and in the home country. Much travel writing implicitly proposes a set of commonsense assumptions to which the reader is supposed to assent. Given the gendered nature of imperialism at a stereotypical level, it is quite clear that information produced within this context will itself be profoundly gendered.

Although travel writing has often been considered as if it were simply describing the process of travel, it is clear that it simultaneously affirms or contests imperial presence. Pratt's work details the way in which particular types of knowledge were produced within particular forms of imperial rule.[23] She suggests that during the 19th century there were two factors that led to the development of certain types of travel writings concerned with the description of inland exploration: demands within capitalism for raw materials, and the beginning of intense rivalry between European powers, expressed through seizure of land. At the same time there was a profound change in European "planetary consciousness" which was intimately linked to changes in views of knowledge, particularly in the scientific sphere. She describes this as "a version marked by an orientation toward interior exploration and the construction of global-scale meaning through the descriptive apparatuses of natural history. This new planetary consciousness . . . is a basic element constructing modern Eurocentrism, that hegemonic reflex that troubles westerners even as it continues to be second nature to them."[24] What characterized Linnaean typologies of natural history and work within those methodologies in the 19th century was their universal scope. This view of natural history led

Europeans to travel all over the globe in search of specimens, and, according to Pratt, "No more vivid example could be found of the way that knowledge exists not as a static accumulation of facts, bits or bytes, but as human activities, tangles of verbal and non-verbal activities."[25] She notes that travel writing was a way in which scientific knowledge was mediated to a wider public. Thus travel writers were "central agents in legitimising scientific authority and its global project alongside Europe's other ways of knowing the world."[26] Within this type of knowledge, specimens are named by Europeans and extracted from their environment; in the process of naming them and setting them within a classificatory system, they are transformed from chaos into an order that is European. Thus, those writers who produce scientific knowledge are fundamentally connected to European imperial expansion and the promotion of a view of the world that sees European activities as fundamentally civilizing. Knowledge here is given the appearance of a simple neutral endeavor at an individual level, but in fact it is very much a part of imperialism; in this way, scientific knowledge can present itself as free from the taint surrounding the commercial and political expansion that it underwrote. The naturalist figure may have had some appeal to women travelers since it seemed so innocent, in relation to "an assumed guilt of conquest," as Pratt puts it; however, imperial expansion made possible naturalist travels and sums up much colonial "longing for a way of taking possession without subjugation and violence."[27] Thus, women's travel writing, although often portrayed by critics as somehow outside of the production of specifically imperial knowledges, is still implicitly producing knowledge that impacts upon the colonial presence.

WHAT DIFFERENCE DOES GENDER MAKE?

A key assumption underlying much of the theoretical work on travel writing is that men's and women's texts are fundamentally different. This may be one of the many reasons why women's travel writing has been so completely ignored in general accounts or why, when general accounts are written, women's texts are ghettoized into a separate chapter.[28] Many critics assert that women's texts are formally different. For example, Stevenson states that "women travellers developed strategies of accommodation not confrontation or domination and [wrote] richly eclectic loosely structured narratives of their discoveries about the continent, its people, and their own psyches."[29] Even Pratt seems to concur with this formal distinction, since she characterizes female travel accounts as not structured on the "goal-directed, linear emplotment of conquest narrative," noting that instead they are "emplotted in a centrepetal fashion around places of residence from which the protagonist sallies forth and to which she returns."[30] Pratt asserts that women are more concerned with the presentation of their own identity and their sense of personal independence rather than the production of scientific knowledge and the relating of adventure narratives. She asserts that the stress laid on the domestic sphere and description of that sphere in women's travel narratives is not simply a reflection of different public and private spheres for men and women, but represents a different "mode of constituting knowledge and subjectivity."[31] Pratt does not go into any detail concerning the way in which these knowledges are differentially produced, and it is my aim in this chapter to investigate if this is in fact the case.

The assumption that women's texts are necessarily different from men's has been the subject of heated debate, particularly indebted to current debates about essentialist versus postmodernist feminisms.[32] This debate has focused on whether it is politically useful to maintain the category "woman," since its use seems to bring about the elision of differences that are the result of race, class, and sexual orientation. However, while it is essential to question the heterogeneity of the category "woman" and to foreground some of the exclusionary practices that have developed within feminism itself because of the use of the term, it is still necessary to realize that women as a group are generally treated in a discriminatory way. However, at the same time, it is essential to realize that discrimination is meted out to women of different classes and of different races in different ways, and is reacted to in different ways. As Judith Bennett states, "Women have not been merely passive victims of patriarchy; they also colluded in, undermined and survived patriarchy. But neither have women been free agents; they have always faced ideological, institutional and practical barriers to equitable association with men (and indeed other women)."[33] In a similar way we cannot assume that British middle class women necessarily react in a homogeneous way within the imperial context, such that we could describe women's travel writing in isolation from men's writing or vice versa.

The imperial context is one where gender roles are polarized in ways in which perhaps they are not to the same extent in the home country. The empire is generally considered to be a place of masculine endeavor, where heroic individual males behave in adventurous ways, exploring undiscovered countries and subduing the inhabitants. As Martin Green states, "Adventure seems to mean a series of events, partly but not wholly accidental, in settings remote from the domestic and probably from the civilised . . . which constitute a challenge to the central character. In meeting this challenge he performs a series of exploits which make him a hero, eminent in virtues such as courage, leadership and persistence."[34] Like many other writers on the empire, Green sets the imperial character outside the private, domestic sphere and pictures him behaving in a strictly masculinist, adventuring, and heroic manner. The adventure hero is characterized in stark contrast to stereotypical versions of the "native" and the British female. As Rebecca Stott states, "Imperialist discourse is . . . a man-made discourse, expressing male fantasies, fears, anxieties. It is a discourse that emphasises the importance of male camaraderie and which implicitly warns of the debilitating effects of women."[35] Although the 19th century was a period when gender roles were fairly polarized, it seems that the empire was coded as a place where extreme forms of masculine behavious were expected, even if that is not what happened in reality. In early accounts of colonial discourse, this masculinization of empire was not much commented on and was accepted as common sense; in more recent accounts of empire, especially those written by feminist theorists, there has been a concern not only with a gendering of women's writing (something that has always happened) but also with a gendering of the overall, seemingly gender-neutral colonial entreprise. Thus, for example, Blake can assert that just as women's travel texts are often read as if they were only about the individual and not about colonial expansion, so certain male writings are read as if they were only about colonial adventure, when in truth they are also about proving individual manhood, and a particular type of colonial manhood at that.[36] Rather than seeing the narratives written by males as neutral and related to colonial expansion, we need to view all writing during this period as inextricably gendered, at both an individual and a state level (if we can assume that it is possible to disentangle these two levels within the imperial context). It is also necessary for us to examine the gender stereotypes that infiltrate our interpretative frameworks.

This concern with a particular type of imperial activity has led to the reprinting of certain examples of women's travel writing that accord with the masculinist norms of the adventure narrative; therefore, those texts that contain strong adventuring heroes are reprinted, whereas those where the character is a more retiring feminine one are rarely reprinted.[37] As Kroller states, certain critics have been "determined to rework Victorian narratives to tell a very specific feminist success story."[38] This has been part of a move to reevaluate the Victorian period and challenge the notion that women could not travel without chaperones; however, it has had the effect of affirming the elision between heroic adventuring and imperialism. As Chaudhuri and Strobel state, "Recent colonial nostalgia is notable in its efforts to co-opt feminist consciousness and activism. In an increasingly conservative political climate it is hardly surprising to find feminism manifested as an interest in famous 'heroic' white women in colonial settings."[39] And as this quotation shows, much of the early feminist work on these "eccentric" women travelers explicitly excised any mention of the colonial setting from their analyses, stressing instead the independence and heroic qualities of the women travelers themselves as individuals.

In the imperial context, apart from a few eccentric female representatives, women seemed to function mainly at a symbolic level, rather than occupy any real conceptual or physical space.[40] It is almost as if women served as a moral justificatory power for the empire: their pure representations were found in all sorts of public arenas where the empire was displayed. It is surprising therefore that their actual presence within the imperial context seems to be viewed so negatively. In account after account, one finds reiterations of the "fact" that once the memsahibs arrived in India, relations with Indians ceased to be friendly. Yet at the same time, at a symbolic level, women were seen to be both the empire's weakest element, since they were the subject of feared attacks by "natives" and they served as the supposed justification for vicious retribution after rebellions such as the Indian Uprising of 1857.[41] As Strobel shows, Western women themselves were the site of contradictory feelings of racial superiority and vulnerability, and for Western men they often served as the site of the projection of their own sexual feelings about colonized males. Thus, within the imperial context there is a clash and an elision of the symbolic and the actual, where women within the imperial setting were constantly confronted with norms that had developed at the symbolic level and that were impossible to live within.

A distinction should be made between women settlers and women travelers, since there seems to be quite a fundamental difference between the two groups. Women settlers, for example, the memsahibs in India, were subject to even stricter class and hierarchy rules than those that operated on them within Britain; this occured partly because of the need to assert a strong cultural identity as a community in the face of overwhelming different communities – the maintenance of this structure fell largely to women. Travelers, however, were not seen as necessarily a part of these communities and could behave in a slightly eccentric way. Their accounts are usually significantly different from those produced by settlers, especially in the way in which they describe being treated as honorary men. Settler women, especially in India, were often treated as if they were in purdah. Women travelers managed to travel alone or with "native" men as guides in ways settler women would have found difficult or impossible.

There has started to develop a substantial literature about women's travel writing. Most of the early work is descriptive in nature.[42] Some later critics have tried to examine the way that these texts can be reclaimed as examples of earlier feminism, or constituted as different voices to the conventional imperialist voices of male writers. For example, Stevenson states, "Women travelers ventured into the controversial male arena of foreign policy and struggled to find an acceptably feminine voice for their angry and trenchant criticism of British imperial policy towards Africans."[43] She argues that this critical position stems from the fact that the situation of the colonized mirrored their own situation as women and that their protests over colonial activity were in fact displacements of "their anger into positive social action for the good of others."[44] This approach has serious flaws in that the methodological approach to the texts is wholly evaluative and has to ignore a great many texts by women that are equally imperialist. As Strobel states, "I do not see Western women merely as cultural imperialists, the good cop to the bad cop of the military and colonial administration." She is rather worried by the "current resurgence of colonial nostalgia and its particular manifestation of portraying heroic white women in colonial settings, a kind of converse of the destructive memsahib."[45] Some critics even go so far as to assert that female travel writers "rejected the virulent racism that blights most of the male accounts."[46] It is true that many women travelers did write accounts that either ignored the institutional colonial setting entirely, or were critical of certain excesses; however, the criticisms of colonial rule seem to be very much at the level of single issues rather than wholesale critique, and it is also true to say that many of them even in their silence about colonialism produced a form of knowledge that affirmed colonial presence.

Feminist theorists are now beginning to question the necessity that women's texts will be different, but yet are interested in investigating the differences in the conditions of their production and are explicitly contrasting texts by women with those by men within a similar context.[47] Despite their different relation to the imperial institutions–few women were actually a part of the institutional imperial context except as what Callan calls "incorporated wives"[48]–many of the women were profoundly involved within colonialism, for example, by teaching, by nursing, by writing. Women's position is often rather ambivalent, because as Strobel states, "Women carved out a space amid the options available to them: options for the most part created by imperialism and limited by male dominance (and by class). As participants in the historical process of British expansion, they benefited from the economic and political subjugation of indigenous peoples and shared many of the accompanying attitudes of racism, paternalism, ethnocentrism and national chauvinism."[49]

GENDER AND KNOWLEDGE

Women's relation to knowledge production has always been a troubled one; this is quite clearly the case within the imperial context where women travel writers seem to produce particular forms of knowledge because of societal constraints at a discourse level.[50] Not only do women travel writers have to produce knowledge that will be interesting enough to sell books in the home country, so that their books are structured around unusual events and activities that are not related within male travel accounts (the first woman to reach a certain city, the first woman to climb a certain mountain, the only person to obtain secret knowledge about "Oriental" women, and so on), but they are also producing knowledge about themselves that will be used to judge them as individuals. Their position is one that is negotiated between both the institutional and the individual, the imperial and the home setting. But that is not to say that this knowledge divides so neatly between the institutional and the personal, since even the knowledge of the domestic sphere, or information about correctness of dress, or the like, is also a part of the production of cultural norms within imperialism. In general, the knowledges that are produced are fairly stereotypical when considering women's position in the 19th century. First, women did not produce a great deal of information about strictly institutional and state imperial relations but when they did, as in Mary Kingsley's case, it was often critical.[51] Kingsley criticises governmental intervention in West Africa and states that it would be more advantageous if a trading model were used; she also criticises the missionary activity within West Africa. Her writing is perhaps exceptional but is part and parcel of a larger discursive practice whereby middle-class British women were able to adopt a tone of high moral concern; thus Florence Dixie was able to criticise the British government for keeping prisoner the Zulu leader Cetshwayo.[52] However, at the same time, a great deal of racist knowledge was also produced. Kingsley considered black people inferior to white people and wrote extensively of their childlike nature and difference from a superior Western norm. Callaway and Helly have shown that the type of text that was produced by women who were openly imperialist tends not to be studied.[53] This accords with my findings that frequently critics will simply pass over imperialist knowledge in women's travel writings when they are trying to position the travel writer as a feminist precursor.

As I mentioned earlier, Pratt has shown that scientific knowledge characterized the imperial adventure more than any other type of knowledge. Because of women's problematic relation with scientific knowledge and their virtual exclusion from higher education until the late

19th century, women travel writers often produced knowledge within their texts of a very particular and safe feminine type, such as information about flowers and butterflies. However, as Pratt has shown, this type of knowledge is imbricated within the process of imperialist expansion, and at the same time that its production displays to the reader a safe, feminine persona for the narrator, it also produces a vision of the colonized country as a storehouse of random flora and fauna waiting for the civilizing ordering of the narrator with her Western science.

A significant number of women travelers investigated the status of women in the colonized country; this had a variety of effects, as Chaudhuri and Strobel have shown. Here women travelers drew on a supposed moral high ground in order to challenge practices such as child marriage, the killing of twin children, the burning of widows (suttee), clitoridectomy, and purdah. At the same time they present "native" treatment of women as barbaric, these critical writings also had the result of falsely presenting Western women as being relatively free from patriarchal oppression. As Hatem states, "By thinking of themselves as all-powerful and free vis-a-vis Egyptian women, Western women could avoid confronting their own powerlessness and gender oppression at home."[54] They could also avoid confronting the ways in which the power they had derived from imperial relations, rather than from their own individual or gender position. These knowledges of "native" women simply reaffirmed the colonial view that British society was best and that societies could be judged on their level of civilization according to the degree they approximated the idealized British treatment of women. Furthermore, women travel writers often adopted a maternal role in relation to indigenous women, a role that challenged neither the imperial assertion of superiority nor the type of knowledge that asserted that "natives" were childlike. It also provided the women travelers with a textual role for their persona that was fundamentally safe. But as Strobel states when discussing the reforms that British women tried to encourage in India, "Carried out, as they most often were, in the absence of a critique of colonialism, such reforms mistakenly identified women's problems as a result only of indigenous patriarchal relations, rather than the result of the interaction of these indigenous relations with colonial exploitation and gender oppression."[55] And as Sinha states, "The so-called degraded plight of native women was an excuse that the Anglo-Indians used to justify denying all natives their political rights."[56] Thus women who wrote about "native" women and argued for reform conformed to their role in writing about "feminine" concerns and were part of a production of knowledge that resulted in larger scale oppression of colonized subjects as a whole. The reforms that were attempted were channeled directly through the colonial authorities and thus reinforced the view that only the imperial powers could do something about the way that members of another culture lived. In effect, by concentrating on the production of knowledge about colonized women and criticizing their plight from a "humanitarian" point of view, these women reinscribed the view that Britain was more civilized than other countries and had the right to act as a moral arbiter in such matters. This type of seemingly critical knowledge also provided a space for British women within the imperial entreprise as a whole, so that they could be imperial citizens while remaining thoroughly within the stereotypical discourses of femininity and motherhood. Thus, rather than the empire being a thoroughly masculine place, it seems that it also had a feminine identity; the production of a type of moral knowledge by females seems an essential part of the justification by the imperialist power of its own presence.

Furthermore, it must be remembered that we cannot simply focus on the production of these knowledges; at the reception side of the equation they were also judged and contested by reviewers, critics, and readers. Travel writing has always had a problematic relation to the truth, but many women's travel texts were challenged and edited when their information did not fit in with stereotypical norms.[57] Thus, in order to examine the relationship between gender and knowledge, we must be aware of a vast array of different and complex factors that act upon the production of knowledge, so that we can see texts not as containing a simple unitary message for which the author is wholly responsible, but rather as a complex negotiation between the author and the discursive frameworks that imperialism constructed and maintained.

FANNY PARKES: WANDERINGS OF A PILGRIM

At this point, I would like to concentrate on one woman traveler in order to exemplify some of the points I have raised about the production of knowledge. In 1850 Fanny Parkes wrote an account of her stay in India, *Wanderings of a Pilgrim in Search of the Picturesque during Twenty-Four Years in the East, with Revelations of Life in the Zenana.* She had traveled to India with her husband, who was in the Indian Civil Service, and in her book she describes both her residence in India and the various travels she undertook alone or accompanied by male companions. In this text, Parkes produces a great deal of conventional knowledge about India, but she also produces herself as a particular type of feminine subject. Her title sets the book within a firm context of the picturesque, and this means that she can justify the inclusion of myriad unconnected events and pieces of information without recourse to a firmly structured narrative. This picturesque element is a profoundly imperialist move, since all of the scenes that are related are totally decontextualized: no history is given – the narrator simply responds to sights and events and it is only the narrator who is a stable position of knowledge within the text. She describes her interest in natural history and relates her many quests to collect various animals, for example, baby alligators, tigers, and fossils. This arbitrary specimen collecting is paralleled by her collecting of pieces of information about India. She does not set any of these diverse elements into their context: they are presented simply because they are of interest to the overarching personality of the narrator. A further element in the title which is of interest is that she claims that she will reveal unknown knowledge about the *zenana,* the enclosed spaces which some Indian women occupied, and which only women could enter. In writing about the zenana, as I will show, Fanny Parkes marks herself as an imperial subject and also contributes to the imperial task of revealing the secrets of the colonized country.

In the book Parkes sets herself firmly within "Orientalist" knowledges, in that she dedicates her book both to her mother and to the Hindu god Ganesh and she writes her name on the flyleaf in Arabic/Persian script. Most of the knowledge she displays is of this eclectic amateur type, whereby snippets of information that she finds interesting are displayed without an overall framework of knowledge about the different cultural environments within which they make sense or normally occur, for example, she frequently cites Indian proverbs and Hindustani songs. However, she is acute enough to realize that her Persian calligraphy is not accurate and states clearly that she is only a simple pilgrim rather than a scholar.[58] But despite this self-effacement, which could be analyzed as the production of a feminine self, she uses her position of alignment with the "natives" through her knowledge of their customs and beliefs to pose herself as apart from other Westerners. For example, when she visits the Taj Mahal, she states:

> Crowds of gaily-dressed and most picturesque natives were seen in all directions. . . . They added great beauty to the scene . . . whilst the eye of taste turned away pained and annoyed by the vile round hats and stiff attire of the European gentleman and the equally ugly bonnets and stiff graceless dresses of the English ladies. . . . Can you imagine anything so detestable? European ladies and gentlemen have the band to play on the marble terrace and dance quadrilles in front of the tomb! . . . I cannot enter the Taj without feelings of deep devotion . . . and I could no more jest or indulge in levity beneath the dome of the Taj than I could in my prayers.[59]

Thus, in this passage, she can be seen to be showing herself more in sympathy with Indian culture than with these "ugly" Western people. She even sets herself very much apart from them in spatial terms: they are located at some distance from her and she portrays herself in a devotional and not a recreational space, despite the fact that she must be wearing the same "ugly" garments that she describes. Thus, this aesthetic quality is one which she locates with the Indian people, who become reified as picturesque.

At the same time that she seems to present herself as sympathetic to Indian culture, she also displays conventional imperial knowledge, portraying Indian women as idle (while at the same time commenting on the way that she is waited upon hand and foot): "The idleness of the natives is excessive; for instance, my ayha will dress me, after which she will sleep in one corner of my room for the whole day."[60] Thus her own inactivity, demonstrated by the fact that she is dressed by a servant, is not remarked upon. She also comments extensively on the deceitfulness of servants; however, she imagines that despite their fairly negative condition, they are at least happy. She states, "What happy wretches the natives are"[61] because although they are paid only a small wage they can manage to support themselves easily on this. Much of her book is concerned with relating domestic arrangements, and while this information may not seem to have a direct bearing on imperial rule, it is clear that within the home country, Parkes would not have been able to afford the fifty-four servants that she has to organize in India. This clearly marks the imperial setting as one embedded in power relations.

She provides a great deal of information about Indian women in general and comments that "Women in all countries are considered such dust in the balance, when their interests are pitted against those of men."[62] But it seems as if, again, the information she offers about women is mainly concerned to bolster her own position of authority, for she says, "I know of no European lady who has ever had the opportunity of becoming intimate with native ladies of rank,"[63] as she asserts that she herself did. Most of her statements about the zenana are evaluative rather than simply descriptive. She provides a portrait of life in the zenana that is mainly a straightforward replication of many of the earlier accounts by male travel writers, that is, mostly fantastic and erotic. Thus, she, again, is concerned with the aesthetic qualities of the women, she states, "How much I should like to pay the ladies [of the zenana] a visit and see if there are any remarkably handsome women among them!"[64] It is almost as if she is acting as an envoy of the male readers who would be unable themselves to enter the zenana. She describes one women in the zenana: "Mulka walks straight as an arrow. In Europe, how very rarely does a women walk gracefully bound up in stays, the body is as stiff as a lobster in its shell. . . . A lady in European attire gives me the idea of a German mannekin; an Asiatic in her flowing drapery, recalls the statues of antiquity."[65] This description, while seeming on the surface to be displaying a sympathetic account of Mulka, at the same time manages to reduce her to an aesthetic object (an Asiatic, statue of antiquity) in much the same way that Parkes describes Indian architecture.

Other descriptions of the zenana are highly judgmental, as shown by her disapproval of the fact that one of the women gives opium to the children. In the zenana she visits the daughter of an English officer and a Eurasian woman; she says "I felt ashamed of the circumstances when I saw her chewing *pan* with all the gusto of a regular Hindostanee."[66] This is a complex statement, since she sees this woman very much as an English woman, despite the fact that she is of mixed parentage – here she expresses her distaste at the superimposition of various cultural norms – a seemingly white woman who is behaving in the manner of an Indian woman. She provides other information about Indian women, for example, she attends a suttee and gives a very neutral unemotional account of a woman who jumped from the fire only to be forced back by the crowd. Thus, her accounts of Indian women, while sometimes seeming sympathetic, are very much in line with conventional imperial views, stressing their beauty and at the same time their "degraded" condition.

She comments on certain events that might normally have appeared to be taboo for Western women, for example, when she sees a festival of Churuk Puja that involved bodily mutilation, she remarks: "I was much disgusted but greatly interested."[67] With most of this taboo knowledge she attempts to distance herself from the source of the information; she does not directly report a great deal of it, but instead encloses it within a framework whereby another persona in the text is forced to take the moral responsibility. Thus, at the same time that she safeguards her femininity, she also produces knowledges about India as a place of strange and barbaric customs, which she observes from a distance or is told about, but which does not contaminate her. She manages to distance herself from the sight of sexual images in a temple she visits, stating, "The worship is very impure, I am told."[68] When she reports about the thuggee activities, in which certain secret robber bands engaged in murdering their victims, she is very careful to distance herself from this indelicate subject and includes letters from her soldier informant rather than integrating this knowledge into her own text. She says, "I could not omit inserting the above [Thug] narrative on account of the quiet coolness with which the Thug Oomeid relates the murders committed by himself and his gang,"[69] but while this method permits her to include the narrative, she herself does not engage with the "quiet coolness" of the barbaric Thug; she allows herself a position of objectivity outside the acount by foregrounding her role as narrator.

She frequently relates incidents that would supposedly have been shocking for a feminine British woman, and she allows herself the textual space to produce these descriptions of taboo or shocking subjects by concentrating on her own disgust, rather than the spectacle itself. For example, she states, "I have been more disgusted today than I can express," a remark prompted by witnessing a corpse floating down the river. She had imagined it was a European, but on checking she found that it was in fact an Indian who had been burnt in ghee at the funeral, a process that had turned the skin white: "The most disgusting object imaginable."[70] After describing bear fights she witnessed, she states, "The scene was a cruel one and I was glad when it was over."[71] In this way she shows herself very well aware of the knowledge that should be introduced into a travel text, that is, the text must contain information that is anomalous according to a Western norm, but she is also aware that she, as a feminine woman, cannot avoid compromising her respectability if she does include such information in unmediated form. In this way, Parkes manages both to produce knowledges of India that are quite clearly imperialist while at the same time producing a textual space for herself that is not compromised by the seeming masculinity of such knowledges.

However, simultaneously, she displays a certain amount of awareness that her own behavior is judged by different moral standards. She states, "You cannot roam in India as in Europe or go into places, crowded with natives, without a gentleman; they think it so incorrect and so marvellous, that they collect in crowds to see a *beebee sahiba* who is indecent enough to appear unveiled."[72] This again could be seen as reserving a position of authority for herself, whereby she knows so much about the imperial setting that she can even consider introducing a critique of her own behavior.

CONCLUSIONS

This chapter has attempted to consider some of the complexities surrounding the relations between gender and knowledge within the imperial context. It has not been my aim to assert that women travel writers necessarily produce knowledge in a different way to male writers because it is clear that they share many characteristics with them, but it is also clear that there are certain pressures that act on the production and reception of women's writing in very gender-specific ways. Even those knowledges that seem at first sight to be innocent of the taint of imperialism, such as self-revelation and the simple construction of safe knowledges, are affirmations of colonial rule. Even those knowledges that contest colonial rule do so within a set of discursive constraints that have been instigated both by discourses of feminine behavior and the high moral ground available to women. As such, they do not substantially question the basis of imperial rule.

Perhaps what this type of analysis calls for is less a concentration on women's writing per se, than a reorientation of our views of imperialism, so that we resist the projection of imperial expansion as adventure, and concentrate more on the lived experience of all of those involved in colonial life. Instead of viewing as imperial knowledge only the statistics and manners and customs descriptions of other countries and their inhabitants, it will be possible to analyze those descriptions that have been seen as seemingly trivial, because of their association with the domestic and women's spaces. It is clear that feminist work is beginning to see the production of knowledges about these seemingly trivial elements as just as important in the analysis of colonial discourse as the "heroic" adventures of male travelers.

NOTES

1. See S. Mills, "Gender and Colonialism," conference paper, *Gender and Colonialism* Conference, University of Galway, 1992.
2. E. Said, *Orientalism* (London: Routledge and Kegan Paul, 1978). This work has inspired a whole host of similar studies both directly about the "Orient" and applying the notion of orientalism to other contexts; see, for example, R. Kabbani, *Europe's Myths of Orient: Devise and Rule* (London: Macmillian, 1986).
3. See, for example, M. L. Pratt, "Scratches on the Face of the Earth, or What Mr. Barrows saw in the Land of the Bushmen," *Critical Inquiry 12,* no. 1 (Autumn 1985): 119–143, and *Imperial Eyes: Travel Writing and Transculturation* (London: Routledge, 1991); P. Hulme, *Colonial Encounters: Europe and the Native Caribbean, 1492–1797* (London: Methuen, 1986); R. Radhakrishnan, "Nationalism, Gender and the Narrative of Identity," in *Nationalisms and Sexualities,* A. Parker, M. Russo, D. Sommer, and P. Yaeger, eds. (London: Routledge, 1992), 77–95; N. Chaudhuri and M. Strobel, eds., *Western Women and Imperialism: Complicity and Resistance* (Bloomington: Indiana University Press, 1992); K. Sangari and S. Vaid, eds., *Recasting Women: Essays in Indian Colonial History* (New Brunswick, NJ: Rutgers University Press, 1990); and S. Blake, "A Woman's Trek: What Difference Does Gender Make?," *Women's Studies International Forum 13,* no. 4 (1990): 347–355.
4. I am using the terms "empire" and "imperial" in rather a loose way here to refer to relations between states where one state has dominance over the other, either through trade, economic exploitation, religious activity, or actual invasion or settlement. Thus I am using it as a superordinate term to "colonialism," which I will be using to refer only to colonial settlement.
5. Parker, Russo, Sommer, and Yaeger, eds., *Nationalisms and Sexualities,* 5.
6. This is also partly due to work that has been undertaken recently which

has recognized the very Western nature of the concept of the nation-state; see, for example, B. Davidson, *The Black Man's Burden: Africa and the Curse of the Nation State* (London: James Currey, 1993).

7. Pratt, *Imperial Eyes.*

8. Ibid., 4.

9. Ibid., 6.

10. Hulme, *Colonial Encounters,* 12.

11. Pratt, "Scratches on the Face of the Country."

12. Hulme, *Colonial Encounters,* 21.

13. D. Porter, "Orientalism and Its Problems," in *The Politics of Theory,* F. Barker, ed. (Colchester, U.K.: University of Essex, 1986), 179–193.

14. N. Chaudhuri, "Shawls, Jewelry, Curry and Rice in Victorian Britain," in *Western Women and Imperialism,* Chaudhuri and Strobel, eds., 231–246, quote from p. 232.

15. See, for example, S. Mills, *Discourses of Difference: Women's Travel Writing and Colonialism* (London: Routledge, 1991); P. Barr, *The Memsahibs: The Women of Victorian India* (London: Secker and Warburg, 1976); J. Trollope, *Britannia's Daughters: Women of the British Empire* (London: Hutchinson, 1983); and J. Alexander, *Voices and Echoes: Tales from Colonial Women* (London: Quartet, 1983).

16. M. Strobel, *European Women and the Second British Empire* (Bloomington: Indiana University Press, 1991).

17. Chaudhuri and Strobel, eds., *Western Women and Imperialism,* 4.

18. Sangari and Vaid, eds., *Recasting Women,* 3.

19. Radhakrishnan, "Nationalism, Gender and the Narrative of Identity," 79.

20. Blake, "A Woman's Trek," 353.

21. Ibid., 354.

22. M. Foucault, *The Archaeology of Knowledge* (New York: Harper Colophon, 1972), and *Power/Knowledge: Selected Interviews,* C. Gordon, ed. (Brighton, U.K.: Harvester, 1980).

23. Pratt, *Imperial Eyes.*

24. Ibid., 15.

25. Ibid., 29.

26. Ibid.

27. Ibid., 57.

28. Edward Said mentions only one women traveler in his account in *Orientalism,* and P. Fussell states that he does not mention women travelers since their writing is second-rate. In Pratt's *Imperial Eyes* a separate chapter is devoted to women travelers, where they are treated as a distinct category of writers.

29. C. Stevenson, *Victorian Women Travel Writers in Africa* (Boston: Twayne, 1982), 160.

30. Pratt, *Imperial Eyes,* 157–159.

31. Ibid., 159.

32. See for discussions D. Fuss, *Essentially Speaking: Feminism, Nature and Difference* (London: Routledge, 1990); J. Butler, *Gender Trouble: Feminism and the Subversion of Identity* (London: Routledge, 1990); and T. Modleski, *Feminism without Women* (London: Routledge, 1991).

33. Cited in Chaudhuri and Strobel, eds., *Western Women and Imperialism*, 4.

34. M. Green, *Dreams of Adventure—Deeds of Empire* (London: Routledge and Kegan Paul, 1980), 23.

35. R. Stott, "The Dark Continent: Africa as Female Body in Haggard's Adventure Fiction," *Feminist Review* 32 (Summer 1989): 69–89.

36. Blake, "A Woman's Trek."

37. Virago has reprinted a large number of 19th- and 20th-century travel texts by women, such as Mary Kingsley, Alexandra David-Neel, and Flora Tristan, but other texts such as those by Nina Mazuchelli and Fanny Parkes have remained out of print. Manchester University Press is soon reissuing these texts in a series entitled *Exploring Travel*.

38. E. M. Kroller, "First Impressions: Rhetorical Strategies in Travel Writing by Victorian Women," *Ariel: Review of International English*, 4 (October 1990): 87–99.

39. Chaudhuri and Strobel, eds., *Western Women and Imperialism*, 2.

40. See S. Mills, *Discourses of Difference* and "Gender and Colonialism."

41. For critical accounts, see Strobel, *European Women and the Second British Empire*, and Mills, *Discourses of Difference*.

42. See, for example, A. Allen, *Travelling Ladies: Victorian Adventuresses* (London: Jupiter, 1980) and S. Foster, *Across New Worlds: Nineteenth Century Women Travellers and Their Writings* (Hemel Hempstead, U.K.: Harvester, 1990).

43. C. Stevenson, "Female Anger and African Politics," *Turn of the Century Women* 2, no. 1 (1985): 7–17, 91.

44. Ibid., 93.

45. Strobel, *European Women and the Second British Empire*, ix–x.

46. Frank cited in Strobel, *European Women and the Second British Empire*, 73.

47. Blake, "A Woman's Trek" and "Travel Literature: The Liberian Narratives of Esther Warner and Graham Greene," *Research in African Literature* 22, no. 2 (1991): 191–203.

48. H. Callan and S. Ardener, *The Incorporated Wife*, (London: Croom Helm, 1984).

49. Strobel, *European Women and the Second British Empire*, xiii.

50. See Mills, *Discourses of Difference*.

51. M. Kingsley, *Travels in West Africa* (1897; reprint, London: Virago, 1982).

52. M. Toone, "An Analysis of the Travel writing of Florence Dixie" (Unpublished dissertation, University of Loughborough, Loughborough, U.K., 1990).

53. H. Callaway and D. Helly, "Crusader for Empire: Flora Shaw/Lady Lugard," in *Western Women and Imperialism*, Chaudhuri and Strobel, eds., 79–97.

54. M. Hatem, "Through Each Others' Eyes: The Impact of Colonial Encounter on the Images of Egyptian, Levantine, Egyptian, and European Women, 1862–1920," in *Western Women and Imperialism*, Chaudhuri and Strobel, eds., 33–58, quote from p. 37.

55. Strobel, *European Women and the Second British Empire*, 51.

56. M. Sinha, "Chathams, Pitts and Gladstones in Petticoats: The Politics of Gender and Race in the Ilbert Bill Controversy," in *Western Women and Imperialism*, Chaudhuri and Strobel, eds., 198–116, quote from p. 110.

57. See S. Mills, "A Foucauldian Perspective on Fictionality and Literariness

in Travel Writing" (Ph.D. diss., University of Birmingham, Birmingham, U.K., 1988).

58. F. Parkes, *Wanderings of a Pilgrim in Search of the Picturesque* (London: Pelham Richardson, 1850).

59. Ibid., 356.

60. Ibid., 26.

61. Ibid., 140.

62. Ibid., 62.

63. Ibid., 63.

64. Ibid., 165.

65. Ibid., 383.

66. Ibid., 90.

67. Ibid., 28.

68. Ibid., 195.

69. Ibid., 246.

70. Ibid., 167.

71. Ibid., 178.

72. Ibid., 118.

3

Mapping Authorship and Authority: Reading Mary Kingsley's Landscape Descriptions

ALISON BLUNT

Two months before the publication of her first book, *Travels in West Africa,* in 1897,[1] Mary Kingsley wrote to George Macmillan about including a map:

> It[']s not a question of where *I* have been – or rather where I say I have been [–] so much as a map to show the geographical facts I have stated. Remember, I have said I will not draw my line on it.[2]

Authority seems inseparable from authorship because where Mary Kingsley *says* she has been is more important than where she *has* been. For Mary Kingsley, the primary role of a map was to convey "the geographical facts." These seem to acquire status beyond her authorship, but both despite and because of this produce and reproduce her own authoritative status. Furthermore, the quotation suggests that instead of using a map to legitimate her account, Mary Kingsley was anxious that a map could potentially undermine her authority. In light of this, I will focus on colonial mapping in terms of mapping a linear route.[3] I will examine *Travels in West Africa* to address questions of authorship and authority of and within the text. I will then discuss Mary Kingsley's landscape descriptions to illustrate her textual rather than linear mapping strategies.

On one level, Mary Kingsley's reluctance to map her route seems symptomatic of her tenuous identification as similar to, but different from, male explorers. On another level, it raises questions about mapping travel more broadly. More complex and reflexive than mapping a route might imply, travel can instead be seen as comprised of departure, journey, and return, revealing as much about constructions of "home" as "away." In addition, the journey itself can be seen to blur dwelling and moving over space and time. Mary Kingsley preferred to map landscapes and her position within them in a textual rather than a linear manner. I will discuss her landscape descriptions and interpretations of them to address the inherently spatial ambivalence of her identity as a white woman traveling in the context of imperialism.

I hope to critique linear mapping in three interrelated ways. On a substantive level, I will discuss Mary Kingsley's preference for textual and metaphorical rather than linear, literal mapping. Next I will address what this reveals about subject positionality. This task seems inseparable from epistemological attempts to map Mary Kingsley and other women travel writers. Finally, both of these goals seem to relate to travel itself which exceeds the linearity of mapping a route in metaphorical as well as material ways.

Travel and travel writing were influential in reproducing imperial ideologies of difference.[4] The experiences of individual travelers can be likened to – but not simply assimilated to – imperial power more generally because "they both assert authority over and depend upon the people they encounter. Their narrative representations . . . constitute models for the national relation between Self and Other that is empire."[5] Such representations should, however, be seen as more complex and ambivalent than fixed. For example, a recurrent theme in the study of imperial travel writing has been "the author's multiple persona, which allows him or her to be both accomplice in, and critic of, the business of imperialism."[6] I want to focus on the implications of such positioning for a white British woman traveling in late-19th-century West Africa.

AUTHORIAL AUTHORITY

Imperial expansion provided unprecedented opportunities for white, and at least middle-class, women to travel, with motives including wifely duty to husbands who were officers or officials, missionary zeal, the desire for adventure, and professional interests such as scientific research.[7] By the late 19th century, many women were well known for their travels, largely through their popular writings. Mary Kingsley made two journeys to West Africa in the 1890s, and became a public figure on her return to Britain because of her two books and numerous articles, her lectures, and her vociferous support of the Liverpool trading lobby.[8] Her travels have been cited in most recent accounts of women travel writers. These have included anthologies and bibliographies[9]; descriptive, and often primarily anecdotal accounts, celebrating intrepid, eccentric individuals[10]; attempts to map women travelers onto histories of geography[11]; and, finally, more critical studies exploring notions of gendered subjectivity, imperialism, and the textualization of difference in travel writing.[12] Such interest illustrates the tensions between attempts to write the often unwritten histories of women and the recognition of such histories as discursively rather than individually sited. Mary Kingsley's concern about publishing a map reflected her desire to legitimate herself and her travels, but it is important to go beyond her immediate concern to discern the conditions and constraints shaping legitimation itself.

Poststructuralist insights about textuality replace a humanist celebration of an individual subject with a more discursive and complex engagement with subjectivity itself. According to Roland Barthes, multiple interpretations of a text should be unconstrained by attempts to reveal a single meaning intended by the author:

> As institution, the author is dead: his civil status, his biographical person have disappeared; dispossessed, they no longer exercise over his work the formidable paternity whose account literary history, teaching and public opinion had the responsibility of establishing and renewing.[13]

For Michel Foucault, notions of authorship reflect the critical *"individualization* in the history of ideas, knowledge, literature, philosophy, and the sciences"[14] whereby the figure of the author came to be perceived as existing before and beyond the text. This conspicuous absence from the text was produced by and itself reproduced a position of privileged distance. Foucault has written that the "author-function" reflects the discursive formations pertaining to authenticity and authority. He has further argued that the author-function split from the 18th century onwards when scientific discourse began to legitimize anonymity in the quest for "truth" while literary discourse began to stress the importance of the author to an unprecedented degree.[15] Travel writing seems distinctive in light of this claim because its content and much of its rhetorical apparatus seems to bridge this divide between science and literature, and because the author as narrator is also the traveler.

It is important to destabilize perceptions of a unity of meaning away from an authoritative authorial presence. However, as long as subjectivity continues to be constructed along lines of difference, and as long as power is exercised by defining, legitimating, and exploiting such differences, it does continue – despite Foucault's projection – to matter who is speaking and/or writing. For example – to highlight one element among many constructions of difference – authorial subjectivity can be seen as gendered because the conditions under which men and women write are materially different, the social construction of gender affects how the writings of men and women are read, and the interpretations of texts are influenced by the gender consciousness of individual readers. As Cheryl Walker notes,

> what we need, instead of a theory of the death of the author, is a new concept of authorship that does not naively assert that the writer is an originating genius, creating aesthetic objects outside of history, but does not diminish the importance of difference and agency in the responses of [marginalized groups such as] women writers to historical formations.[16]

It seems more useful to think in terms of *author positionality* to reveal the different sites at which identities are constructed and contested through space and time. This method corresponds to that of Lisa Lowe in her work on the complex and often contradictory sites and meanings of orientalist discourses. She writes that

> discursively constructed positions of otherness are neither fixed nor continuous. Representations of difference and otherness are multivalent, signifying distinct meanings within particular contexts.[17]

Mary Kingsley wrote at "home" and the many published reviews of her books suggest that her gender was the most significant element of her authorship. However, this was inseparable from her authority to travel, which was grounded in constructions of racial superiority in the context of imperialism. I will discuss the spatial ambivalence of such constructions with reference to Mary Kingsley's first book, *Travels in West Africa*. The inseparability of authorship and authority can be seen in two different ways, namely, *of* and *within* the text. In the former case, I will outline the material production of *Travels in West Africa* and reviews of it that assessed the femininity of Mary Kingsley's authorship. In the latter case, I will turn to the plurality of voices adopted within the text itself and the spatiality of their articulation.

AUTHORSHIP AND AUTHORITY
OF *TRAVELS IN WEST AFRICA*

Travel writing can be seen as ordered in a dualistic way between narration and description, with the former first and most important, and the latter second and subordinate. However, by the late 19th century, these two features were often equally important; indeed, travel was often recorded in two separate volumes that reflect this dualism.[18] For Mary Kingsley, *Travels in West Africa* was a largely descriptive narrative about her second journey, appealing to a popular audience, while *West African Studies,*[19] published two years later in 1899, developed her political proposals and presented her research, particularly on fetish. Reviews of *Travels in West Africa* focused on the novelty of a woman traveler, while reviews of *West African Studies* focused on the book's style and content. In the former case, for example, the *Scottish Geographical Magazine* stated,

> This book is quite a new departure in African literature, and, after reading it, one is not surprised at its popularity and extensive sale, for such a sprightly, interesting, vivid, and in some respects audacious, account of travels in Africa, it has never been our lot to read—and the author a lady![20]

Prior to departure, the codes of conduct for women travelers primarily related to appearance and behavior in the face of potential dangers.[21] After stating that "female curiosity apparently has no limits," the *New York Times* characterized Mary Kingsley as conforming to feminine standards:

> The lady for hard work . . . has no liking for bloomers or any masculine garb, but the highest opinion of the advantages of petticoats.[22]

In the following review, Mary Kingsley's femininity in the face of adversity is established by her appearance and emotions:

> Civilisation clung more or less to her skirts at Cape Coast and other settlements; and it was with relief that Miss Kingsley reembarked to fall in love with the wild beauty of Fernando Po, and to explore the Ogowé, a mighty stream watering Congo Français.[23]

For this reviewer to describe the "Ogowé"[24] as "a mighty stream" and for another reviewer to refer to Mary Kingsley's journey as "her walk"[25] minimized her achievements compared with a more masculine tradition of exploration.

To locate a feminine subject in dangerous situations has the potential both to undermine and to reinforce such constructions according to the tone adopted and the behavior depicted. In the following extract from a review of *Travels in West Africa,* the reviewer's amused tone downplays the dangers encountered, suggesting that Kingsley was an eccentric subject who lacked the control and bravery that might be expected from white men establishing imperial power and authority:

> It is not possible to follow the adventurous author through all her perilous situations, and readers must go to the book itself to see how she warded off the attack of a crocodile, tumbled into the water out of a canoe, escaped many other dangers, and was extricated from several awkward predicaments.[26]

The reviewer conveys the idea that rather than displaying the physical, administrative, or intellectual skill of male explorers, Mary Kingsley overcame danger through more behavioral virtues whereby she

> carried a merry heart with her, and the success of this good medicine is shown by the way in which she escaped serious consequences in the course of her extended travels through the most unhealthy parts of Africa.[27]

Travels in West Africa was published in January 1897; by June five editions were in circulation, including an abridged version designed for a wider audience.[28] As early as December 1894, her publisher George Macmillan complained that her voice was masculine in tone, to which Mary Kingsley indignantly replied:

> I do not understand what you mean by "the story being told by a man." Where have I said it was?[29]

In the same letter questions of gendered identity and authorship arose in terms of how she would be named:

> Of course I would rather not publish it under my own name, and I really cannot draw the trail of a petticoat over the Coast of all places – neither can I have a picture of myself in trousers or any other excitement of that sort added. I went out there as a naturalist not as a sort of circus, but if you would like my name, will it not be sufficient to put M. H. Kingsley? – it does not matter to the general public what I am as long as I tell them the truth as well as I can.[30]

However, gendered authorship is one site to locate the discourses of power/knowledge in constructing and constraining authoritative claims to be telling "the truth."

Mary Kingsley based *Travels in West Africa* on diaries and letters she wrote to friends. This method reveals different sites of authorship whereby she wrote about West Africa while in Britain but used her own writings from West Africa as source material. Such personal sources are made more explicitly known in travel writing by women than by men,[31] paradoxically reinforcing notions of an individual author, while at the same time, by highlighting personal, and potentially more emotional contexts, undermining the authority of that author as a supposedly neutral observer.

The influence of individuals besides the author in the production of a text also qualifies notions of authority. *Travels in West Africa* was edited by Henry Guillemard, who had been appointed the first lecturer in geography at Cambridge University in 1888.[32] However, Mary Kingsley denied this level of involvement in her preface; after acknowledging his help she wrote that he

> has not edited it, or of course the whole thing would have been better, but . . . has most kindly gone through the proof sheets, lassoing prepositions which were straying outside their sentence stockade, taking my eye off the water cask and fixing it on the scenery where I wanted it to be, saying firmly in pencil on margins "No you don't," where I committed some more than usually heinous literary crime, and so on. In cases where his activities in these things may seem to the reader to have been wanting, I beg to state that they really were not. It is I who have declined to ascend to a higher level of lucidity and correctness of diction than I am fitted for.[33]

At the same time she adopts this self-effacing tone, Mary Kingsley clearly establishes her individual identity and authority. However in her correspondence with Macmillan her frustration with Guillemard is obvious, suggesting that such a public voice of authority was privately contested. For example, in August 1896 she wrote,

> I would rather take a 200 ton vessel up a creek than write any book . . . [that incorporate Guillemard's corrections, which] make the thing read easier and more patronising and presuming – "appalling" for simply awful – "dwelling" for house [–] "terminals" for ends – "informed us that" for he said and so on.[34]

AUTHORSHIP AND AUTHORITY
WITHIN *TRAVELS IN WEST AFRICA*

Within the text itself, the plurality of voices undermine perceptions of any fixed and stable authorship and authority. Such conventionally mas-

culine roles as scientific observer, explorer, and trader coexist with a more
feminine self-consciousness about appearance and behavior. Such ambiguities of gendered subjectivity can be seen to arise from the temporary license
granted to behave in ways constructed as masculine while traveling but
in many ways remaining constrained by acceptable feminine conduct. Mary
Kingsley's use of humor and irony is particularly significant in destabiliz-
ing any fixed authority for herself as both narrator and traveler.

Cheryl Walker's work on "persona criticism" reclaims authorship in
multiple, intertextual ways and represents "an attempt to connect what
is peculiar in a writer's work to what is shared with others."[35] A persona
is like a mask rather than a monolithic authorial position. Authorship is
comprised of complex and sometimes contradictory meanings beyond fixed
biography. However, such meanings are multiple within a text so that
different personae can be interpreted. For example, Mary Kingsley prioritized three personae in different ways over the course of her travels. These
personae reveal her shifting identities over space and time and illustrate
the inseparable moments of departure, journey, and return comprising travel
as well as the blurring of dwelling and moving on the journey itself. In
this way, positionality makes a journey specifically and travel generally
more complex and ambivalent than mapping a linear route would imply.

To provide a legitimate motive for her journey, Mary Kingsley identified herself as a scientific observer prior to her departure. By the time
of her second journey, she was equipped with a collector's outfit from
the British Museum and claimed that she was traveling to study "fish
and fetish." She returned home with sixty-five species of fish and eigh-
teen species of reptile; indeed three new species of fish were named after
her.[36] While traveling, her most vigorous collecting of fish took place
around Calabar, suggesting her desire for, and scientific legitimation of,
solitary excursions away from the colonial society of this administrative
center.[37] When writing about her scientific status, however, her plurality of voices reveals the ambiguities and self-consciousness of being a woman
within a conventionally male sphere of activity. Most often, irony paro-
died her position as an individual observer as when, for example, she
described a gorilla:

> The old male rose to his full height (it struck me at the time this was a matter
> of ten feet at least, but for scientific purposes allowance must be made for
> a lady's emotions).[38]

When writing about her travels, Mary Kingsley attempted to locate
herself within the masculine tradition of exploration to gain spatial and

behavioral freedoms away from the constraints of femininity. However, clear tensions existed between wanting to be perceived as an explorer while seeking her own form of self-definition.[39] To align herself with Burton, Stanley, Du Chaillu, and De Brazza was to identify with a dated tradition because explorers had, by the 1890s, been largely replaced by imperial administrators and, in the case of West Africa, by traders. Mary Kingsley referred to the relative length of explorations, writing:

> The "arm-chair explorer" may be impressed by the greatness of length of the red line route of an explorer; but the person locally acquainted with the region may know that some of those red lines are very easily made in Africa . . . In other regions a small red line means four hundred times the work and danger, and requires four thousand times the pluck, perseverance and tact. These regions we may call choice spots.[40]

This passage seems defensive in tone, but implies Mary Kingsley's authority as someone who *was* locally acquainted with Africa. She proceeded to advocate the imperialist agenda of exploration whereby the explorer "who makes his long red line pass through great regions of choice spots" and

> attains power over their natives, and retains it, welding the districts into a whole, making the flag of his country respected and feared therein . . . is a very great man indeed.[41]

Mary Kingsley's emphasis on experiential authority, particularly the endurance of hardship, indicates the inadequacy of mapping a linear route. On one level, this relates to her own experiences of travel where she stressed "choice spots" rather than the quantifiable length of her journeys. On another level, travel clearly exceeds a linear route that can be measured and mapped.

On her travels, Mary Kingsley was the first European to cross from the Ogowé to the Rembwé rivers by the route she followed and the first to ascend Mount Cameroon by its southeast face. These expeditions received the most detailed coverage in *Travels in West Africa* even though, for example, the former trip was less than 100 miles, unlike the transcontinental journeys of some male explorers. In the latter case, she identified herself as "the third English*man* to ascend the Peak and the first to have ascended it from the south-east face,"[42] suggesting that such achievements were meaningful in terms of nationality and race rather than gender difference.

Mary Kingsley financed her travels through trading, but she emphasized her identification with this male sphere more in her political role on her return than when writing about her journeys. She referred to "old coasters and sea captains" as "most excellent people, but supremely human. I am one myself now, so I speak with authority."[43] She valued their paternalism, describing traders as "good-hearted, hospitable English gentlemen, who seem to feel it their duty that no harm they can prevent should happen to anyone."[44] Most of all, she valued the opportunities offered to traders for close contact with African people, saying in a lecture:

> The trading method enables you to sit as an honoured guest at far away inland village fires, it enables you to become the confidential friend of that ever powerful factor in all human societies, the old ladies. It enables you to become an associate of that confraternity of Witch Doctors, things that being surrounded with an expedition of armed men must prevent your doing.[45]

This remark suggests that the perceived authenticity that underpins authority could be more successfully achieved by more individual travels than by large-scale explorations. Furthermore, this illustrates that different sites of travel as well as movement within and between them should be stressed. Such sites correspond to the positionality of travelers both on their journeys and in their writings, which is ignored by mapping a single, linear route.

Mary Kingsley assumed different personae to gain temporary license to behave in ways constructed as masculine to authorize her departure, journey, and political return. This license arose from and reflected her position both inside and outside imperial authority as a white woman, whereby constructions of racial superiority could overcome gender inferiority while traveling. The spatial and temporal discontinuities of Mary Kingsley's self-identification as scientist, explorer, and trader reflect the need to broaden an understanding of travel beyond the journey itself. For Van den Abbeele, travel "has always already begun"[46] because it is bounded by points of departure, destination, and return in an arbitrary and retrospective way. Travel involves the familiarization of the unfamiliar at the same time as the defamiliarization of the familiar. "Home" is defined from "away," and, for travel to have taken place, "home" necessarily changes on the traveler's return – as does the traveler. Mary Kingsley prioritized different authoritative personae in different ways prior to departure, when writing about her journeys, and on her return, reflecting my contention that these are all inseparable moments of travel. Although she portrayed herself within the masculine traditions of science, exploration, and trade, all of these roles were undercut by her self-conscious sense of propriety constructed as feminine. Her strategic identification with such personae illustrates the mobilization of constructions of gender difference over space, but the coexistence of masculine and feminine identities highlights ambivalence rather than fixed, centered constructions of "otherness."

TEXTUAL MAPPING:
MARY KINGSLEY'S LANDSCAPE DESCRIPTIONS

Mary Kingsley's landscape descriptions illustrate her preference for textual and metaphorical rather than literal mapping. In this way, travel exceeds a linear route by relating to positionality as well as movement. Mary Kingsley should neither be mapped at the expense of subject positionality nor positioned at the expense of her movement over space and time. This particularly relates to the tensions of being a woman who could claim potential authority within masculine traditions of exploration.

Mary Kingsley's personal, aesthetic enthusiasm was paramount in her landscape descriptions. The subjectivity of her response paradoxically undermined her claims for authority as an objective observer. She, however, claimed *subjective* authority by stressing the individuality of her response:

> To my taste there is nothing so fascinating as spending a night out in an African forest, or plantation; but I beg you to note I do not advise any one to follow the practice. Nor indeed do I recommend African forest life to any one. Unless you are interested in it and fall under its charm, it is the most awful life in death imaginable. It is like being shut up in a library whose books you cannot read, all the while tormented, terrified, and bored. And if you do fall under its spell, it takes all the colour out of other kinds of living.[47]

The landscape seems to possess magical qualities, accessible only to certain "interested" individuals, and seems to exercise power over those individuals rather than submit to their control.

Mary Kingsley located herself emotionally as well as spatially in West Africa, writing, for example, that "I am more comfortable there than in England."[48] Within West Africa, she felt more comfortable traveling through the bush rather than living fixed in settlements, stating that "I dislike West Coast towns as a general rule."[49] She pictured herself becoming part of the landscape in her aesthetic response to it, suggesting that her textual mapping was a potential way of overcoming the distance imposed by literal mapping. For example, when describing the rapids on the Ogowé River, she wrote:

Do not imagine it gave rise in what I am pleased to call my mind, to those complicated, poetical reflections natural beauty seems to bring out in other people's minds. It never works that way with me; I just lose all sense of human individuality, all memory of human life, with its grief and worry and doubt, and become part of the atmosphere. If I have a heaven, that will be mine.[50]

Such personal identification seems contrary to imperial strategies epitomized by the "monarch-of-all-I-survey" genre of travel writing.[51] The former reveals the subjectivity of an observer located within the landscape, while the latter relates to a panoramic gaze objectifying the landscape through the imperial power and authority of an external observer. The latter privileges vision, while the former includes other sensual responses, as shown by Mary Kingsley's references to sound:

Woe! to the man in Africa who cannot stand perpetual uproar. Few things surprised me more than the rarity of silence and the intensity of it when you did get it.[52]

Rather than establish the landscape as a stage for the exercise of the imperial viewer's power, Mary Kingsley's descriptions of West Africa were more likely to prompt self-questioning. At the end of her second journey, she wrote:

As I sat on the verandah overlooking Victoria and the sea, in the dim soft light of the stars, with the fire-flies round me, and the lights of Victoria way below, and heard the soft rush of the Lukola River, and the sound of the sea-surf on the rocks, and the tom-tomming and singing of the natives, all matching and mingling together, "Why did I come to Africa?" thought I. Why! who would not come to its twin brother hell itself for all the beauty and charm of it.[53]

† For Mary Louise Pratt, the "monarch-of-all-I-survey" genre epitomizes the gendering of travel writing whereby men envisioned themselves as explorers mobilizing the masculine heroic discourse of discovery.[54] She cites Mary Kingsley's writings as the main exception because of her use of irony. This difference seems inherently spatial, with Pratt contrasting her "vast and unexplored mangrove swamps . . . with the gleaming promontories her fellow Victorians sought out."[55] Pratt portrays Mary Kingsley as an eccentric, intrepid explorer and perpetuates stereotypical images of women travelers when she tells of her

discovering her swamps not by looking down at them or even walking around them, but by sloshing zestfully through them in a boat or up to her neck in water and slime, swathed in thick skirts and wearing her boots continuously for weeks on end.[56]

Pratt regards Mary Kingsley's descriptions as feminized in their domesticity. She supports this thesis by describing the boat Mary Kingsley steered down the Rembwé as "a combination [of] bedroom and kitchen" and by characterizing Mary Kingsley as a "domestic goddess."[57] Pratt reinforces notions of Mary Kingsley as an eccentric individual rather than addressing the discursive complexities and ambiguities of gendered subjectivity. For example, Mary Kingsley clearly relished her solitude but this desire for solitude violated codes of appropriate feminine conduct, and her responsibility in steering the boat seems contrary to constructions of feminine passivity, suggesting that traveling gave her the authority to adopt more conventionally masculine behavior.

Mary Kingsley visualized the landscape of the Rembwé by describing:

the great, black, winding river with a pathway in its midst of frosted silver where the moonlight struck it; on each side the ink-black mangrove walls, and above them the band of stars and moonlit heavens that the walls of mangrove allowed one to see.[58]

But such magnificence was only imagined under cover of darkness because "by daylight the Rembwé scenery was certainly not so lovely, and might be slept through without a pang."[59] Her imagination of the landscape differs from the literal and textual strategies of male exploration and domination which depended to a large extent on vision and surveillance.[60]

MATERIAL AND METAPHORICAL SUBJECT POSITIONALITY

The ambivalence of Mary Kingsley's position within imperial discourses of power and authority is clear, but this should be extended to her gendered subjectivity. It is persuasive to locate Mary Kingsley in a "swampy world"[61]—part of but separate from imperialism—but this location reduces the ambivalence of her identity. Mary Kingsley herself used a topographic metaphor to view Africans inhabiting swamps far below the peaks of Western "civilization":

I do not believe that the white race will ever drag the black up their own
particular summit in the mountain range of civilisation . . . alas! for the energetic reformer – the African is not keen on mountaineering in the civilisation
range. He prefers remaining down below and being comfortable. He is not
conceited about this; he admires the higher culture very much, and the people who inconvenience themselves by going in for it – but do it himself? No.
And if he is dragged up into the higher regions of a self-abnegatory religion,
six times in ten he falls back damaged, a morally maimed man, into his old
swampy country fashion valley.[62]

    This quotation raises questions about Mary Kingsley's own position
as a white woman traveling through literally and metaphorically colonized
landscapes. Interpreting such a metaphor also raises questions about
metaphors of travel more generally.[63] Metaphor is inherently spatial in
connecting two seemingly disconnected ideas to illuminate meaning, with
the term itself originating from the Greek word meaning to transfer or
transport. However, both the spatiality of metaphor and the distinctive-
ness of travel are often downplayed.[64] I will outline metaphors of, first,
theory as travel, and, second, travel as theory. With reference to Mary
Kingsley's travels generally and her topographic metaphor more specifically, I will argue that such metaphors should be informed by feminist
spatial imagery and the ambivalence of subject positionality.

    In the case of theory as travel, travel can represent the movement of
ideas and theory away from a point of origin to a new destination, with
their content changing over space and time.[65] In another way, James
Clifford has proposed the use of "travel" as a translation term for comparative cultural studies whereby the blurring between dwelling and traveling is revealed, such that "constructed and disputed *historicities*, sites of
displacement, interference, and interaction, come more sharply into
view."[66] Travel should be seen as diverse, incorporating voluntary but
also forced movement, and experienced differently along lines of race, class,
and gender.[67] Cultural critique oriented around ideas of travel should be
theoretically informed and substantively grounded to avoid "theoretical
tourism on the part of the first world critic, where the margin becomes
a linguistic or cultural vacation, a new poetics of the exotic."[68]

    In the case of travel as theory, the critical distance and perspective of
travel relate to both seeing and knowing. This, however, is rooted in a
distinctly masculine tradition whereby the traveler/theorist is able to move
beyond home rather than be constrained within it.[69] It also relates to the
Enlightenment project of all-encompassing vision through the eyes of an
individual, supposedly rational, viewer, similarly implying a white masculine subject.[70] Travel seems potentially liberating – at least for the white

male traveler/theorist – because of the opportunities for transgression and questioning of ideas formulated at home. However, such transgression is bounded because, in Van den Abbeele's words, "the very understanding of . . . error as 'wandering' implies a topography or a space of wandering."[71] The risks of travel are potentially alienating and include "becoming a foreigner in one's own land in the case of literal travel, [and] becoming a stranger in one's own time in scholarly travel."[72] A feminist critique of the metaphorical significance of travel would highlight gender inequality imposed by patriarchal power and authority. Notions of "home" and "away" should be deconstructed to illustrate unequal male and female access to travel and, by metaphorical extension, to theory.[73] Furthermore, different, distinctively gendered meanings of "home" should be explored.[74] The metaphorical significance of travel should not be isolated from other forms of spatial imagery. Most importantly, travel as metaphor should be seen as inseparable from the spatial imagery of positionality and marginality shaping the ability of people to travel.

Feminist spatial imagery can stimulate a reinterpretation of Mary Kingsley's position as a white woman traveling through colonized landscapes.[75] Returning to her topographical metaphor, Mary Kingsley's consignment of Africans to metaphorical swamps reflects her position of racial superiority in the context of imperialism. Without reference to this metaphor, however, Mary Louise Pratt locates Mary Kingsley in more literal swamps to emphasize her gendered identity. Her position as a white woman traveling in the context of imperialism seems inherently ambivalent, and this in turn seems essentially spatial in literal and metaphorical ways.

The spatiality of ambivalent subjectivity should not, however, be confined to literal and metaphorical swamps. For example, Mary Kingsley's ascent of Mount Cameroon potentially implicates her in masculine and imperial discourses, but, by ambivalently doing so, reveals the complexities and contradictions of her place within such discourses. She locates herself outside the masculine endeavor of mountaineering, stating that "verily I am no mountaineer,"[76] but admires and likens its dangers to those of her own travels:

My most favourite form of literature . . . is accounts of mountaineering exploits . . . as long as the writer will walk along the edge of a precipice with a sheer fall of thousands of feet on one side and a sheer wall on the other; or better still crawl up an *arête* with a precipice on either. Nothing on earth would persuade me to do either of these things myself, but they remind me of bits of country I have been through where you walk a narrow line of security with gulfs of murder looming on each side, and where in exactly the same way you are as safe as if you were in your easy chair at home, as long as you get sufficient holding ground: not on rock in the bush village inhabited by murderous cannibals, but on ideas in those men's and women's minds; and these ideas . . . give you safety.[77]

Just as mountaineering skills can overcome the dangers of the natural world, so, for Mary Kingsley, her intellectual skills could overcome the dangers of the human world, and she presents both as textually gripping for an audience at home.

Despite her lack of identification with mountaineers, Mary Kingsley did climb Mount Cameroon during her second journey in West Africa. From her earliest sightings of Mount Cameroon, Mary Kingsley both identified with and distanced herself from a masculine tradition of exploration:

> Now it is none of my business to go up mountains. There's next to no fish on them in West Africa, and precious little good rank fetish, as the population on them is sparse – the African, like myself, abhorring cool air. Nevertheless, I feel quite sure that no white man has ever looked on the great Peak of Cameroon without a desire arising in his mind to ascend it.[78]

If the panoramic vision achieved by mountaineering epitomizes the "monarch-of-all-I-survey" genre of travel writing, Mary Kingsley's contradictory position in terms of constructions of race and gender can be discerned. Even though she perceives such temptation to climb Mount Cameroon as universal for colonizing men, Mary Kingsley stresses her individuality and authority by ironically characterizing her weakness in succumbing to it:

> Do not . . . imagine that the ascent is a common incident in a coaster's life; far from it. The coaster as a rule resists the temptation of Mungo [Mah Lobeh, or Mount Cameroon] firmly, being stronger than I am; moreover, he is busy and only too often fever-stricken in the bargain. But I am the exception, I own.[79]

Mary Kingsley's account of her ascent illustrates the ambiguities of being constructed as both "inside" and "outside" and moving between patriarchal and imperial discourses. Her description of her ascent lacks the lively enthusiasm and good humor of the rest of *Travels in West Africa*. For example, her ability to identify with the masculine, imperial trope of panoramic vision is undermined when her view is obscured by mist. Furthermore, this obscured vision seems to enhance the natural beauty of the scene in her eyes, as she perceives it in aesthetic rather than strategic terms:

The white, gauze-like mist comes down from the upper mountain towards us: creeping, twining round, and streaming through the moss-covered tree columns. . . . Soon . . . all the mist streams coalesce and make the atmosphere all their own, wrapping us round in a clammy, chill embrace; it is not that wool-blanket, smothering affair that we were wrapped in down by Buana, but exquisitely delicate. The difference it makes to the beauty of the forest is just the same difference you would get if you put a delicate veil over a pretty woman's face or a sack over her head. In fact, the mist here was exceedingly becoming to the forest's beauty.[80]

It is particularly interesting that Mary Kingsley here employs an objectifying, masculine metaphor. The landscape is feminized but its attraction lies in veiling rather than unveiling. From the peak, however, Mary Kingsley's view is fully obscured by thicker, less aesthetically appealing mist. This symbolically reflects her own position as attempting but unable fully to achieve masculine and imperial vision:

There is in me no exultation, but only a deep disgust because the weather has robbed me of my main object in coming here, namely to get a good view.[81]

Mary Kingsley's ascent of Mount Cameroon ironically and ambivalently locates her both inside and outside a masculine, imperialist tradition of exploration, conquest, and surveillance, illustrating the complexities and contradictions of subject positionality.

Mary Kingsley's vulnerability to weather conditions illustrates her immediate, literal, and textual presence in the landscape, unlike the distance and control implied by linear mapping of a route. This symbolically reflects her ambivalent position as a white woman traveling in the context of masculine, imperial discourses. Rather than counter Mary Louise Pratt's siting of Mary Kingsley in swamps by simply describing her on a mountain, I hope that by stressing the spatiality of ambivalent subject positionality, fixity and movement are kept in tension instead of in isolation.

CONCLUSIONS

Mary Kingsley's landscape descriptions relate to the significance of mapping authorship and authority on three inseparable levels. On a substantive level, they illustrate her preference for textual and metaphorical rather than literal mapping. The ambivalence of her subject positionality as a white woman traveling in the context of imperialism seems inherently spatial. The textual plurality of voices, and her use of irony and humor, relate to her adoption of different personae and their prioritization over space and time. Such strategic identification reflects Mary Kingsley's perceived need to legitimate authority within male spheres of activity while retaining feminine codes of conduct. Overall, such tensions reflect the decentering of authorship away from a singular, unified whole toward discontinuous author positionality.

This substantive level is inseparable from authoritative claims to be able to map Mary Kingsley and other women travel writers in epistemological terms. It is insufficient either to map Mary Kingsley in a single, linear way or to confine her to specific locations. Rather, the tensions between these alternative mapping strategies can expose the tensions between movement and fixity that characterize travel and travel writing. In addition, such tensions also relate to writing histories of women. Instead of celebrating individual subjects, it is more helpful to address constructions of subjectivity. More specifically, to refer to subject positionality highlights the inherent spatiality of such constructions, which are ambivalent rather than fixed over space and time.

Finally, travel itself exceeds the linearity of mapping a route in metaphorical as well as material ways. Travel is shaped by departure, journey, and return, and blurs movement and dwelling. In this way, travel is as much about constructions of "home" as "away." This is materially significant for travel writing because it is generally written from the distance of "home" for an audience at "home." Mary Kingsley's concern about publishing a map and her refusal to map her route illustrate her vulnerability in establishing authority for her travels and writing. She instead claimed authority by adopting different personae in her travel writing. Her landscape descriptions illustrate her tenuous position as similar to, yet different from, an exploratory tradition constructed as masculine. Rather than impose a singular, linear map, researchers should recognize the ambivalence of women travel writers positioned both inside and outside imperial power and authority, and therefore adopt multiple, textual, and/or metaphorical mapping strategies.

For Mary Kingsley, authorship was important at "home" and related most often to questions of gender identity. However, the ability both to travel and to write about travel required authority which, for a white woman traveling in the context of imperialism, was primarily grounded in constructions of racial difference. This dichotomy should be deconstructed to reveal the inherently spatial ambivalence of subject positionality both between "home" and "away" and between dwelling and traveling on the journey itself.

ACKNOWLEDGMENTS

I am grateful to Robyn Dowling, Derek Gregory, and Anna Skeels for their helpful comments on this chapter.

NOTES

1. Mary Kingsley, *Travels in West Africa: Congo Francais, Corisco and Cameroons* (London: Macmillan, 1897). This has been most recently reprinted in 1986 by Virago Press, London; all page references are to this edition.

2. Mary Kingsley to George Macmillan, November 25, 1896. These letters are part of Macmillan Archive 54914 at the British Library. Mary Kingsley's concern about a map arose from her desire to be distanced from the inaccurate names and spelling of already published maps that might make her vulnerable to criticism from "aged blind armchair geographers" (Mary Kingsley to George Macmillan, January 2, 1896.) Despite her concerns a map was included in *Travels in West Africa.*

3. See Chapter 1 of this volume for a more detailed discussion of colonial mapping strategies.

4. Sara Mills, *Discourses of Difference: An Analysis of Women's Travel Writing and Colonialism* (London: Routledge, 1991). Sara Mills emphasizes the spatiality of discourses of difference, as discussed in Chapter 1 of this volume. Also see Sara Mills's chapter in this volume.

5. Susan Blake, "A Woman's Trek: What Difference Does Gender Make?," *Women's Studies International Forum 13,* no. 4 (1990): 347–355, quote from p. 348.

6. Eva-Marie Kröller, "First Impressions: Rhetorical Strategies in Travel Writing by Victorian Women," *Ariel 21,* no. 4 (1990): 87–99, quote from p. 87.

7. Jane Robinson, *Wayward Women: A Guide to Women Travellers* (Oxford: Oxford University Press, 1990).

8. See Alison Blunt, *Travel, Gender, and Imperialism: Mary Kingsley and West Africa* (New York: Guilford Press, 1994), for further discussion.

9. See, for example, Leo Hamalian, *Ladies on the Loose* (New York: Dodd, Mead and Co., 1981); Robinson, *Wayward Women;* and Marion Tinling, *Women into the Unknown: A Sourcebook of Women Explorers and Travellers* (New York: Greenwood Press, 1989).

10. Including Alexandra Allen, *Travelling Ladies* (London: Jupiter Books, 1980); Dorothy Middleton, *Victorian Lady Travellers* (London: Routledge and Kegan Paul, 1965); Mary Russell, *The Blessings of a Good Thick Skirt: Women Travellers and Their World* (London: Collins, 1988); and Catherine Stevenson, *Victorian Women Travel Writers in Africa* (Boston: Twayne, 1982).

11. Dorothy Middleton, "Some Victorian Lady Travellers," *Geographical Journal 139* (1973): 65–75. For more recent interest, see Mona Domosh, "Toward a Feminist Historiography of Geography," *Transactions of the Institute of British*

Geographers, n.s., *16* (1991): 95–104; the reply to this article, by David Stoddart, in the same journal, "Do We Need a Feminist Historiography of Geography– And if We Do, What Should It Be?," 484–487; and, finally, also in the same journal, Mona Domosh, "Beyond the Frontiers of Geographical Knowledge," 488–490.

12. See, for example, Dea Birkett, *Spinsters Abroad: Victorian Lady Explorers* (Oxford: Basil Blackwell, 1989); Blake, "A Women's Trek"; Blunt, *Travel, Gender, and Imperialism;* Kröller, "First Impressions"; Sara Mills, "Discourses of Difference," *Cultural Studies 4,* no. 2 (1990): 128–140; and Mills, *Discourses of Difference.*

13. Roland Barthes, *The Pleasure of the Text,* R. Miller, trans. (New York: Hill and Wang, 1975), 27.

14. Michel Foucault, "What Is an Author?," in *Textual Strategies: Perspectives in Post-Structuralist Criticism,* Josue V. Harari, ed. (Ithaca, NY: Cornell University Press, 1979), 141–160, quote from p. 141.

15. Ibid.

16. Cheryl Walker, "Feminist Literary Criticism and the Author," *Critical Inquiry 16,* no. 3 (1990): 551–571, quote from p. 560.

17. Lisa Lowe, *Critical Terrains: French and British Orientalisms* (Ithaca, NY: Cornell University Press, 1991).

18. Mary Louise Pratt, "Fieldwork in Common Places," in *Writing Culture: The Poetics and Politics of Ethnography,* James Clifford and George Marcus, eds. (Berkeley: University of California Press, 1986), 27–50.

19. Mary Kingsley, *West African Studies* (London: Macmillan, 1899).

20. *Scottish Geographical Magazine 13,* no. 4 (April 1897): 215–217.

21. Lilias Campbell Davidson, *Hints to Lady Travellers at Home and Abroad* (London: Illife and Son, 1889). This alphabetical guide from "accidents" to "yachting" includes ninety-one entries, ranging from "etiquette" to more starkly material concerns such as "teapots" and "wedges for doors." Overall, this text attempted to inform women how to maintain respectability while violating the codes of society by traveling beyond the domestic sphere. For an overview of conduct literature, see Nancy Armstrong and Leonard Tennenhouse, eds., *The Ideology of Conduct: Essays in Literature and the History of Sexuality* (New York: Methuen, 1987).

22. *New York Times,* February 13, 1897.

23. *Illustrated London News,* February 6, 1897.

24. I am using Mary Kingsley's spelling for what are now the Ogooué and Remboué rivers.

25. *Morning Post,* January 14, 1897.

26. *Morning Post,* January 21, 1897.

27. *Geographical Journal,* March 9, 1897, p. 324.

28. Both of Mary Kingsley's books are very long; including appendices, *Travels in West Africa* has more than 700 pages and *West African Studies* has more than 600 pages.

29. Mary Kingsley to George Macmillan, December 18, 1894.

30. Mary Kingsley to George Macmillan, December 18, 1894.

31. Stevenson, *Victorian Women.*

32. D. R. Stoddart, *On Geography and Its History* (Oxford: Basil Blackwell, 1986). Stoddart writes that Guillemard was a naturalist who wrote an account of his travels in, among other places, Japan, New Guinea, and Borneo from 1882 to 1884. He resigned his lectureship after only six months, writing later that this was due to failing health, poor teaching equipment, and the lack of a lecture room.

33. Kingsley, *Travels in West Africa,* xx.

34. Mary Kingsley to George Macmillan, August 20, 1896.

35. Cheryl Walker, "Persona Criticism and the Death of the Author," in *Contesting the Subject: Essays in the Postmodern Theory and Practice of Biography and Biographical Criticism,* William H. Epstein, ed. (West Lafayette, IN: Purdue University Press, 1991), 118.

36. Katherine Frank, *A Voyager Out: The Life of Mary Kingsley* (Boston: Houghton Mifflin, 1986).

37. Dea Birkett, "An Independent Woman in West Africa: The Case of Mary Kingsley" (Ph.D. diss, University of London, 1987). Also see Dea Birkett, *Mary Kingsley: Imperial Adventuress* (London: Macmillan, 1992).

38. *Travels in West Africa,* 268.

39. Birkett, *An Independent Woman.*

40. *Travels in West Africa,* 353.

41. Ibid., 353.

42. Ibid., 550; italics added.

43. Ibid., 514.

44. Kingsley, *West African Studies,* 13.

45. "A Lecture on West Africa" by Miss Mary Kingsley in *Cheltenham Ladies College Magazine* 38 (Autumn 1898): 264–280, quote from p. 267.

46. Georges Van den Abbeele, *Travel as Metaphor: From Montaigne to Rousseau* (Minneapolis, MN: University of Minneapolis Press, 1992), xvii and 1.

47. Kingsley, *Travels in West Africa,* 102.

48. Ibid., xxi.

49. Ibid., 347.

50. Ibid., 177.

51. Mary Louise Pratt, *Imperial Eyes: Travel Writing and Transculturation* (London: Routledge, 1992).

52. Kingsley, *West African Studies,* 62.

53. Kingsley, *Travels in West Africa,* 608.

54. Pratt, *Imperial Eyes.*

55. Ibid., 213.

56. Ibid.

57. Ibid., 214.

58. Kingsley, *Travels in West Africa,* 338.

59. Ibid.

60. See Chapter 1 in this volume for further discussion of the importance of vision and visibility to imperial power and authority.

61. Kingsley, *Travels in West Africa,* 108.

62. Ibid., 680.

63. See Janet Wolff, "On the Road Again: Metaphors of Travel in Cultural Criticism," *Cultural Studies* 7 (1993): 224–239, for an introduction to such metaphors.

64. As by Wolff, who seems, I think, to be discussing mobility generally rather than travel specifically.

65. Edward Said, *The World, the Text, and the Critic* (Cambridge, MA: Harvard Unversity Press, 1983), 11.

66. James Clifford, "Traveling Cultures," in *Cultural Studies*, Lawrence Grossberg, Cary Nelson, and Paula A. Treichler, eds. (London: Routledge, 1992), 96–116.

67. See, for example, bell hooks's critique of Clifford in which she states: "From certain standpoints, to travel is to encounter the terrorizing force of white supremacy"; bell hooks, "Representing Whiteness in the Black Imagination," in *Cultural Studies*, Grossberg, Nelson, and Treichler, eds., 338–346, quote from p. 344.

68. Caren Kaplan, "Deterritorializations: The Rewriting of Home and Exile in Western Feminist Discourses," *Cultural Critique 6* (Spring 1987): 187–198, quote from p. 191.

69. Meaghan Morris, "At Henry Parkes Motel," *Cultural Studies 2*, no. 1 (1988): 1–16, 29–47.

70. Van den Abbeele, *Travel as Metaphor;* also see Genevieve Lloyd, *The Man of Reason: "Male" and "Female" in Western Philosophy* (London: Methuen, 1984).

71. Van den Abbeele, *Travel as Metaphor*, 47.

72. Ibid., 50.

73. It is also important to note the wide currency of a sense of "home" and "homelessness" in postcolonial criticism. See, for example, Homi Bhabha, "The World and the Home," *Social Text 31–32* (1992): 141–153; Paul Carter, *Living in a New Country: History, Travelling and Language* (London: Faber and Faber, 1992); Rosemary Marangoly George, "Traveling Light: Of Immigration, Invisible Suitcases, and Gunny Sacks," *Differences, 4*, no. 2 (1992): 72–99; and Edward W. Said, *Culture and Imperialism* (New York: Alfred A. Knopf, 1993).

74. As shown by Minnie Bruce Pratt's account of her different "homes" in space and time, as discussed in Chapter 1 of this volume.

75. For an overview, see Geraldine Pratt, "Commentary: Spatial Metaphors and Speaking Positions," *Environment and Planning D: Society and Space 10* (1992): 241–244. She identifies three sets of spatial metaphors in current use: those drawing on the rhetoric of mobility, those emphasizing marginality and exile, and those representing the borderland as a place.

76. Kingsley, *Travels in West Africa*, 594.

77. Ibid., 329.

78. Ibid., 549.

79. Ibid., 550.

80. Ibid., 570.

81. Ibid., 594.

4

Encounters with West African Women: Textual Representations of Difference by White Women Abroad

CHERYL McEWAN

During the 19th century West Africa was often imagined by Europeans as the antithesis of Europe.[1] It was the most nefarious corner of the "Dark Continent," a place of violence, where human life was cheap and immorality rife. An extreme climate and a harsh physical environment ensured that the area was colored the deepest black on maps of the geography of disease; its dense forests were impenetrable and mysterious. Its "chaos" and "savagery" contrasted with the "order" and "civilization" of Europe. It was the focus of European and indigenous slave trading. West Africans were believed to be steeped in cannibalism, human sacrifice, infant marriage, and polygamy. These images of West Africa were promoted not only in travelogues, missionary literature, and popular novels, but also in scientific debates. For example, James Hunt's polygenist belief that Africans were a separate species created a split in the Ethnological Society and led to the establishment of the Anthropological Society in 1863. Thomas Henry Huxley's *Man's Place in Nature* (1863) suggested that Africans were the "missing link" between the anthropoid apes and civilized (white) "man" kind. In *The Origin of Civilisation* (1870), John Lubbock argued that Africans did not represent the starting point of social evolution, but were below that starting point.[2] Scientific debates, along with accounts from explorers and missionaries, ensured that Africa was perceived as the "dark continent" and Africans as "savages."

Such images were usually constructed through the gender relations that were central to imperial discourse. Their narratives contained conscious and unconscious motives for imperialism; savagery was constructed as inherent in the landscapes and societies of West Africa, and provided justification for the twin tools of European imperialism, the civilizing mission and the Christianizing mission. This depiction of West Africa thus fulfilled the strategic need of proimperialists. It also arose from the Victorian desire for titillation from tales of savagery and immorality in far-off exotic places.[3] In both popular travel literature and fiction and in the journals of scientific explorations barbaric West Africa provided the backdrop for the heroic deeds of imperialists. In this process of "othering," the landscapes of West Africa were feminized and the language of imperialism was imbued with sexual metaphor: West Africa was penetrated, conquered, subdued, and controlled.[4] It provided British[5] explorers with a sexual playground free from the constraints of Victorian morality or the presence of British women.

British women were not only excluded from these tales of heroes and adventure, they also seemed to be physically excluded from West Africa. It was a land considered unsuitable for colonization by Europeans, who did not thrive there; it was "No place for a White Woman."[6] At first sight there certainly seemed to be few white women traveling to West Africa during the 19th century. However, several British women went to West Africa to undertake very different roles during this period. Mary Slessor was a Scottish Presbyterian missionary, brought up in the slums of Dundee, who spent almost 40 years (1876 to 1915) in the forests of Calabar, in southeast Nigeria. Slessor came to identify Calabar as "home," and rather than perceive herself as a traveler in a "foreign" land, she considered herself a member of the communities in which she lived. This is important in considering her relationships to, and with, the landscapes and peoples of Calabar. She did not publish a book, but she did write many articles, letters, and reports for the *Missionary Record* and the *Women's Missionary Magazine*. Mary Kingsley was a member of a renowned literary family. She achieved fame in her own right as a travel writer and expert on West African affairs, despite spending only 18 months in West Africa (1893 to 1895). Her major publication was *Travels in West Africa* (1897), which was succeeded by two more books[7] and many articles. Constance Larymore was the wife of a colonial military administrator. She traveled with her husband first through southern Nigeria, then through northern

Nigeria at the time of its "pacification" in the early years of the 20th century. She wrote an account of her travels, *A Resident's Wife in Nigeria* (1908).

Several recent studies have focused upon white women's various experiences of empire.[8] Such studies have raised the importance of the interplay between gender, race, and class in the liberation and empowerment of women abroad. They have also questioned constructions of a singular "other," and emphasized the complexities of constructions of racial and gender difference in white women's contributions to imperial perceptions of "otherness." In the light of such studies, this chapter explores the ways in which constructions of gender and racial difference enabled Kingsley, Slessor, and Larymore to acquire authority and influence in British imperialism in West Africa. Particular attention is paid to their encounters with, and subsequent descriptions of, the women of West Africa, and how their own perceptions of racial difference challenge the construction of a singular "other."

A feature of 19th-century narratives about Africa was the anonymity of the indigenous peoples; their individuality was often ignored so that they faded into the background and became part of the overall picture of savagery. African women were particularly anonymous. Very few travel accounts mentioned African women, and those that did tended to reinforce the twin stereotypes of the oppressed wife in a polygamous household, or the lascivious female, associated with the prostitute in Britain.[9] African societies were condemned for condoning infant marriage, for producing child-mothers, for treating women as slaves when they were adults, and for subjecting widows to trial by ordeal. The comparative nudity of West African women was believed to indicate their unrestrained sexuality. The few descriptions of African women that did exist were thus formulated within the framework of enduring stereotypes. Little effort was made to describe African women within the context of their own cultures. This chapter analyzes the relationships that Slessor, Kingsley, and Larymore shared with their West African counterparts. The complex relationships between race, gender, and class are examined through their portrayals of West African women, as are the ways in which these descriptions were enabled or constrained by notions of gender in Victorian Britain. The mapping of their identities in their textual representations, and how they re-created and redefined themselves in their juxtapositions with West African women, is considered. Finally, the extent to which these textual representations and constructions of difference over space empowered their authors are examined.

EXTERNAL OBSERVERS OR INTERNAL ALLIES?:
THE RELATIONSHIPS BETWEEN BRITISH
AND WEST AFRICAN WOMEN

Gender, as well as race, was a significant factor in allowing British women travelers access to West African societies: they presented little threat to the authority of African men; their status as women facilitated easy and frequent access to African women; and they were thus able to consider their lives from within the context of African culture and customs. As Kingsley wrote, "I openly own that if I have a soft spot in my feelings it is towards African women; and the close contact I have lived in with them has given rise to this, and, I venture to think, made me understand them."[10] Consequently, West African women feature extensively in the texts of Victorian women writers. However, only Slessor's representations of West African women differed from her representations of West African men. Slessor often represented West African women as allies in her fight against what she perceived as the abuses and injustices of polygamy.[11] She considered Ma Eme, the wife of a prominent ruler in Okoyong, to be her closest ally in helping her to prevent the ill-treatment of women.[12] The fact of her gender enhanced Slessor's relationships with West African women. Both Larymore and Kingsley were travelers in West Africa and, unlike Slessor, at the time of their journeys they did not consider West Africa as "home."[13] Gender may have facilitated their access to West African women, but they remained observers from without, and their accounts of West African women were no different from their accounts of West African men. Geographical and textual "closeness" to West African women was predicated on the imperial authority they derived from their status as *white* women. This gave them privileged access to West African women that was often denied to British men.

Kingsley believed that the only way to understand West Africa and its peoples was to observe from the inside, to see "things as they are, with all the go and glory and beauty in them as well as the mechanism and the microbes."[14] Therefore, although she spent much time at mission stations and colonial offices, she also spent time alone in African villages. In this way she fostered relationships with West African women during her travels in the French Congo. In her publications, lectures, and articles, these relationships with West African women are evident. Kingsley witnessed the customs of women in different West African societies, and described in great detail their roles within village life and local economies. Like other women travelers, she paid particular attention to the different practices of dressing, ornamentation, and hairdressing.[15] In such descriptions, Kingsley's position seems to be one of a detached, objective observer. This has led some commentators to doubt Kingsley's proximity to the

Africans whom she described: a paradox exists between Kingsley's self-proclaimed "closeness" to West African women, and the distance she maintained as a scientific observer. Birkett suggests that much of her knowledge was in fact secondhand, based on the work of other anthropologists (R. E. Dennett, Edward Tylor), missionaries (particularly Robert Nassau), and explorers (De Brazza, Du Chaillu, and Richard Burton).[16] Although it is true that she drew heavily on the works of such experts, Kingsley's own comments suggest that she developed real relationships with West African women. She wrote, "I own I like African women; we have always got on together. True, they have made some spiteful remarks on my complexion, but I must ignore these in the face of the thousand kindnesses for which I am their debtor."[17]

Constance Larymore traveled over 3,000 miles with her husband, a major in the British Army who was responsible for delineating the boundaries of the newly formed northern Nigeria. She was allowed to enter the harems of the emir of Bida, becoming the first Western woman to do so. This is perhaps a reflection of Larymore's powerful status in West Africa. As the wife of a major in a region that had been conquered by the British military forces,[18] she had considerable influence, but her white skin gave her authority independent of that of her husband. She therefore gained a privileged insight into a facet of Nigerian life that remained murky and mysterious in the Victorian imagination. Larymore's role as the wife of an active agent of British imperialism tended to keep her separate from local populations. In her account of her travels,[19] her position as observer from without is apparent, and there seems to have been little interaction between herself and the women she observed. Her status and social class forced her to maintain a "respectable" distance between herself and Africans. As in the case of Kingsley, we are presented with a paradox between Larymore's (geographical) "closeness" to West African women, and the distance that existed between her the observer and the women she observed. Her upper-class status maintained a distance between herself and West African women.

Mary Slessor, perhaps, took the greatest interest in the women of West Africa.[20] In 1878 Salisbury drew up a treaty with the rulers of Duke Town, the administrative center of Calabar, banning twin murder, human sacrifices, trial by ordeal, and the enforced mourning of widows. However, this treaty was practically impossible to implement outside Duke Town. Slessor took it upon herself to enforce the treaty. In her opinion, the lives of West African women could only be improved by raising the women's own low view of their status in society. She was intent on living in West African villages, which meant moving away from the coastal towns of Calabar, and traveling into the interior, as yet unexplored by Europeans. This pioneering style has prompted comparisons with David Livingstone. Like Livingstone, Slessor was converted to an African life-style but had little success converting Africans to Christianity. Her descriptions of the lives of West African women were a product of this integration into West African societies. Unlike Kingsley and Larymore, Slessor actively intervened in West African societies.

TEXTUAL CONSTRAINTS AND THE MAPPING OF IDENTITIES IN WOMEN'S NARRATIVES

The construction of identities in the narratives of Kingsley, Slessor, and Larymore is inherently linked to textual constraints in both the production and the reception of these narratives.[21] One of the major textual constraints upon these women was the justification for their presence in West Africa. As Frank argues, "In an age when a woman could scarcely ride alone in a railway carriage from Brighton to London, she would certainly be called upon to explain why she was off to the mouth of the Niger or the source of the Nile."[22] It is significant that each of these three women adopted the motive of "duty" for traveling to West Africa. For the most part, this duty was constructed as feminine and private, but quite often there was a blurring of the distinctions between private and public duty. Slessor's justification for being in West Africa was defined in terms of her duty to the church, which can be seen as a public duty. Following the death of Livingstone in 1873, she felt that it was her duty to continue his work in bringing Africans into the fold of the Christian religion. However, Slessor also considered her work a private duty that was grounded in the family. She was fulfilling her mother's wishes, who had intended to send her eldest child, John, to Calabar as a missionary, a plan aborted by his premature death in New Zealand. Larymore's "duty" was also grounded in the family. She had gone with her husband to India, and felt it her duty to uproot herself once more and follow him to West Africa. Although essentially a private "duty," here too there is a blurring between distinctions of public and private duty in Larymore's role in West Africa. Having no defined role other than "wife," she performed a necessary public service of studying and observing life in West Africa, and then passing on her advice to other prospective colonial wives in her one publication. One of the reasons Kingsley gave for traveling to West Africa was a duty to her dead father. George Kingsley had contemplated going out to West Africa in order to complete his anthropological research, but never did; Kingsley fulfilled this feminine, private duty by continuing her father's work on sacrificial rites. However, by suggesting that she was contributing to scientific knowledge, Kingsley justified her travels in the sense that they fulfilled a public duty.

The use of duty as a reason for traveling to Africa, however, did not hide the inner impulses that prompted these women to travel, the private needs that flowed beneath the veneer of an essentially private duty. Being in West Africa was a liberating experience, and the juxtaposition between private duty and private pleasure often produced conflicting voices within their texts. This was particularly evident in the work of Kingsley. Several commentators have discussed the conflicting voices in *Travels in West Africa*, and Mills in particular has tied these in with the constraints shaping the text. As Mills points out, the external constraints concerning the reception of the text led Kingsley to adopt a multiplicity of conflicting voices, both masculine and feminine, objective and subjective, in her struggle to create the image of a scientifically accurate explorer while maintaining her "femininity." As Alison Blunt points out in Chapter 3, Kingsley assumed multiple identities throughout *Travels:* she was at once an ichthyologist and an enthnologist, identities she maintained in her other publications.[23] She deliberately adopted a scientific, objective, detached, masculine voice to lend credence to her text; she did not wish to be seen as just another "globetrotteress."

The masculine voice is particularly evident in Kingsley's descriptions of West African women. For example, she wrote:

> The "Fanny Po" ladies are celebrated for their beauty all along the West Coast, and very justly. They are not however, . . . the most beautiful women in this part of the world. . . . I prefer an Elmina, or an Igalwa, or a M'pongwe, or – but I had better stop and own that my affections have got very scattered among the black ladies on the West Coast, and I no longer remember one lovely creature whose soft eyes, perfect form, and winning, pretty ways have captivated me than I think of another.[24]

It is clear from the descriptions in *Travels* of the women of West Africa that Kingsley's responses were of a personal and sensual nature, but textual constraints and notions of femininity made it difficult for her to express this reality. Consequently, her sensual response to West African women could only be expressed through the adoption of a masculine, objective voice, suggestive of a sexual attraction and addressed to a masculine audience.[25] She was constrained by the inescapable fact of her gender to deny the scientific nature of her travels, arguing that she was merely "skylarking" or "puddling about,"[26] and that she in fact had very little

knowledge of scientific methodology.[27] Nonetheless, Kingsley made positive claims for the role of women in anthropological fieldwork, arguing
that her gender was an important factor in allowing her access to West
African women. Personal relationships and subjective inquiry gave her
a privileged insight into the lives of African women that was denied to
male travelers. However, as a single woman traveling in West Africa, she
repeatedly felt the need to emphasize her own femininity, particularly
with regard to her appearance and clothing.[28] In this way she countered
the masculine voices she was forced to adopt to describe her adventures,
but the tensions between objective/masculine and subjective/feminine voices
are apparent throughout *Travels*.

Unlike Kingsley, Larymore did not have the difficulty of explaining
or justifying her role in West Africa, for this was defined for her by her
husband's role in northern Nigeria. As a wife traveling with her husband,
she required no further justification for being in West Africa other than
duty. *A Resident's Wife in Nigeria* is dedicated to "the Sahib," her husband.
Larymore was an "incorporated wife" in the sense that her presence in
Nigeria was defined solely by her husband's employment[29]; her travels
were dictated by her husband's changing responsibilities and locations and
she had little personal control over them. The constraints controlling Larymore's text are clear. *A Resident's Wife* is a travelogue; Larymore was an
observer rather than an analyst. Unlike Kingsley, she did not adopt a scientific standpoint from which to explain what she saw: she merely described
her experiences. The text is primarily concerned with descriptions of her
"feminine" pursuits, particularly her attempts to grow flower gardens and
to recognize Nigerian flora. She said little about the rigors involved in traveling 3,000 miles on horseback through the sub-Saharan region, nor the
debilitating effects of the climate.

Unlike Kingsley and Slessor, Larymore was reticent in making claims
for her own achievements. Both of the former emphasized the fact that
they had traveled in areas as yet unexplored by Europeans, and, as noted
in Chapter 3, Kingsley staked a claim to being the first European to cross
overland between the Ogowé and Rembwé rivers, and another to being
one of the few to ascend Mount Cameroon. The only claim that Larymore made was that "no Englishwoman yet had gone where I meant
to go, or done what I hoped to do: we knew little or nothing of the conditions of life before us except that it was rough, *very* rough."[30] She was
the first British woman to travel extensively around northern Nigeria and
to write about her experiences, but her femininity prevented her from adopting the voice of the explorer/discoverer/adventurer. The construction of
her text testifies to these constraints; Part I is primarily concerned with

describing what she saw during her travels, while Part II is divided into sections giving advice on "The Home," "The Household," "Dogs, Poultry and Cows," "The Garden" (subdivided into sections on "The Flower Garden," "The Lawn," "Trees and Shrubs," "The Verandah Garden," and "The Vegetable Garden"), "The Stable," "Camp Life," and "What to Wear." Larymore was further justifying her travels, and validating her text, in grafting on advice to other potential women travelers and settlers in Nigeria. As Frank argues, Larymore's book thus represented a transition from the traveler's account to the tourist's guidebook,[31] but its significance lay in the fact that her advice was restricted to the domestic sphere. Like Kingsley, she was concerned with presenting herself as the most feminine of women despite her unconventional life-style.

The distinction between public and private writings is an important one in terms of women's writing, particularly their travel writing. The textual constraints that controlled published narratives were not present in private correspondence, where women were often freer to express their opinions regarding even the most taboo of subjects in Victorian society. That textual constraints controlled published narratives becomes clear when one compares the opinions expressed in print to those explained in private correspondence. For example, Kingsley excluded descriptions of the practice of female circumcision from her published narratives. This custom was a fundamental ceremonial rite in many parts of West Africa, but none of the women discussed here referred to it. Kingsley was aware of its existence, but did not allude to it in any of her anthropological studies; neither could she bring herself to describe it to the anthropologist E. B. Tylor: instead she hinted at the custom in letters to his wife, in the hope that she would communicate the information back to Tylor.[32] Her views on miscegenation were also confined to her letters.

The conflict between public and private writings is even clearer in the work of Slessor. In her reports published in the missionary magazines she was a narrator, and, like Larymore, confined herself to describing her environment and her own work, without veering toward the masculine world of analysis and critique, politics and science. She made constant reference to the state of her health, assuring her readers that she was well. The picture she offers is of a woman happily carrying out the work of the church in Africa, and enjoying some success. The picture of Slessor revealed in her correspondence is very different. She was often sick with fever, and on occasion close to death. She suffered from erysipelas, lost her hair, and had heart trouble. Her discomfort is evident in several of her letters and in her surviving diaries. However, her health problems were not reported in the *Missionary Record* or the *Women's Missionary Magazine*. This was partly because Slessor felt she had a mission to complete and did not want to be recalled to Britain. On one of her few furloughs, when her superiors expressed doubts about her returning to Africa, she announced, "If ye dinna send me back, I'll swim back."[33]

She was conscious of her status as one of the few single women missionaries in Africa, and did not want this status confused with notions of weakness and unsuitability. Furthermore, Slessor did not want to represent herself as a hero figure in the mold of Livingstone. It was important that she remained within the bounds of acceptable feminine behavior as defined by the Church of Scotland, an institution initially against her proposal to travel inland, and later opposed to the idea of her living in an African-style hut.[34] She tempered her role as a pioneer by assuming a maternal presence in West Africa. For example, she wrote of her excursion into Okoyong:

> I hope to get a room at several of the villages, so that they will feel they are looked after. At first they did not seem to know whether they should repulse me, but the medicine . . . has made the whole place mine. Every chief, more or less, has been under my care, or some of his people have been, and they have expressed in various ways their appreciation of my services. No white person need fear to go anywhere now.[35]

Slessor's adoption of African children was symbolic of her wider adoption of the people of Calabar, who referred to her as "Ma."[36] She pictured herself as a mother figure and the saver of twins rather than as an explorer.

Slessor was a modest and shy person,[37] but she felt that her work in Calabar was important. Thus she was at times highly critical in her letters toward the Church of Scotland for not providing the necessary backup to allow her to continue her travels into the interior. She wrote, "Do you at home realise that while you are giving for extension, we are closing stations for want of workers?"[38] She often criticized both the church and the British government for what she saw as their ethnocentrism and their patronizing attitude toward Africans, but again her anger, which at times was vitriolic, was confined to her private correspondence and diaries. Indeed, she gained a reputation among the colonial administrators in Nigeria at the turn of the century for being difficult, obstructive, and cantankerous,[39] a very different image from the one represented in the missionary magazines, where her freedom to express her opinions was limited.

Although constraints often shaped the way these women wrote, text also served to some extent to empower the authors. The act of describing in itself represented the position of power enjoyed by women writers: they appropriated West African women, filling their narratives with descriptions of those silenced by the imperialism that had facilitated their own liberation. Their published texts gave them audiences and authority that would have been difficult to acquire otherwise, and their own liberation in West Africa was achieved at the expense of the liberation of West Africans. This is a significant consideration when analyzing how these women represented West African women and their life-styles.

REPRESENTATIONS OF WEST AFRICAN WOMEN

Many indigenous customs within West African societies were used by Westerners to portray African women as oppressed and downtrodden, particularly polygamy, human sacrifice, and the violence perpetrated by secret societies. However, the access that British women had to West African women meant that they sometimes challenged the ethnocentric assumptions concerning the latter's lives.

The Victorian reverence for the virtuous wife meant that polygamy was perceived as an immoral means of maintaining the subservience of African women. According to the prevailing view, African wives in polygamous marriages were treated as chattels. Kingsley's understanding of polygamy was considerably different, though it was also revealing of her own prejudices. When asked in an interview, "I suppose, Miss Kingsley, that the African woman is a very degraded specimen of humanity?" Kingsley replied:

> Not all together; her position has been greatly exaggerated by travellers and as most of them were men they had small opportunity for judging. As a woman I could mix freely with them and study their domestic life, and I used to have long talks . . . and gleaned a lot of information. I believe, on the whole, that the African married woman is happier than the majority of English wives.[40]

Although presenting polygamy in a favorable light, her response to the question of African women being in a state of degradation was suggestive of Kingsley's underlying racist beliefs. She challenged the notion that polygamy was a repressive institution for women, arguing that from her experience in West Africa, she was

> compelled to think polygamy *for the African* is not an unmixed evil; and that at *the present culture-level of the African* it is not to be eradicated. . . . It is perfectly

impossible for one African woman to do the work of the house, prepare the food, fetch water, cultivate the plantations, and look after the children at-tributive to one man.[41]

In other words, although polygamy was unacceptable for "civilized" Eu-ropeans, it was quite acceptable, and perhaps inevitable, for "uncivilized" Africans. Such an attitude was deeply patrician, revealing Kingsley's be-lief in polygenesis and European superiority. In her view, polygamy was of benefit to African women when placed in the context of the state of African society, which she saw as inferior to that of Europe. It reduced the burden of labor, allowing women time to become involved in domes-tic economies and trade. Furthermore, Kingsley argued that although Afri-can societies granted sexual freedom to men while denying it to women, the burden of coping with the sexual demands of one man was shared in polygamous households, as was the burden of childbearing. While a West African woman was breast-feeding a child, the husband was not allowed any sexual contact with her. According to Kingsley, therefore, African women had considerable rights and freedom within marriage. For her, the image of the downtrodden African wife was an erroneous one when placed in the overall context of African society.

Slessor's position on polygamy is unclear, since she rarely mentioned it in her reports. This may be an indication of the textual constraints that existed at the time of her writing. She had spent many hours in the wom-en's compounds, and yet did not describe her experiences there in her reports. Her male predecessors had written lengthy reports about polyga-my and the "debasing" effect it had on society,[42] but it may have been unacceptable for a woman to allude to such descriptions. She wrote of polygamy in her private correspondence and was sympathetic to King-sley's defense of the custom.[43] It seems that Slessor's primary concerns lay in eradicating what she saw as the more barbaric aspects of West African customs, such as twin murders and human sacrifice. However, she ad-hered to the demands of her church in allowing only men with one wife to become members of her congregation in West Africa, the standard policy of the mission in attempting to undermine the custom. She also support-ed wives who fled from their polygamous marriages to become Christi-ans. In this way, Slessor took a small but significant stand against polygamy.

Kingsley's rebuttal of the myth of the oppressed African wife was up-held by Constance Larymore; in *A Resident's Wife in Nigeria,* she wrote that while among the trading women in the market at Kabba the tender-hearted philanthropist would have to seek far and long in this merry crowd for the "downtrodden women of Africa" and the "black sister of slavery," of whom one seems to have heard. There is not much that indicates subjection or fear about these ladies, sitting at graceful ease among their loads, or strolling about in the hot sunshine.[44]

Like Kingsley, Larymore believed that African women were the driving force behind indigenous trade and economies, exercised great power within the villages, and contributed to the maintenance of public order.[45] She wrote, "I have a strong conviction that (in spite of the laments indulged in by good people at home, over the sad position of the downtrodden woman of Africa) the ladies rule the villages and set the public tone."[46] However, she did have some preconceptions about the state of women in harems. This is reflected in her complete surprise at what she found after having obtained permission to enter the harem of the emir of Bida. She found the harem to be a community of women and children of all ages, and was amazed to find them "all laughing, clapping their hands, calling greetings and salutations incessantly." This was not the scene of lasciviousness that she had expected. The women did not mob her in their excitement at seeing their first white woman. Instead, "their perfect courtesy, that fine characteristic of the African people, prevailed to restrain them. There was no . . . pushing, or crowding."[47] Larymore's descriptions of the harem were, therefore, quite different from many contemporary portrayals.[48] Melman argues that this was a separate, feminine experience of the harem,[49] but Larymore's experiences as a *white* woman make her descriptions all the more relevant.

Like polygamy, the secret societies of West Africa were often portrayed in a negative light. They were considered the sole domain of men, and inherently linked to witchcraft and cannibalism through which villages, and, in particular, women were terrorized. Kingsley, while recognizing the fear that the secret societies inspired, did not believe that they were completely disadvantageous to West African women. She argued that secret societies were not religious but judicial. Men's societies existed to keep the women in check, and arose "from the undoubted fact that women are notably deficient in real reverence for authority, as is demonstrated by the way they continually treat that of their husbands."[50] (Whether Kingsley sees this as a positive attribute is somewhat unclear.) She cited the existence of women's secret societies, and suggested that they were testimony to the rights of African women within their villages. Kingsley wrote that women's secret societies were just as powerful and exclusive as those of the men: "A man who attempts to penetrate the female mysteries would be as surely killed as a woman who might attempt to investigate the male mysteries."[51] For Kingsley, the secret societies were a means of maintaining social harmony, and were therefore of benefit to the women, rather than a means of terrorizing them.

The most feared secret society was the Egbo of Nigeria, whose members were believed to have the power to transform themselves into wild animals to attack people. The Egbo runners brought fear upon the villages, and any woman found on the streets as they passed through was attacked or molested. Slessor's way of dealing with the Egbo was to confront them, exercising the power that her white skin allowed her. One of her adopted children, Daniel, described how she attacked the Egbo runners.[52] Slessor wanted to break the spell of fear that the Egbo held over the women of Calabar, and she made every effort to dispel the superstitions concerning the powers of the Egbo runners, ignoring the charms they left to obstruct her path and confronting them whenever possible.

For British women, the treatment of widows was perhaps the most difficult aspect of the lives of African women to confront. West African women were often required by tribal laws to undergo trials by ordeal, ritual sacrifice, or enforced mourning upon the death of their husbands. Such customs were alien to the sensibilities of Western women. However, Kingsley, for the most part, was able to suspend judgment in order to explain these customs from the point of view of the African. She argued that "cruelty" toward widows emanated from the fear of witchcraft and was therefore an understandable part of African law, rather than an expression of misogyny. The fear of witchcraft meant that the first people suspected of a man's death were his wives, who were tried. Kingsley explained that for the African, the confinement of widows was a means of protecting the soul of the dead man, which remained around the house until the burial. She wrote that, contrary to the impression given by missionary reports, the period of mourning ended with the burial of the husband, and that the widow(s) was then free to marry again.[53]

Some ethnic groups sacrificed wives at funerals so that they would accompany their husband to the underworld, ensuring that he did not arrive as a pauper (a man's wealth was measured by the number of wives he had). According to Kingsley, a Calabar chief had explained to her that the British government's rigorous suppression of this custom meant that men went into the next world as paupers, and "added an additional chance of his going there prematurely, for his wives and slaves, no longer restrained by the prospect of being killed at his death and sent off with him would, on very slight aggravation, put 'bash in his chop.' "[54] In other words, he would be poisoned. Kingsley suggested that the threat of ritual sacrifice thus helped to maintain social order. For other tribes that believed in reincarnation, such as those around the Niger Delta, women were sent down with their husbands to determine the class of the reincarnated soul. There was a great fear that a person would be reincarnated as a slave if he were sent down without his wives. Kingsley adopted the stance of the anthropologist in attempting to rationalize such customs by referring to the point of view of the West African. The paradox between distance and "closeness" is again apparent, with Kingsley becoming the detached scientific observer, but claiming that her knowledge was based on her "intimate" relationships with West Africans. The tensions of being inside and outside imperial discourses are also apparent. Kingsley was attempting to challenge some of the ethnocentric assumptions about West African customs, but she was forced to adopt the voice of the external observer, gazing from a position of authority upon the subjects of British imperialism to give credence to her observations and opinions.

The descriptions of West African women by British women writers were often influenced by their awareness of their own position within British society. As women, they were considered by most Victorians, and indeed by themselves, to be inferior to men. (As Kingsley wrote, "A great woman, mentally or physically, will excel an indifferent man, but no woman has ever equalled a really great man."[55]) As African women were "othered" by racial difference, so British women were "othered" by gender difference, and thus they often felt an affinity with African women. As Frank argues, "The legacy of sexual oppression paradoxically fostered these women's identification with the subjected Africans whose lower station facilitated their own liberation in Africa."[56] Gender allowed Kingsley to identify with West African women when she wrote of "the inextinguishable thirst for knowledge, so long as that knowledge is forbidden, which characterises our sex."[57] (Here she drew an analogy between her own attempts to gain scientific knowledge and the African women's attempts to discover the secrets of the men's societies.) Furthermore, in Kingsley's texts there was even the hint of envy for her West African counterparts. She argued that West African women were hostile to Europeanization because it would threaten many of their existing rights. The law of *mütterecht* made the tie between the mother and the children closer than that between the father and the children; Europeanization would reverse this system. Between husband and wife there was no community of goods under African law: each had a separate estate; again, this was very different from Victorian law, which ceded everything to the husband.[58] For many Western women traveling in West Africa it soon became clear that despite the perceived horrors of polygamy, infant marriage, secret societies, and cruelty toward mothers of twins and widows, in some ways West African women had many more rights, freedoms, and much more influence in everyday life than certain Western discourses suggested, and in the opinion of Kingsley, than British women themselves had in Victorian society.

EMPOWERMENT THROUGH TEXT: WHITE WOMEN'S ROLES IN THE BRITISH EMPIRE

British women were empowered by the fact that within the empire status was determined by race as well as by gender. Notions of gender were closely linked to notions of race; Africa as a continent and the African people themselves were commonly feminized by the literature of empire; women and Africans were both "othered." In West Africa, however, British women often became "honorary men," were treated no differently by the Africans than were British men, and were often referred to as "Sir."[59] This feeling of authority manifested itself in the condescending tone sometimes adopted by Larymore. For example, on one occasion she referred to Africans as "light-hearted children,"[60] but this reaction was based more on class than on race. She treated Africans no differently than she would have treated servants in Britain. She described her African servants as

> all lazy and stupid . . . ignorant of the first principles of order and cleanliness, and, unmistakenly, considering Missis rather a bore when she insists on trying to inculcate these . . . but I must not omit to say that I have only *very rarely* found any one of them in the least degree untruthful, and that I know them to be absolutely honest.[61]

Therefore, Larymore's condescending response to West Africans was based upon her upper-class status, and her authority derived from this status. It was an attitude rarely found in Slessor, hailing as she did from the slums of Dundee, and only occasionally in Kingsley, whose own mother was a housemaid before she married into the illustrious Kingsley family. However, as Blake argues,

> The substitution of a sense of class superiority undermines the premises of empire. It transforms the cliché that Africans are childlike from a justification of imperialism to an attitude toward servants. It allows . . . [them] . . . to acknowledge the social distinctions Africans themselves make and to regard African society as parallel to English.[62]

It is significant that these women escaped some of the constraints that were apparent in British society. For example, because she was forced to adopt a masculine voice, Kingsley was able to describe such taboo subjects as cannibalism, human sacrifice, polygamy, and the liquor traffic in West Africa. Although Larymore was a "dependent wife" whose social identity was drawn from her husband's work and rank, and whose travels were structured according to his changing duties and repostings,[63] she retained some autonomy by publishing a book based on her own experiences. The literature of empire was extremely popular during the 19th century and beyond, and this gave women writers access to large audiences.

The audiences for the views of the women discussed here were very different. In the case of Slessor, her audience ranged across class barriers, but was restricted to Scottish Presbyterians. Although publication figures for the *Missionary Record* do not exist, it can be assumed that it was very widely read throughout the major industrial towns of Scotland where the Church of Scotland was particularly strong. Its sister publication, the *Women's Missionary Magazine,* for which Slessor was a prolific writer, had an average monthly publication for 1902 of 27,800 and thus gave her access to a considerable female audience.[64] The potential audience for a work such as Larymore's was also large. There existed a fascination with empire among leisured middle- and upper-class women in Britain, which was an extension of the Victorian desire for tales of adventure in far-off, "exotic" locations. The tales of "the daughters of Albion" who were busy establishing "little Englands" around the world were extremely popular.[65] There is more evidence regarding the popularity of Kingsley's work. Her audience was a varied one, incorporating those interested in travel narratives from the empire and those engaged in commerce, science, and politics. The first edition of *Travels in West Africa* ran to 1,500 copies, and was reprinted eight times up to 1904, with reprint runs totaling 7,500. *West African Studies* was published in 1899 in an edition of 2,000 copies. It was reprinted in 1901 in an edition of 1,500 copies.[66] She also published articles in the influential periodicals of the time, such as the *Fortnightly Review* and the *Spectator,* and she was widely reviewed in both the national and the provincial press. Potentially large audiences added to the influence that these women, particularly Kingsley and Slessor, commanded as a result of their publications.

Following her return from Africa in 1895 and the publication of *Travels in West Africa,* Kingsley became a celebrity in Britain. She also acquired a great deal of influence. Her book ensured that she was widely regarded at the time as *the* expert on the affairs of West Africa, and demands were placed upon her for further publications and lecture tours. She established contacts with intellectuals such as E. B. Tylor and James Frazer, colonialists such as Sir George Goldie, future colonial governors such as Frederick Lugard and Matthew Nathan, representatives of the trading fraternity such as John Holt and Alfred Lyall, and members of the Colonial Office, including Joseph Chamberlain himself. This "networking" was enabled by the fame that she acquired through the publication of *Travels.*[67] Consequently, Kingsley came to exercise considerable influence within political circles, despite being outside them, particularly with regard to the debate surrounding the administration of the West African colonies and the formulation of Indirect Rule.[68] She also influenced the debate surrounding issues of education in West Africa, and helped lay the foundations for cultural relativism in the field of social anthropology.[69] Following her death while working as a nurse in South Africa during the Boer War, W. T. Stead wrote in the *Review of Reviews:*

> What a pity it is that Miss Mary Kingsley died before the Pan-African Conference was held! It is one more count of the indictment of Humanity against this hateful South African War, that it should have cost us the life of the only Paleface who could make the Black Man intelligible to Europe![70]

Kingsley's influence was, therefore, widespread, and had its origins in her first publication.

Slessor acquired influence in both Scotland and West Africa, but through different means. Her influence in Calabar was based on her proximity to West Africans and on her reports in the *Missionary Record* and the *Women's Missionary Magazine.* The great interest that she inspired, as a result of her reports and as a woman living alone in the unexplored forests of West Africa, gave her a great deal of influence within the Church of Scotland. The Foreign Missions Board was aware of the influence of her reports in the missionary magazines, and members wrote to her asking for more, a "sketch of anything connected with your work – any of your observations or your experiences."[71] Her knowledge of Calabar and her importance to the church meant that she was able to implement many of her own policies. If the church opposed her suggestions, Slessor's African lifestyle and her independence from the need of church funds, which she deliberately fostered through trading, meant that she could go ahead with her plans regardless of their protests. This influence can be discerned from the fact that Slessor's journeys into the interior were mapped out by herself, rather than by the Mission: she herself decided when and where she went. On one occasion when the church opposed her ideas (possibly concerned with opening up new villages in Ikpe) she threatened to sever com-

pletely her ties with the Mission. The response from the church was con-
ciliatory, arguing that it was "far too proud of you to dream of such a
thing, and if there is a difference of opinion there will be many a solution
thought of before that!"[72]

Such influence allowed Slessor to make substantial achievements in
West Africa, particularly with the women of Calabar. She was determined
to show that African women could escape the compounds and command
their own lives, if given the opportunity. They already kept local economies functioning, and Slessor believed that if they had their own land
they could be independent. They had no rights within the harem, and
if rejected they often starved. Slessor sheltered such women. Her attitude
is summed up by a scribbled comment in one of her Bibles against the
passage where Saint Paul lays down the rules for the subjection of wom-
en: she wrote, "Na! Na! Paul, laddie! This will no do!"[73]

Unlike Kingsley and Larymore, Slessor actively intervened to prevent
excessive cruelty to women, and was allowed to do so because she considered Africa her *home,* she *lived* in Calabar as well as *traveled* around it. This
geographical location in West Africa meant integration and eventually
influence within Calabar societies. She believed her successful interventions to prevent floggings and human sacrifices were enabled because she
was a woman, and therefore proved no threat to the authority of the
elders.[74] Her understanding of indigenous laws and customs persuaded
Consul MacDonald to appoint her as vice-consul in 1892,[75] the first
woman to acquire such a position in the British Empire, and to grant to
her the powers of a magistrate. Such an appointment was acceptable to
the people of Okoyong, since Slessor often ruled in accordance with African laws, when other Europeans would not have done so.[76]

The ultimate aim of Slessor's work was to establish a women's settlement, and she advocated training schools for women where they could
achieve independence and self-confidence. She gained the trust of the people
among whom she lived by forging friendships with women close to the
chiefs and elders, in the hope that they would use their influence and enable her to pursue her policies and ideas. Slessor apparently repaid this closeness of West African women, for when she became a magistrate, it was
widely rumored that no woman ever lost a case in her court.[77]

Slessor's dream of creating a women's settlement was realized in 1908
when a site near Use became available. She purchased the land in the name
of her adopted African daughters and built a refuge for widows, orphans,
the mothers of twins and their children, and refugees fleeing the harems.
Her financial independence from the Church of Scotland, which was based
on her trading with the people of Calabar to generate an income, meant

that she could build this refuge without the consent of the church. For the first time women had a place to go to outside the societies that had rejected them. Furthermore, a training center was established to educate women and girls in traditional industries, crafts, and farming. Slessor disagreed with the quasi-religious education promoted by the Mission, and believed that training in traditional methods was best suited to West Africa.[78] Again, she pursued her own policies independent of advice from the Mission. Slessor ensured that her settlement was located near large potential markets; the goods produced were thus exchanged for materials such as medical supplies, books, and writing equipment, and the settlement became self-sufficient.[79] The establishment of the women's settlement was typical of Slessor's efforts to improve the lives of West African women: she did not attempt to attack overtly existing customs, but provided an alternative, both to these customs and to the official solutions offered by the Church of Scotland.

As well as acquiring authority herself and, in turn, helping West African women attain some autonomy, Slessor also empowered a few women in Scotland. At the end of the 19th century it was still relatively unusual to find single women Protestant missionaries in Africa, and as Hunt argues, their presence was actively discouraged.[80] However, not only was Slessor an inspirational figure to other Scottish women, she also vigorously encouraged them to work in West Africa. She complained in the *Missionary Record* and the *Women's Missionary Magazine* about the lack of women volunteering to continue her work at the stations she had founded; it was imperative that others took over these stations in order that she continue her progress into the interior. As a result of such complaints, Charlotte Crawford of the Women's Foreign Mission Board agitated on Slessor's behalf in Scotland to send more women to West Africa. Several women answered Slessor's call, including her four protégées: Martha Peacock, Beatrice Welsh, Mina Amess, and Agnes Arnot. Slessor believed that Africans should run their own out-stations, under the initial supervision of traveling white missionaries, and the presence of these women not only consolidated her work but proved such ideas to be tenable. Slessor thus provided a valid reason for other British women to broaden their horizons and travel to West Africa.

CONCLUSION

The West Africa of the Victorian imagination during the 19th century was a place constructed essentially by British men for a masculine audience.

British women are remarkable only for their absence in descriptions of West Africa at this time. However, running parallel to this masculine literary tradition was the genre of women's travel writing,[81] which created novel pictures of West Africa based on the experiences of the British women who traveled there. I have focused on the texts of three women who wrote about their experiences in West Africa. There were many other women during the 19th and early 20th centuries who published details of their travels in West Africa,[82] and certainly many more who wrote letters and the like but who did not publish accounts of their travels, among them missionaries, teachers, and the wives of administrators. Although reputed to be "No Place for a White Woman," many British women in various guises traveled in West Africa during the 19th century, and the depictions of the people and places experienced by these women provide an interesting addition to, and in some cases a challenge to, the descriptions of male travelers. They also provide a valuable insight into the ways in which women, who were to varying extents marginalized in their own societies, acquired influence and authority in West Africa as a consequence both of their gender and of their white skins.

In the case of Kingsley, Larymore, and Slessor, I have placed particular emphasis on their experiences of, and with, West African women in the course of their narratives. Gender, as well as race, was a significant factor in this, allowing these women closer contact with West African women, especially in the women's compounds and in the harems. It was also a result of the textual constraints that were placed upon their descriptions. Women tended to be excluded from political and scientific discourse, and their texts were thus directed more toward descriptions of landscapes and people. It is therefore not entirely unexpected that women travel writers should choose to devote extensive passages to their West African counterparts, and thus have a greater concern for the subject of their enquiry. Nevertheless, the descriptions by Kingsley, Larymore, and Slessor reveal their own interest in the lives of West African women, and the information that they imparted about the role of women within West African societies and economies, particularly in the case of Slessor and Kingsley, was invaluable to subsequent policies in colonial education and administration.[83] Furthermore, the exploration of how these women negotiated racial, gender, and – to a lesser extent – class differences within the theater of empire raises important questions about the construction of a singular "other." It is perhaps more a case of the "other within" (predicated primarily on gender but also on social class) developing their own notions of the "other without" (predicated on racial difference).[84]

Despite textual constraints, these women managed to partially break out of the mold prescribed for them by a patriarchal Victorian Britain. Kingsley adopted masculine voices in her text, and although this in itself is indicative of the constraints operating upon her writing, it also allowed her to describe and discuss subjects that would otherwise have been inaccessible. It also facilitated her subsequent involvement in the realms of science and politics. The very act of writing allowed Larymore a voice and an audience while many other "incorporated wives" remained silent and invisible. It provided her with a stage upon which to challenge some of the assumptions made about the women of West Africa, and also an opportunity to encourage other British women to travel within the empire, albeit in the guise of model wives. Slessor acquired influence within West African societies, and often challenged the authority of the Church of Scotland and the colonial government. She gave the women of Calabar the opportunity to achieve autonomy, and indirectly did the same for a few women in Scotland by encouraging them to carry on her work in West Africa.

Despite their own liberation in the course of their travels and through the subsequent re-creation of their experiences in their publications, none of these women championed women's rights in Britain. Kingsley vociferously denied reports in newspapers that she was a "New Woman," but this denial may be further evidence of the constraints shaping her texts, and cannot be viewed without consideration of her great desire to be taken seriously in scientific and political circles. She felt that association with the women's rights movement would undermine her position of influence with the men of trade, science, and politics who had become her acquaintances. She could not afford to alienate her audience by being identified with radical "shrieking females."[85] Larymore made no claims on the behalf of women in her text, and encouraged other women to follow her example of remaining loyal to her husband, supporting him in his efforts on behalf of the empire, and making herself of some use while accompanying him on his travels. Although Slessor devoted a great deal of energy to the cause of West African women, she remained remote from debates about the rights of British women. In a letter to a friend she wrote, "I have enjoyed the old world gentlewomen, who after all are more to my taste than the new woman. I'm far too old for the new clever independent hand I fear."[86]

The importance of the writings of these three women lies in the fact that their descriptions of West African women reveal ways in which they were themselves empowered in the British Empire on the grounds of racial difference. Their descriptions were more revealing of their own prejudices and beliefs than they were about the lives of West African women, but their texts provided an important counterbalance and complement to those of male travelers.

Not only did these portrayals by white women travelers disrupt Orientalist images of non-European women, but they were also founded on completely different relationships with these women. As Melman argues:

> Travel and the encounter with systems of behaviour, manners and morals, most notably with the systems of polygamy, concubinage and the sequestration of females, resulted in analogy between the polygamous Orient and the travelling women's own monogamous society. And analogy led to self criticism rather than cultural smugness and sometimes resulted in an identification with the other that cut across barriers of religion, culture and ethnicity. Western women's writings on "other" women then substitutes a sense of solidarity of gender for sexual and racial superiority.[87]

This was particularly evident in the narratives of Kingsley and Slessor, and apparent to a lesser degree in Larymore's work. The exploration of the negotiation by these women of race, gender, and, to a lesser extent, class differences within the theater of empire raises important questions about the construction of a singular "other."

Furthermore, the lives of these women inform contemporary debates about the real and the perceived marginality of Victorian women.

ACKNOWLEDGMENTS

This chapter was written when I was a graduate student, funded by the British Academy, in the Department of Geography at Loughborough University of Technology. I am grateful to the editors, Alison Blunt and Gillian Rose, and to Morag Bell and Mike Heffernan, for their helpful comments on earlier drafts of this chapter.

NOTES

1. Patrick Brantlinger, "Victorians and Africans: The Genealogy of the Myth of the Dark Continent," *Critical Inquiry 1,* no. 12 (1985): 166–203.

2. Ibid.

3. Malak Alloula, *The Colonial Harem* (Manchester, U.K.: Manchester University Press, 1986); Rana Kabbani, *Europe's Myth's of Orient: Devise and Rule* (London: Macmillan, 1986).

4. Rebecca Stott, "The Dark Continent: Africa as a Female Body in Haggard's Adventure Fiction," *Feminist Review,* no. 32, (Summer 1989): 69–89.

5. This chapter focuses explicitly on the writings of British women writers, and their work is thus framed within British imperialism in West Africa.

6. Helen Callaway, *Gender, Culture and Empire: European Women in Colonial Nigeria,* (London: Macmillan, 1987), 4–8.

7. Mary Kingsley's major publications were *Travels in West Africa* (London: Macmillan, 1897) and *West African Studies* (London: Macmillan, 1899), together with the more minor publication of *The Story of West Africa* (London: Horace Marshall, 1900).

8. For example, see Dea Birkett, *Spinsters Abroad: Victorian Lady Explorers* (Oxford: Blackwell, 1989) and *Mary Kingsley: Imperial Adventuress* (London: Macmillan, 1992); Susan L. Blake, "A Woman's Trek: What Difference Does Gender Make?," *Women's Studies International Forum 13,* no. 4 (1990): 347–355; Shirley Foster, *Across New Worlds: Nineteenth Century Women Travellers and Their Writings* (London: Harvester Wheatsheaf, 1990); Katherine Frank, *A Voyager Out: The Life of Mary Kingsley* (London: Hamish Hamilton, 1986), and "Voyages Out: Nineteenth-Century Women Travellers in Africa," in *Gender, Ideology, and Action,* Janet Sharistanian, ed. (Westport, CN: Greenwood Press, 1986); and Margaret Strobel, *European Women and the Second British Empire* (Bloomington: Indiana University Press, 1991) for analyses of the different experiences and accounts of women travel writers. See Hilary Callan and Shirley Ardener, eds., *The Incorporated Wife* (London: Croom Helm, 1984) and Helen Callaway, *Gender, Culture and Empire: European Women in Colonial Nigeria* (London: Macmillan, 1987) for discussion of the experiences of the wives of colonial administrators. Billie Melman, *Women's Orients: English Women and the Middle East, 1718–1918* (London: Macmillan, 1992) explores English women travelers' relationships with the Middle East. Sara Mills, *Discourses of Difference* (London: Routledge, 1991), discusses the texts of women travel writers from a Foucauldian perspective. Mona Domosh, in "Toward a Feminist Historiography of Geography," *I.B.G. Transactions 16,* no. 1 (1991): 95–105, uses the work of women travel writers in her argument in favor of a feminist historiography of geography.

9. Brantlinger, "Victorians and Africans."

10. Kingsley, *West African Studies,* 2nd ed. (London: Macmillan, 1901), 320.

11. M. D. W. Jeffreys, "Mary Slessor – Magistrate, Part 1," *West African Review* (June 1950): 629.

12. W. P. Livingstone, *Mary Slessor of Calabar,* 6th ed. (London: Hodder & Stoughton, 1916), 71.

13. Later in her life Kingsley on occasion referred to West Africa as "home," for example, in "A Lecture on West Africa," *Cheltenham Ladies Magazine 38* (1898): 280.

14. Kingsley to Macmillan, n.d., Macmillan Papers, British Library.

15. For example, see Kingsley, *Travels in West Africa,* 5th ed. (London: Virago, 1982), 21, 46–48, 72, 222–224, 341, 531.

16. See Birkett, *Mary Kingsley,* 148.

17. Kingsley, *West African Studies,* 387–388.

18. Constance Larymore, *A Resident's Wife in Nigeria* (London: Routledge, 1908).

19. Richard H. Dusgate, *The Conquest of Northern Nigeria* (London: Frank Cass, 1985).

20. Slessor was particularly concerned with the quality of life for West African women. She herself had been accustomed to hardship. Her father was a violent man who eventually drank himself to death. The streets of Dundee were often places of crime and violence, fuelled by massive unemployment, and on a number of occasions she was threatened with violence on her way to church. Such an upbringing may have provided the impetus to improve the lives of African women.

21. Mills, *Discourses of Difference.*

22. Frank, "Voyages Out," 70.

23. Kingsley referred to herself as an ethnologist in the following publications: Introductory chapter to R. E. Dennett, *Notes on the Folklore of the Fjort* (London: Nutt, 1898); "A Lecture on West Africa," *Cheltenham Ladies Magazine,* no. 38 (Autumn 1898): 264–280; "The Forms of Apparitions in West Africa," *West Africa 14,* no. 35 (1897): 331–342; "The Fetish View of the Human Soul," *Address to the Folk Lore Society* (1897): 138–151; "West Africa from an Ethnologists Point of View," *Transactions and Annual Report—Council of the Liverpool Geographical Society* (1898): 58–73. She referred to herself as an ichthyologist in "Travels on the Western Coast of Equatorial Africa," *Scottish Geographical Magazine 12* (1896): 113–124; and "The Ascent of Cameroon's Peak and Travels in French Congo," *Transactions and Annual Report—Council of the Liverpool Geographical Society* (1896): 36–52.

24. Kingsley, *Travels in West Africa,* 5th ed., 72.

25. Mills, *Discources of Difference,* 157–158.

26. Kingsley, *Travels in West Africa,* 5th ed., 8.

27. Ibid., 101, 141.

28. For example, see Kingsley, *Travels in West Africa,* 5th ed., 502.

29. Callan and Ardener, *Incorporated Wife.*

30. Larymore, *A Resident's Wife,* 1–2.

31. Frank, "Voyages Out," 89.

32. Kingsley to Mrs. Tylor, December 7, 1896, E. B. Tylor Papers, Rhodes House, Oxford, U.K. Kingsley wrote: "Now if *you* would turn ethnologist I could tell you a lot of queer things that have very important bearings on what we will call the external skeleton of the ceremonials."

33. James Buchan, *The Expendable Mary Slessor* (Edinburgh, Scotland: St. Andrew Press, 1980), 24.

34. Buchanan to Slessor, January 13, 1905, MS 7661, United Presbyterian Papers, Foreign 3, 394, National Library of Scotland.

35. *Missionary Record,* October 1890, p. 304.

36. Livingstone, *Mary Slessor,* xii.

37. Jessie F. Hogg, "Mary M. Slessor," *Women's Missionary Magazine of the United Free Church of Scotland,* February 1915, pp. 53–54.

38. M. Slessor, "Present Opportunity in Ibibio," *Women's Missionary Magazine of the United Free Church of Scotland,* December 1908, p. 256.

39. Provincial Commissioner of Eastern Province to Falk, September 12, 1910, Edward Morris Falk Correspondence, mss. Afr. s. 1000, Rhodes House, Oxford, U.K.

40. Frank, *A Voyager Out,* 219.

41. Kingsley, *West Africa Studies,* 662; italics added.

42. For example, see Hope Waddell, report in *Missionary Record,* 1848, p. 169, and a report on the state of the missions, *Missionary Record,* 1851, p. 88.

43. Slessor to Irvine, December 12, 1903, St. Andrew's Hall Missionary College library, Selly Oak, Birmingham, U.K.

44. Larymore, *A Resident's Wife,* 116.

45. There is a long tradition in Africanist travel literature of describing the roles that women played within local economies and societies. For example, Duveyrier (1864) expounded the matriarchal nature of the Touareg society; see Michael Heffernan, "The Limits of Utopia: Henri Duveyrier and the Exploration of the Sahara in the Nineteenth Century," *Geographical Journal 155,* no. 3 (1989): 342–352.

46. Larymore, *A Resident's Wife,* 286.

47. Ibid., 28–29.

48. For analyses of accounts of harems by European male travelers, see Alloula, *The Colonial Harem;* Kabbani, *Europe's Myth;* Melman, *Women's Orients;* and Edward W. Said, *Orientalism* (London: Peregrine, 1978).

49. Melman, *Women's Orients,* 1.

50. Kingsley, *Travels in West Africa,* 5th ed., 526.

51. Kingsley, *West Africa Studies,* 527.

52. Daniel Slessor to Thomas Hart, November 30, 1948, Slessor Papers, MacManus Galleries, Dundee Museum, Dundee, Scotland. Slessor wrote that the Egbo "tremble because she a woman, of what power they cannot say, can dare to even come here, let alone attack without the fear of instant death."

53. Kingsley, *Travels in West Africa,* 5th ed., 483–484, 487–491, 516.

54. Kingsley, *West Africa Studies,* 489.

55. Kingsley, "The Development of Dodos," *National Review,* March 1896, p. 71.

56. Frank, "Voyages Out," 72.

57. Kingsley, *Travels in West Africa,* 5th ed., 527.

58. Kingsley, *West Africa Studies,* 322.

59. Kingsley, *Travels in West Africa,* 5th ed., 502.

60. Larymore, *A Resident's Wife,* 29.

61. Ibid., 207.

62. Blake, "A Women's Trek," 348.

63. Callaway, *Gender, Culture, and Empire,* 165.

64. *Women's Missionary Magazine of the Free Church of Scotland,* July 1903, p. 154.

65. Jane Robinson, *Wayward Women: A Guide to Women Travellers* (Oxford: Oxford University Press, 1991), 200.

66. Information courtesy of Macmillan Publishers, Ltd. Both books were reissued in the 1960s by Cass, and *Travels in West Africa* was reprinted in 1972, 1982, and 1987.

67. Deborah Birkett discusses Kingsley's "networking" strategy in "An Independent Woman in West Africa: The Case of Mary Kingsley" (Ph.D. diss., School of Oriental and African Studies, University of London, 1987), 219, 268; *Mary Kingsley* (London: Macmillan, 1992); and in a review article, "Networking West Africa," *African Affairs 2,* (1987): 115–119.

68. For accounts of Kingsley's influence in the political arena, see Catherine Barnes Stevenson, *Victorian Women Travel Writers in Africa* (Boston: Twayne, 1982); Anthony I. Nwabughuogu, "The Role of Propaganda in the Development of Indirect Rule in Nigeria, 1880–1929," *International Journal of African Historical Studies 14*, no. 1 (1981): 65–93; Kenneth Dike Nworah, "The Liverpool 'Sect' and British West Africa Policy, 1895–1915," *African Affairs 4*, (1971): 349–364; Robert D. Pearce, *Mary Kingsley: Light at the Heart of Darkness* (Oxford: Kensal Press, 1990); and Bernard Potter, *Critics of Empire* (London: Macmillan, 1961).

69. Robert D. Pearce, "Missionary Education in Colonial Africa: The Critique of Mary Kingsley," *History of Education 17*, no. 4 (1988): 283–294.

70. August 1900, p. 131.

71. Buchanan to Slessor, July 7, 1902, November 10, 1902, MS. 7658, 7659, United Presbyterian Papers, National Library of Scotland.

72. Stevenson to Slessor, June 4, 1912, MS. 7952, United Free Church Papers, National Library of Scotland. Slessor got her own way and continued her progress in opening up stations in Ikpe.

73. Buchan, *Expendable Mary Slessor,* 103.

74. Church of Scotland Overseas Council, *Mary Slessor of Calabar* (1978), 10–11.

75. Carol Christian and Gladys Plummer, *God and One Redhead. Mary Slessor of Calabar* (London: Hodder & Stoughton, 1970), 90.

76. Jeffreys, "Mary Slessor," 802–805.

77. Ibid., 629.

78. Caroline Oliver, *Western Women in Colonial Africa* (Westport, CN: Greenwood Press, 1982), 118–119; Elizabeth G. K. Hewat, *Vision and Achievement, 1796–1956. A History of the Churches United in the Church of Scotland* (Edinburgh: Nelson, 1960), 203.

79. Jubilee Booklet, *The Life of Mary Slessor, Pioneer Missionary, 1840–1915* (Edinburgh: Nelson, 1948), 13.

80. Nancy Rose Hunt, " 'Single Ladies on the Congo': Protestant Missionary Tensions and Voices," *Women's Studies International Forum 13*, no. 4 (1990): 395–403.

81. There is a debate as to whether a specifically feminine genre can be posited. However, as Foster (*Across New Worlds,* 18–19) argues, although women travelers wrote within the framework of "colonialist" and "imperialist" discourses, the tensions and paradoxes that existed in their texts render them distinct from those of male travelers. For example, although women were sometimes forced to adopt masculine voices, the confessional nature of travel writing by women, and its emphasis on self-effacement and self-mockery, support the argument for a separate, distinct genre.

82. See, for example, Mary Church, *Sierra Leone; or, The Liberated Africans* (London: Longman, 1835); Zélie Colvile, *Round the Black Man's Garden* (Edinburgh, Scotland: Blackwood, 1893); Mrs Henry Grant Foote, *Recollections of Central America and the West Coast of Africa* (London: Newby, 1869); Anna Hinderer, *Seventeen Years in the Yoruba Country* (London: Seeley, Jackson & Halliday, 1872); and Elizabeth Melville, *A Residence at Sierra Leone* (Reprint, London: Cass, 1968).

83. The ideas of both Slessor and Kingsley on traditional education were adopt-

ed in the 1920s, and Kingsley's had been an important voice in advocating the policy of Indirect Rule in West Africa, subsequently applied by Lugard to Nigeria.

84. Melman, *Women's Orients,* 5 1.

85. Kingsley's own words, quoted in Barnes Stevenson, *Victorian Women Travel Writers,* 147.

86. Slessor to Partridge, Use, January 1, 1908, Slessor Papers, Dundee City Library.

87. Melman, *Women's Orients,* 7–8.

5

Colonizing Gender in Colonial Australia: The Eliza Fraser Story

KAY SCHAFFER

Anyone who knows anything about Australia will tell you that it's a "man-zone" country.[1] It is not, of course, except by a facile but enduring reputation. A myriad of white masculine images of Australian national identity pervade popular film and the media as well as the literary and historical representations of the academy. This is one reason why Eliza Fraser is remarkable within an Australian frame. In 1836 Mrs. Fraser was shipwrecked off the northeastern coast of Australia, thus becoming the first white woman to encounter Aborigines and to tell her (less-than-sympathetic) tale. Although of some local interest in the 1830s, her story receives scant attention in mainstream historical texts. But as a 20th-century figure of legend – represented as a captive victim who seduced and then betrayed her convict rescuer – Mrs. Fraser has taken on nearly mythical status in Australia, as anyone who has read Patrick White's novel *A Fringe of Leaves* (1976), or seen any of Sidney Nolan's paintings from his *Mrs. Fraser* series (1947–1964), or viewed the David Williamson and Tim Burstall film *Eliza Fraser* (1976) could attest.[2]

Her story is legendary today: but the legend has little to do with the actual woman or the historical event in which she figured. I suggest, however, that what is known of the woman as a historical agent pales in significance next to the textual production of "Eliza Fraser" as a colonial and postcolonial object of power/knowledge.[3] What is known of the event is less significant than its representation in the various discourses in which it is situated. In the 19th century the significance of the Eliza Fraser story was understood with reference to imperialism, Christianity, the natural science of evolutionism, and Victorian sexual politics. Controversy surrounding the event contributed to the evolution of Australia as a nation, beyond its status and identity as an outpost of empire. In the 20th century, the legend surrounding Eliza Fraser became enmeshed within the aesthetic, ideological, and political networks supporting Australian nationalism. Throughout the time in which the story has circulated within so-called high and popular culture, it has operated as a means of regulating racial, class, and gender divisions, the effects of which can be traced within Australian cultural politics today.

This chapter, then, will examine the Eliza Fraser story not as a historical event but as a foundational fiction aligned to the maintenance of a colonial empire and to the making of the Australian nation. Focusing on the 19th century, it will attend to a variety of texts that reproduce her story in various ways: government documents, histories, ballads, handbills, and newspaper reports. The analysis aims not to get at the "truth of the thing," but to examine Mrs. Fraser's position(s) in the narratives and that of other speakers, writers, and commentators; to examine her construction as a victim of native savagery; and to explore the ways in which different forms of narrative contribute differently to colonial constructions of race, gender, and class divisions and hierarchies. The chapter will also examine the ways in which the texts have been read and received as representations that uphold or resist conflicting notions of imperial, colonial, or national authority. The approach assumes that there is no guarantee of knowledge beyond the textual representations of the event. The event, through narration, becomes placed in a number of fields of meaning, themselves embedded in Western, rationalist, imperial discourses of history.[4] There is no way to recover the real, no "real" outside of representation to recover.

First, a brief account of the story, offered here in order to construct a ground from which it will be possible to speak, and to give my readers a point of reference/departure. In 1836 Eliza Fraser, the English wife of an ailing Scottish ship captain, James Fraser, accompanied her husband on what was to prove to be a fatal voyage to the antipodes. The couple left their three children behind at the Orkney Islands off the north coast of Scotland in the care of the Presbyterian minister. Their brig, the *Stirling Castle,* was a merchant ship that carried goods and emigrant passengers from England to the colonies. On the return voyage the vessel was wrecked on a reef 500 miles off the present Queensland coast. The crew spent six treacherous weeks at sea in two leaky lifeboats, one of which abandoned the captain's party. Members of the longboat that included Captain and Mrs. Fraser eventually landed on what is now called (after the captain) Fraser Island, but only after the crew threatened to "draw lots" if the captain, who was mortally afraid of native violence, did not pull ashore. Mrs. Fraser and seven men eventually survived the ordeal.

The survivors spent six weeks on the island. While "in captivity" among "natives"[5] Mrs. Fraser experienced severe personal hardship, as well as witnessing the spearing and death of her husband and the sufferings of several other crew members before being rescued "from a fate worse than death" during a corroboree (an Aboriginal dance festival held at night) by the convict John Graham, who had volunteered his services as part of an official government rescue party that set out from the penal settlement at Moreton Bay. Years later, runaway convict David Bracefell claimed that he had rescued Eliza and walked her some 100 miles back to Moreton Bay before she turned on him, threatening to report him for his abuse of her person. This has been the version favored by some Queenslanders and built into the legend of Eliza Fraser, but it appears to be without historical foundation. After the rescue, Mrs. Fraser was returned to Moreton Bay, where local residents nursed her back to health before she departed for Sydney. In Sydney she gave several interviews to the press about her experiences before meeting Captain Alexander Greene of the *Mediterranean Packet,* marrying him, and accompanying him back to England. On arrival in England, she appealed to the authorities (first in Liverpool and then in London) for funds, representing herself as "Mrs. Fraser," a poor widow woman without a farthing, despite the fact that she had received £400 and two trunks full of clothing donated by the citizens of Sydney. She also gave further interviews to the press which by now had taken on a wildly exaggerated air. A subscription fund was set up by the lord mayor of London which attracted some £500 before news reached the city from Liverpool that her claims were somewhat inflated. She was accused of being an ingenious imposter and of perpetrating fraud. A Commission of Inquiry followed, and resulted in the lord mayor transferring the money to a trust fund for Mrs. Fraser's children under guardianship of the Protestant minister at Stromness. Details of the inquiry were reported daily in the press and later resulted in the publication of the first "official" history of the event, *The Shipwreck of the Stirling Castle* (1838), written by John Curtis, a court reporter for the *Times.* The last reference to Mrs. Fraser concerns a woman (who may have been an actress) who appeared as a sideshow attraction in Hyde Park, admission 6d.

One can map Mrs. Fraser's journey from the isolation of the Orkney

Islands, through a treacherous voyage to the new Australian colony, through shipwreck, captivity, and rescue on Fraser Island, followed by recovery at Moreton Bay and Sydney, and finally to notoriety in Liverpool and London. At each point in her journey different interests were brought to bear on her story: those of the colonial government and the British naval authorities, the mutinous crew, her convict rescuers, the colonial settlers in Australia, and the public in Britain. At each point along the way, what identity(ies) it was possible for her to assume, what she meant to others, and how she was able to represent herself and be represented were all dependent on her geographic locations, their political contexts, and the network of power relations in which she and her story were embedded.

NARRATIVE CONSTRUCTIONS

Mrs. Fraser gave three different reports of her ordeal to a number of different audiences: she filed an official report with the commandant at Moreton Bay, gave interviews to the local press in Sydney, and prepared an extended sensationalized account that was released to the popular press upon her arrival in Liverpool. The later account was published as a classic captivity narrative in the United States, appeared in ballad form on handbills and as a penny dreadful in London, and was picked up and circulated by the colonial press throughout the English-speaking world. She also gave testimony at the London Inquiry, along with Baxter, the second officer, and seaman Darge, one of the mutinous crew, and was interviewed further by John Curtis in the preparation of his book-length defense of Mrs. Fraser-Greene against charges of fraud. The plethora of materials the event generated contributed to an expanding discursive network supporting new knowledges and sustaining the imperialist impulse of the West.

At Moreton Bay all survivors were interviewed by the commandant and official statements were taken. Eliza's report is about 1,500 words in length. Two-thirds of the narrative details the shipwreck and performance of the captain and crew, while the final third summarizes events that occurred on the island and describes her treatment by the "natives." In the main the document attends to the mutinous behavior of the crew. This involved their refusal to rescue food and valuables from the *Stirling Castle* and led to the parting of the pinnace from the longboat with Mrs. Fraser's twelve-year-old nephew on board. Later, on the island, the remaining crew abandoned Eliza, the captain, the first mate, the second mate, and the steward to their fate after taking possession of firearms, ammunition, and navigational instruments. The report is clearly addressed to an official government audience for which Mrs. Fraser speaks not only for herself but also for her dead husband. It attempts to relieve the captain of responsibility for mismanagement or wrongdoing. The report successfully led to the punishment of the surviving crew members, all of whom had previously received a hero's welcome. In this narrative, although the "natives" are accused of treating the party "with the greatest cruelty," there is no mention of the "savagery" and "barbarism" that creeps into subsequent accounts.

The second account of Mrs. Fraser's ordeal resulted from interviews by local journalists in Sydney who reported her story to the public via the local press. These accounts, which pay considerably more attention to her encounters with the natives on the island, are more sensational. They detail the spearing and death of the captain; the death of the first mate, Brown, after he was tortured and burnt; and the stripping and intense privations of Eliza prior to her rescue by the convict John Graham under the guidance of Lieutenant Otter. For the first time a clear delineation of "us" and "them" categories emerges. The terms "cannibals" and "savages" are employed to describe the natives and Mrs. Fraser is represented as an innocent victim of fate's outrageous fortune, miraculously rescued by Divine Providence. These press reports tell the local public what it wants to hear. They titillate the colonial imagination with a depiction of the horrible sufferings of a vulnerable woman and incite fear of the savage "others" at the fringes of the new society, fear that would lead later to bloodshed and the near-extinction of the indigenous population of Fraser Island. A subscription campaign was launched by the bishop of Sydney for Mrs. Fraser and other members of the surviving crew, although only she would benefit from it. An outpouring of sympathy, hospitality, and generosity for Mrs. Fraser followed, as the citizens of the new colony attempted to rescue not only the woman but their own reputation for maintaining a civilized and ordered bourgeois life in the antipodes. As news filtered through to Sydney about the crew's mutiny and possible cannibalism among them, sympathy began to shift from the party of eight survivors to Eliza alone.

Although Mrs. Fraser gave three official reports of her ordeal, it is the third one, first published in the London *Courier* on August 19, 1837, and later adapted (with lurid illustrations) as a penny dreadful and advertised on handbills similar to those that announced her sideshow performance in Hyde Park, which reached the English-speaking colonial world in the form of a classic captivity narrative. Other London, provincial, and colonial papers were quick to reprint this account. Its preface draws the readers' attention to.

the deplorable case of Mrs. Fraser and others, who have miraculously survived an awful shipwreck, and the cruelties practiced on them by the savages
of New South Wales, amongst whom they were thrown, and by whom the
majority of the ship's crew have been enslaved in lowest bondage, and in
short tortured to death, by means at which the old Inquisition of Spain might
blush.[6]

It contains tales of warfare between native tribes and refers to their savagery
and cannibalism in ways that had not been reported to the official government administrators after the event and could not be corroborated by other
crew members. It includes fantastic descriptions of events, including reports
of grotesque, blue-haired natives and a gruesome tale of the torture and
beheading of one James Major whose body was said to have been eaten
by natives and his head preserved for use as a figure bust for one of their
canoes. It was this sensational and melodramatic version of the story that
appeared in *Alexander's East India and Colonial Magazine* and the *Army and
Navy Chronicle* (Washington, DC) in September and October 1837, followed by publication in the tabloid magazine *Tales of Travellers* (London,
1837), and was later repeated in an editorial in the *Sydney Gazette* (January
1838). In the words of a recent historian, "This one article set black/white
relations in the Wide Bay area [of Queensland] back at least a hundred
years."[7]

Within months the Americans had published an "Americanized" version of the captivity narrative, complete with tepees, squaws, Indian chiefs,
tomahawks, bows and arrows, and crude illustrations. The illustrations
detail Captain Fraser's death and Eliza's conveyance to the chief's "hut
or wigwam," which suggests to the reader that "fate worst than death"
(miscegenation) that the American captivity genre made famous. The narrative contains all the elements of the genre, albeit laced with the melodramatic elements associated with the sentimental novel. Some indications
of its tone can be detected in the introduction, which appeared on the
title page along with two suggestive illustrations. It reads:

[After the wreck the crew] were driven to and thrown on an unknown island, inhabited by Savages, by whom Captain Fraser and his first mate were
barbarously murdered, and Mrs. Fraser . . . [was] for several weeks held in
bondage, and after having been compelled to take up her abode in a wigwam
and to become the adopted wife of one of the Chiefs, Mrs. F. was provident-
ly rescued from her perilous situation.[8]

Here the crew, which is quickly reduced to a woman, is plunged into a perilous ordeal, from which it (but textually only "she") is miraculously rescued. The lone woman is the classic victim of the captivity narrative. It is her vulnerability that excites sympathy and incites the instincts of revenge against the barbarous enemy within colonial discourse. This sensational text proceeds to establish Mrs. Fraser's credentials as a reluctant narrator, unprepared for her performance, having had an "indifferent education" and deprived of the aid of her husband. But this constructed autobiographical author promises a "plain, unvarnished tale; exaggerating nothing, but recording truly and faithfully the particulars" of her ordeal, an ordeal in which she moves from "a state of content and enviable happiness, to that of inconceivable wretchedness" before being "miraculously rescued" from her "bondage." The natives appear in the text as types, marked by their violence, their physicality, and their orality. The husbands are "lazy" or "naturally very indolent," the squaws are "savage monsters" who nonetheless "perform the most laborious duties . . . cheerfully . . . without complaint or murmur." All the natives yell, whoop, and howl. Unlike the classic captivity narrative, however, this one revolves around the death of Captain Fraser (or his "savage/brutal murder" at the hands of "remorseless demons," to be true to the text). This moment produces a climax in the text that plunges Eliza into chaos. Threats of sexual violation are signaled by a crisis of narrative address: "Alas, it is impossible to reflect on what I endured . . . to imagine the shock of horrors to come. . . . The reader cannot have any idea of the horrors I suffered." More horrors follow, until, finally, Eliza is rescued "not from the devouring jaws of a ravenous lion, but from the hands of a savage ruffian, far more to be dreaded!"

The American version differs only in minor details from those published in England and in the colonial magazines. American commentators have suggested that its interest may have been motivated by the outbreak of the Seminole Wars between the colonists and the Indians of Florida, Nat Turner's slave rebellion and, beyond the local interest, America's Manifest Destiny: "Inevitably, these patterns included the notion that the Pacific was yet another American frontier."[9] With these publications Mrs. Fraser becomes a figure of display for an imperial/colonial audience and her story a myth by which the popular imagination understood the civilized world by means of its difference from the savage "others" at its margins. In terms of the construction of social space, Mrs. Fraser's captivity narrative provided for a widespread Western colonial audience the justification for control by the West over the rest of the world.

HISTORICAL ACCOUNTS

At the same time, other historical records appeared. John Curtis's book-length defense of Eliza, *The Shipwreck of the Stirling Castle,* was published in England in 1838 and reprinted in 1841. In Australia, a mild local interest in the story was revived with the rescue of the escaped convict David Bracefell, who in 1842 was brought back to Moreton Bay by a party of explorers intent on land settlement. He reported that he (not John Graham) had rescued the said Eliza and had walked her back to Moreton Bay (some 100 miles away) in the hope of a pardon and possibly a reward but that the ungrateful lady had turned on him at the edge of civilization, threatening to complain of him to the authorities. One of the explorer party, Henry Stuart Russell, includes this reminiscence in his memoirs, *The Genesis of Queensland,* published to commemorate the centenary of Queensland in 1888.[10] Here, within an Australian colonial context, Eliza becomes a foil to Bracefell, her British duplicity standing out against his convict heroism. These historical texts of Curtis and Russell provide a reference point for 20th century postcolonial constructions of Eliza Fraser in Australia that turn the tale into a romance, with David Bracefell as her rescuer. They present Eliza as an unreliable narrator, a seductress, and a betrayer of men—repetitions of which have won her near mythical status on an international scale in the 20th century.[11]

In the 19th century, however, Curtis's history became the official account of the event and a reference point for future commentators. Curtis's book is a polysemic text of empire. Throughout the text he engages in a spirited defense of Eliza Fraser that serves to disguise the wider social, political, and ideological implications of this first engagement between the innocent, saintly, white, female victim and her encounter with a savage "otherness" at the margins of the British Empire.[12] The main text attempts to reconstruct events that occurred on Fraser Island by telling Eliza's story through a series of divergent voices. At the same time, extensive footnotes create for the reader a subtext through which Curtis addresses the fields of navigation, emigration, and the legal system, as well as presents a wealth of anthropological, geological, and scientific information. Within these two textual spaces there is a negotiation between doubt and certainty, between Eliza's dubious story of captivity and the verities of scientific truth. The text utilizes a number of narrative modes including direct address, debate, description, exhortation, the scientific treatise, the diary, and the epistolary novel. It also succumbs to a series of narrative crises. The promise of new disclosures and proofs concerning Mrs. Fraser's veracity and innocence of wrongdoing is constantly subverted by tangential textual delays that occur in the footnotes and all-but take over the page. These diversions occur particularly before the disclosure of possible evidence of rape or cannibalism, hinted at but never quite proven.

An irony here is that the scientific verities are wildly inaccurate. Curtis's description of Fraser Island Aborigines, for example, was lifted from an 1827 ethnography of Port Jackson Aborigines in New South Wales; his descriptions and illustrations of ritual cannibalism and other burial practices are derived from sailor's tales of the South Pacific possibly brought back by Captain Greene, Eliza's new husband, who captained whaling vessels around the coast of New Zealand and wrote sensational traveler's tales for the colonial magazines. The text is connected to empire in diverse ways. Curtis relates in the preface that his aims are to justify Mrs. Fraser's cause; to tell the story of the wreck, captivity and rescue; to encourage missionary work among the natives; to promote emigration; and to enhance anthropological and geographical knowledge.[13]

It has been argued that this text contributed to the emigration and settlement of Australia's northeastern seaboard, to the extension of racial colonization, and to the imposition of Christianity through the mission movement in Australia, which later in the century virtually wiped out the native population of Fraser Island. The text was published in 1838, a year after the founding of the British and Foreign Aboriginal Protection Society and in the same year as the Sydney-based Aboriginal Protection Society came into existence, a society that established the term by which native peoples would be uniformly categorized as "Aborigines" and through which their affairs would be managed.[14] The calls that Curtis made to the builders of empire would be heeded, in part, in Mrs. Fraser's name. Indeed, the first official expedition to Fraser Island and surrounding coastal areas in 1842 was mounted ostensibly to bring back the runaway convicts whom Mrs. Fraser had encountered. It resulted in the first official survey of the land for white settlement, the European naming of landmarks (including Fraser Island), and the demarcation of possible sights for capital expansion of the pastoral and timber industries. What followed brought about the settlement wars of the 1850s, white colonization, and the disruption and dispersal of traditional Aboriginal culture in the area.

MRS. FRASER AS A HISTORICAL AGENT

To what degree can Eliza Fraser be considered a historical agent? To what degree is "she" here at all? What the foregoing discussion has demonstrated is the degree to which the woman and the historical event collapse into a number of discontinuous fields of meaning into which they are placed. Mrs. Fraser's stories to the press, her sensational trial in London, her side-show performances, and the popular literature they invoke all serve to provide the British people as well as the citizens of colonial Australia with a foundational fiction that marks the boundaries between civilization and the wilderness. Not Mrs. Fraser, but her story in its various guises pro-vides the white, male Western hero of progress the space in which to perform a "rescue" operation through which he marks the boundaries be-tween colonizer and colonized, man and his "others"–an operation that protects the idea of "a people" through the exclusion of native inhabitants on an alien, yet-to-be-claimed, physical, psychic, and mythically constructed landscape. Mrs. Fraser has a voice, but it is a voice made present through the masculine constructions of "woman." The natives have no voice and can only be present in the form of representations of their difference from their "civilized" observers, a difference that marks the boundaries of civili-zation. Imaginary projections of the ideas of woman, race, and sexuality motivate the circulation of her tale. "Woman" and her "others" function to guarantee the constructed status, identity, and authority of the British peoples, and later of the Australian nation. Mrs. Fraser is there, but only in the spaces allowed her by her commentators and constructed through categories of femininity already available to her for self-representation, and to her popularizers for the edification/titillation of her various audiences.

What can be said of "Mrs. Fraser" in the narratives that bear her name? They require us to locate her in a number of positions. It is not enough to view Eliza Fraser only and essentially as a woman. If we locate Eliza Fraser within the various discourses of power, we can see that she was complicit with the politics of domination. She became a conduit of the Empire, regardless of what her personal motivations may have been. Ad-ditionally, the meaning of "Eliza Fraser" differs depending on the con-texts of her narratives and their intended audiences. From the moment she entered history, she was already situated within the discourses of power–patriarchy, imperialism, Christianity, and capitalism–but in a number of contradictory ways. From the outset, gender, but also class, relations dominate. She was the captain's wife, traveling on a trading ship that also took emigrant families from Imperial Britain to colonial Australia. But there were no emigrants on board at the time of the wreck, no passengers who could have helped her uphold the captain's rank, authority, and po-sition. Given the power vested in ship's captains in the 19th century, and given the condition of her particular husband, her insistence on his authority in her first official report should not be surprising. During the wreck and its aftermath the captain was ill. Mrs. Fraser attempted to act as his represen-tative. But the crew would have none of it. Despite her superior class position and the aililng condition of her husband, whose rank she attempted to uphold, the crew would not obey her. They called her the "She Captain" and threatened to drown her.[15] When she attempted to collect water for her husband, the water vessel was forcibly taken from her hands. What power was not available to her at the time through social practice, however, was supplied textually in her official report after the event, and concretized by the punitive actions of the colonial administrators at Moreton Bay.[16] In addition, the Caribbean steward from the brig remained faithful to her throughout the voyage.[17] If the crew would not rescue her trunks of clothing and the special food she had prepared for the captain, he would and did, thereby alienating himself from the crew, denying his own limited space of freedom, and upholding relations of dominance and submission marked by race and class.

Once on the island, her race takes on significance, for she was a white woman among the natives. But she was no conqueror. Placed in the care of the women without the company or protection of her husband or any of the crew, without language or knowledge of their customs, she was quickly subjected to their authority. In this situation, her race (a white woman among Aborigines); her class status (one of assumed middle-class authority amid a working-class crew); her patriarchal position (wife of an ailing captain and aunt to the ship's second mate) were to no avail. But race, class, and gender hierarchies are restored in the historical constructions of the event. Indeed, her identity as constituted through these hierarchies of race, class, and gender impels the necessity of History itself.

There are other complications, recorded by the histories but for which no evidence exists, which influence the ways it has been possible to read and thus place the historical Eliza. Michael Alexander, her 20th-century historian of note, reports that although descended from Derbyshire tenant farmers, she was born and raised in Ceylon.[18] She thus would have been an early daughter of the British Raj. No archival evidence has been found to support Alexander's claims, but that is inconsequential. His claims influence the reading of Eliza by subsequent commentators, which in turn feeds the discourses of colonialism with regard to race and class. In addition, they supply a historical interpretation that she herself (like the other white women of the Raj?) was sensual and indulgent, thus providing a motive for the crews' hostility to her. Then there are the biological contingencies of her situation. Mrs. Fraser's third sensational account maintains that she was pregnant when she left Liverpool and gave birth five days after the wreck to a child who drowned shortly after birth. If this is so, she would then have been in a postpartum condition during the time of her so-called captivity, a condition that could be used to explain her treatment by the natives, her position among the women, and her availability to the men of the group.[19] These factors also have bearing on and interact with her gender position as read by future commentators, sometimes in contradictory ways.

SPATIAL DELINEATIONS OF POWER

These race, class, and gender distinctions also have relevance when we consider the spatial dynamics of power. An emigrant ship was a microcosm of class and power relations in England. Its space was assumed to be a unitary social space promoted as a community but divided, policed, and regulated along the boundaries of power. The captain, although he may have come from a lowly class background at home, was by rank the supreme authority on board his vessel. Vested with the judicial powers of arrest and punishment, he also possessed religious and secular power to baptize, marry, and bury while at sea.[20] His authority was mapped out in the spatial arrangements on board – in the distance between the captain, first- and second-class passengers, and the (lowly) crew. These spatial arrangements confer an illusive power, one that must be constantly policed and enforced by social practice. The captain's quarters occupied the poop deck, at the apex and at the rear of the ship, mirroring his position at the apex of its command structure, his gaze directed out and down upon his empire. The crew, on the other hand, were billeted in the worst accommodation, in the forecastle before the mast, and denied access to space allocated (albeit differentially) to the passengers. According to Hassam, "The division of space on board ship work[ed] primarily on the basis of exclusion, of excluding different groups from certain areas of the ship, and this in turn [led] to contestations of space which provide both the focus for the bringing into being of the captain's power and a focus for the affirmation and maintenance of social identity."[21] In the case of the *Stirling Castle,* even though incapacitated by ill health, it was possible for Captain Fraser to maintain his control, status, and class position while the ship was at sea prior to the wreck, despite the absence of passengers whose place might have further enhanced his authority. But the wreck initiated a disintegration of the social order and a breakdown of borders and boundaries, both physical and ideological. Try as she might, Eliza could not step into her husband's shoes. Her good health and her desire to command the vessel on behalf of the captain were no substitute for masculinity. She was no match for a mutinous crew.

After the wreck, the shift in power relations becomes clear with the division of crew into the two lifeboats. Although larger, the longboat, into which the captain was put with his wife, was less seaworthy. He attempted to enforce his command by placing the first mate in charge of the longboat and his second mate in charge of the pinnace. Clearly, his command of these spaces was as important as his naval command. His personal authority broke down, however, when the second mate became ill and was transferred to the longboat, his twelve-year-old nephew was pressed into the service of the mutineers, and a seaman took command of the pinnace, which abandoned the party. On another level, Mrs. Fraser attempted to demand respect for her own and the captain's status by insisting that her/their possessions be brought on board. The crew refused but the faithful mulatto steward rescued them for her from the brig. She thus extended the space occupied by the couple through the presence of two large trunks in the longboat. This act also established a domestic woman's space on board the vessel: the trunks were all that she had to represent "home," although they were mightily resented by the crew. She was afforded no privileges, however, as the crew demanded that she bail water for both herself and her ailing husband. This is the space in which she was said to have given birth, knee-deep in water, attended by the first mate who eventually wrapped the drowned child in his shirt and commended it to the deep.

On the island another configuration of spatial relations evolved, designed in this instance to separate the survivors from the natives. To the survivors the island was wholly alien space, roughly mapped only as coastline on navigational charts and never before inhabited (or known to be inhabited) by white Europeans. Here the shipwreck victims stayed together, interacting tentatively with the natives, bartering clothing for food, knowing themselves and their identity as Britons primarily through their group identity, their proximity to one another. They clung to the shoreline, making their way south, until surrounded by natives and divided among several small groups. Mrs. Fraser was left alone until taken up by a party of women. This was a new social space, totally outside the boundaries of European knowledge, beyond the gaze of the Father's Law. If it can be said that Mrs. Fraser was "in captivity" with the natives, her captivity was as much related to the alterity of this space as it was to the physical controls and constraints placed upon her. Socially and symbolically she was "nowhere" and that spatial positioning robbed her of an identity. What is captivity outside the symbolic order and the rule of the Father's Law? Where there is no Law, there can be no identity.[22] Mrs.

Fraser's subjection was effected through her location and absorption in the space of "otherness."

But not completely. When she was found, her rescuer John Graham reported that the only article of clothing on her person was a tangle of vines around her waist which "her dead and most lamented husband had put on" in which she had hidden her wedding ring and earrings.[23] These become emblematic words for Patrick White and his novel, *A Fringe of Leaves*. Thus, readers of the history are reminded at the point of her rescue of the symbolic presence of her husband through the fringe of leaves that inscribes her body within patriarchy and calls attention to her status as female, protecting herself and her "femininity" from total dissolution.

FOUNDATIONAL FICTIONS

I want to return to the 19th-century origins of the story and to study it as a liminal narrative, that is, a narrative arising from first contact between Europeans and the indigenous people, Europeans and the foreign land occurring in an alien situation that has no predetermined meaning. These liminal stories of first contact, which in Australia would include tales of shipwreck, captivity, and convict escape, could be said to have several important, although discontinuous, effects. Through newspaper articles, oral histories, and local legends they incite the popular imagination and provide initial constructions of racial, class, and gender differences in and for the colony. Through rescue expeditions, they make possible the first mappings of the land, producing a new Western geography, a social production of space. At least two types of official governmental and academic interest follows in the wake of these historical events. The governmental interest concerns colonial policies and practices. Knowledge of the shipwreck and captivity led to further geographic expeditions, observations of Aboriginal life, missionary work, penal surveillance and punishments, as well as the institution of social, ethical, and moral values – all of which change the character of colonial life. The other academic, historical, and ethnographical interest in Mrs. Fraser's ordeal feeds information into broader Western academic classification systems and taxonomies (natural history, philology, ethnography, cartography). These create, maintain, and/or reinforce race and gender hierarchies, legitimize the "natural superiority" of Western rule in colonial empires, *and* provide the structures, ideologies, and institutions of power utilized to constitute the new nation state.

FORMATIONS OF THE NATION-STATE

My conclusions are informed by a number of relevant postcolonial and feminist writers whose critiques open up a new set of questions concerning the construction of the postcolonial nation-state. Postcolonial theoretical perspectives suggest that the basis for a contemporary politics of both global and national power relationships can be found in the complex web of 19th century power relations embedded in the discourses of colonialism. In *Nation and Narration,* for example, Homi Bhabha argues that discourses establish the cultural boundaries of a nation, containing the thresholds of meaning that must be crossed, erased, and translated in the processes of cultural production. He and other contributors to the anthology analyze the concept of nation *as* narration, exploring ways by which strategies invoked within poststructuralist theories of narrative knowledge – textuality, discourse, enunciation, *écriture,* "the unconscious as a language" – might be evoked to open up the ambivalent margins of nation-space.[24] Feminist postcolonial writers suggest further that through an analysis of colonial discourse it is possible to trace the dynamics of contemporary Western knowledge through an analysis of its categories and assumptions that marginalize women, natives, and others.[25] In the main, these theoretical perspectives concern colonial discourses that emerge in so-called Third World countries previously under the control of imperialist forces. My examination of the Eliza Fraser story and the recent cultural critiques of a number of other Australian postcolonial commentators indicate that, at least in part, they provide appropriate frameworks for analysis of settler societies like Australia as well.[26]

AUSTRALIAN NATIONAL IDENTITY
AND THE ELIZA FRASER STORY

The idea of nation, as I argued in *Women and the Bush,* emerges out of social and cultural constructions that posit identity through difference.[27] If the nation is an imagined community, as Anderson maintains,[28] the maintenance of a coherent identity relies on historical narratives that posit and secure its continuance. In the case of Australia, the dominant mythical structure out of which concepts of national identity arise is figured with reference to the white, native-born, Australian male and his battle with the land/Aborigines/"others," framed against the English parent culture. Although women are said to be absent from the annals of Australian history, the idea of the feminine figures metaphorically as the category of difference from the masculine, in a play of masculine sameness and of feminine difference. The white Australian native son battles against a hostile feminine environment, an "enemy to be fought." Sometimes actual women are the enemy, but more often the category is filled in by fire, flood, and drought, and by the presence of Aborigines, the Chinese, and other migrants. Man posits his identity as "Australian" in opposition to his "others"–women, natives, the land–that which "he" is not.

Although it is generally assumed that Australian national identity emerged in the decade of the 1890s, it could be argued that that decade fused elements already nascent in the underlying imaginings of the colonial state. My analysis of the Eliza Fraser story leads in this direction. As a character in a 19th-century drama of empire she can be figured as masculine and given status and authority. In 20th-century Australian versions of the story she is located within the despised British parent culture as a betrayer of her underdog rescuer. In both the 19th- and 20th-century accounts, however, whether directed toward mass culture or a high-minded academic audience, "Eliza Fraser" marks the territory of a superior white civilization. Her story polices the borders of difference within colonial, neocolonial, and postcolonial frameworks of meaning. Her story provides an instance of the nation's representational work: how it understands racial and gender differences, what happens on their sites of contestation, and what are their changing political effects. Analyzing her story in this way significantly alters present dominant understandings of Australian nationalism and the rise of the nation-state. In addition, such a reading challenges the historical assumptions that geography is simply the ground on which historical events take place. Finally, the Eliza Fraser story provides a specifically Australian context for the wider exploration of postcolonial perspectives that mark the field of cultural studies in an intranational arena.

NOTES

1. This is the title of a chapter and the name that Anne Summers coins for Australia as an object of analysis in her pioneering feminist history, *Damned Whores and God's Police* (Ringwood, Australia: Penguin, 1975).

2. The 20th-century representations of the legend have been critically examined by Jim Davidson in "Beyond the Fatal Shore: The Mythologization of Mrs Fraser," *Meanjin* 3 (1990): 449–461, and by me in "Australian Mythologies: The Eliza Fraser Story and Constructions of the Feminine in Patrick White's 'A Fringe of Leaves' and Sidney Nolan's 'Eliza Fraser' Paintings," *Kunapipi 11*, no. 2 (1989): 1–15. In addition to these studies, a historical biography of Eliza Fraser

is being prepared by Yolanda Drummond, a New Zealand writer, and promises to include the New Zealand connection (Eliza reputedly migrates to New Zealand with her second husband in the 1840s). A master's thesis on the history of the Cooloola area, which includes Fraser Island, is in preparation by Elaine Brown through the History Department, University of Queensland.

3. See Michel Foucault, *The Order of Things: An Archaeology of the Human Sciences,* Alan Sheridan, trans. (London: Tavistock, 1970) and *Power/Knowledge: Selected Interviews and Other Writings, 1972–1977,* Colin Gordon, ed., and Colin Gordon, Leo Marshall, John Mepham, and Kate Sopor, trans. (New York: Pantheon, 1980).

4. For an insightful explication of this perspective, see Robert Young, *White Mythologies: Writing History and the West* (London: Routledge, 1990), 1–19.

5. I use the term within quotation marks in the first instance to indicate an ironic distance from its 19th-century significations. Although Eliza and subsequent narrators viewed the event as a captivity, from another perspective it could be seen as her salvation. She was not held captive. Her life, although harsh from her perspective, nonetheless paralleled that of other female members of the group. The term "native" was employed in 19th-century British accounts as a racist expression of inferiority to refer to what were in this instance members of three different clans of the Kabi language group. The term "native" is in the process of being rescued to some degree in the 20th century by indigenous peoples, as the debates in Australia over native title legislation demonstrate. The term "Aboriginal" (another totalizing racist signifier) did not come into existence until 1838 when, with the foundation of the Aboriginal Protection Society, it was introduced to designate indigenous peoples of colonized territories throughout the British Empire.

6. Anon., "Disastrous Wreck of the Ship 'Stirling Castle,' Bound from Sydney, New South Wales, to Singapore," *Alexander's East India Colonial Magazine 14,* part 82 (1837): 258.

7. Neil Buchanan and Barry Dwyer, *The Rescue of Eliza Fraser* (Noosa, Queensland: Noosa Graphica, 1986), 42.

8. Anon., *Narrative of the Capture, Suffering, and Miraculous Escape of Mrs. Eliza Fraser* (New York: Charles Webb and Sons, 1837), 1.

9. See James Levernier and Hennig Cohen, eds. comps., *The Indians and Their Captives* (Westport, CN: Greenwood Press, 1977), 267.

10. Henry Stuart Russell, *The Genesis of Queensland* (London: Vintage Books, 1888; reprint, Toowoomba, Queensland, Australia: Vintage Books, 1989), 257–258.

11. The legend both in Australia and overseas took shape as a result of Sidney Nolan's first international exhibition in London in which a series of "Mrs Fraser" paintings were included. Colin MacInnes's introduction to the catalogue *Sydney Nolan: Catalogue of an Exhibition of Paintings from 1947 to 1957 Held at the Whitechapel Art Gallery, London, June to July, 1957* (London: Whitechapel Gallery, 1957) summarizes the story in the following way:

Mrs Fraser was a Scottish lady who was shipwrecked on what is now Fraser Island, off the Queensland coast. She lived for 6 months among the aborigines,

rapidly losing her clothes, until she was discovered by one Bracefell, a desert-
ing convict who himself had hidden for 10 years among the primitive Australians. The lady asked the criminal to restore her to civilisation, which he
agreed to do if she would promise to intercede for his free pardon from the
Governor. The bargain was sealed and the couple set off inland.

At first sight of European settlement, Mrs Fraser rounded on her benefactor
and threatened to deliver him to justice if he did not immediately decamp.
Bracefell returned disillusioned to the hospitable bush, and Mrs Fraser's adventures aroused such admiring interest that on her return to Europe she was
able to exhibit herself at 6d a showing in Hyde Park.

This is the legend surrounding the event to which both Michael Ondaatje and
Andre Brink had reference. It forms the basis for Andre Brink's South African
novel, *An Instant in the Wind* (London: Minerva, 1976) and for Michael Ondaatje's
long poem, *The Man with Seven Toes* (Toronto: Coach House Press, 1969).

12. For more extensive treatment of the London media coverage of the ship-
wreck, see Kay Schaffer, "Eliza Fraser's Trial by Media," *Antipodes (US)*, (Decem-
ber 1991): 114–119, and Kay Schaffer, "Captivity Narratives and the Idea of
Nation," in Kay Schaffer, Kate Darian-Smith, and Roslyn Poignant, *Captured Lives:
Australian Captivity Narratives* (London: Sir Robert Menzies Centre for Australian
Studies, University of London, 1993), 1–17.

13. John Curtis, *The Wreck of the Stirling Castle* (London: George Virtue, 1838),
preface.

14. John Stratton, "A Question of Origins," *Arena 89* (1989): 134.

15. In the official report Mrs. Fraser singles out one member of the defiant
crew by name, a Henry Youlden, who "curses" Eliza and takes rainwater from
her which she had collected for her ailing husband. His words are the only ones
to appear in direct quotation: "Damn you, you She-Captain, if you say much
more I'll drown you." Youlden's side of the story would emerge a decade later,
in an article published in the New York *Knickerbocker Magazine,* ostensibly written to warn would-be gold prospectors about the dangers of a voyage to Australia, but also no doubt to vindicate himself from the charges brought against him
by Mrs. Fraser. See Henry Youlden, "Shipwreck in Australia," *Knickerbocker 41,*
no. 4 (1853): 291–300.

16. Within a 20th-century Australian nationalist context, of course, these behaviors of the recalcitrant crew toward Mrs. Fraser (as a representative of English
colonial authority) would be read as heroic. Youlden's article to an American public
also details to his mind the unjust punishments meted out to the crew whom
he represents as able, sober, and responsible actors caught in an irrational power
struggle with the captain's party and a hostile public.

17. Various survivors including Mrs. Fraser, Baxter, and seamen Hodge and
Darge commented on Corallis's devotion to Mrs. Fraser; see Curtis, *Wreck of the
Stirling Castle,* 30, 49, 174.

18. Michael Alexander, *Mrs Fraser on the Fatal Shore* (London: Michael Joseph,
1971), 8. Yolanda Drummond, a New Zealand researcher who is preparing a bi-

ography of Eliza Fraser, has located a copy of the book by Robert Gibbings, John Graham, Convict, 1824, in the possession of one of Eliza Fraser's descendants in New Zealand which contains a marginal note, written by a great-grandson. In response to Gibbings's contention that Mrs. Fraser had lived all her life in the Orkney Islands, he responds: "Wrong. She came from Ceylon where her parents lived." Drummond suggests that this is the source for Alexander's claim. See "Progress of Eliza," *Royal Historical Society of Queensland Journal 15,* no. 1 (February 1993): 16.

19. These considerations are taken up in Elaine Brown, "History of the Cooloola Region" (MA thesis [in progress], History Department, University of Queensland). Drummond casts doubt on the whole story, see "Progress," 17, 20–21.

20. See Andrew Hassam, " 'Our Floating Home': Social Space and Group Identity on Board the Emigrant Ship," *Working Papers in Australian Studies,* no. 76 (London: Sir Robert Menzies Centre for Australian Studies, University of London, 1992), 3.

21. Ibid., 7.

22. This discussion assumes a Lacanian psychoanalytic understanding of the subject. According to Lacan, and also to psychoanalytic French feminist thought, each of us takes on our personal, social, and cultural identity within a network if social and symbolic meanings organized by and through language. In a phallocentric culture, masculinity (or what Lacan calls "the Father's Law") is the overriding signifier of status, power, and authority for the Self (whether one is born biologically male or female). What this means is that identity is constituted through language that takes masculinity as its norm. Both men and women can occupy the cultural position of a masculine subject, that is, one who has power, status, and authority, but women will also be marked as different, and inferior. The feminine position (a category that can include the lower class, Aborigines, convicts, and other "deviant" types) is designated as inferior, lacking, "other". If subjectivity is constituted through one's position(s) within the symbolic order of culture, then finding oneself in a totally alien environment would constitute a site of nonmeaning/nonidentity. See Jacques Lacan, "The Mirror Phase," *New Left Review 51* (1968): 71–77, and Helene Cixous, "Laugh of the Medusa," *Signs 1,* no. 4 (Summer 1976): 879.

23. From John Graham's log, quoted in Robert Gibbings, *John Graham, Convict* (London: J. M. Dent, 1956), 98.

24. Homi Bhabha, "Introduction: Narrating the Nation," in *Nation and Narration,* Homi Bhabha, ed. (London: Routledge, 1990), 4.

25. See, for example, Mary Louise Pratt, *Imperial Eyes: Travel Writing and Transculturation* (London: Routledge, 1992); Gayatri Chakravorty Spivak, "Can the Subaltern Speak? Speculations on Widow Sacrifice," in *Marxism and the Interpretation of Culture,* Cary Nelson and Lawrence Grossberg, eds. (London: Macmillan, 1988), 271–313. Gayatri Chakravorty Spivak, "Subaltern Studies: Deconstructing Historiography," 197–221, and "A Literary Representation of the Subaltern: A Woman's Text from the Third World," in *In Other Worlds: Essays in Cultural*

Politics, 241–268 (New York: Routledge, 1988); Marianna Torgovnick, *Gone Primitive* (Chicago: Chicago University Press, 1990); and Trinh T. Minh-ha, *Woman, Native, Other* (Bloomington: Indiana University Press, 1989).

26. Relevant here is the work of Bill Ashcroft, Gareth Griffiths, and Helen Tiffin, eds., *The Empire Writes Back: Theory and Practice in Post-Colonial Literatures* (New York: Routledge, 1989); Gareth Griffiths, "Imitation, Abrogation and Appropriation: The Production of the Post-Colonial Text," *Kunapipi 9*, no. 1 (1987): 13–20; Sneja Gunew, "Denaturalizing Cultural Nationalisms: Multicultural Readings of 'Australia,' " in *Nation and Narration*, Homi Bhabha, ed. (London: Routledge, 1990, 99–120; Sneja Gunew, "PMT (Post Modernist Tensions): Reading for (Multi)cultural Difference," in *Striking Chords: Multicultural Literary Interpretations*, Sneja Gunew and Kateryna Longley, eds. (Sydney: Allen and Unwin, 1992): 36–46; and Stephen Meucke, *Textual Spaces: Aboriginality and Cultural Studies* (Sydney: University of New South Wales Press, 1992).

27. Kay Schaffer, *Women and the Bush: Forces of Desire and the Australian Cultural Tradition* (Sydney: Cambridge University Press, 1988), 8–15.

28. Benedict Anderson, *Imagined Communities: Reflections on the Origin and Spread of Nationalism* (London: Verso, 1983, 1991), 16, 145.

6

Gender, War, and Imagined Geographies: United States Women and the ''Far-Flung'' Fronts of World War II

JUDY BARRETT LITOFF
DAVID C. SMITH

St. Louis Railroad Station – July 29, 1944

It's 1:25 A.M. and here I sit, practically alone, waiting for 8:00 A.M. . . . Oh yes, I missed my train in Cincinnati this morning by two minutes. . . . Another girl missed the train, too, and we had a gay time walking around Cincinnati. . . . All my life I've wanted something interesting like this to happen to me, and it has. . . . This is really a trip for the books. — FRANCES ZULAUF to Lt. Robert Zulauf[1]

Edgewood, Rhode Island – October 23, 1944

We, too, have our maps in the "bulkhead" over the kitchen radiator. I have just put up the new geographic map of your part of the world and have just put the pins in Leyte. . . . There over on the opposite wall, between the windows and the cupboard side of the sink, I have "Germany" and have just put the pin in Aachen. It looks marvelous and yet the unconquered territory still looks huge! — SAIDEE R. LEACH to Lt. (J.G.) Douglas Leach[2]

The cataclysmic events of World War II altered and expanded the geographical horizons of women in the United States in ways that were unimaginable prior to the outbreak of hostilities. Traveling to remote areas, meeting new people, taking on new jobs, encountering different ways of life, and establishing homes in unknown locations provided immense opportunities for women to extend their geographical centers and states of knowledge. This was particularly true for the more than 350,000 women who joined the WACS (Women's Army Corps), WAVES (Women Accepted for Volunteer Emergency Service, Navy), SPARS (Semper Paratus/Always Ready, Coast Guard), Marine Corps Women's Reserve, Army Nurse Corps, Navy Nurse Corps, American Red Cross, United Service Organizations, and Women Airforce Service Pilots. In addition, mothers, wives, sisters, and daughters vicariously followed the routes of loved ones who were stationed at distant postings around the world.

In their letters to friends and loved ones, United States women regularly commented on their changing and expanding horizons. They provided detailed descriptions of their growing sense of their place in the world, and they solicited information from correspondents about new and unusual experiences. Letter writers mapped out the events of their daily lives in their letters as they sought to prepare loved ones for the changes they were undergoing. Indeed, the billions of letters exchanged during the wartime years helped to minimize the distinctions between the separate domains of the letter writers and their recipients.

The significance of letter writing and the rapid and regular delivery of the mail was never more poignantly clear than during World War II. Magazine covers, feature and news articles, thousands of advertisements, government posters, greeting cards, advice manuals, as well as novels, short stories, and popular songs, all depicted the mail as an important morale builder. Although the mail inevitably included reports of deaths, wounds, prisoners of war, the occasional "Dear John" or "Dear Jane" letter, as well as the "I thought you ought to know" letter, the myriad ways that the mail and morale motif was emphasized make it clear that letter writing was extraordinarily crucial to a nation caught up in the throes of war.[3]

Throughout the wartime period millions of people were on the move in the United States as one of the major demographic shifts in American history took place. The U.S. Census Bureau estimated that 15,300,000 civilians moved during the war, over half of them across state lines. People hurried to new jobs opening up in shipyards and war plants. Families sought out the precious times they could steal together "for the duration" or for as long as would be granted them at the military bases where loved ones were in training.[4]

Service wives often traveled thousands of miles to be with their husbands. They journeyed from small North American towns to sophisticated metropolitan centers and back again. A reporter for the *New York*

Times Magazine described these women as "wandering members of a huge unorganized club." They recognized each other on sight; exchanged views on living quarters, babies, and allotments; expressed pride in their husbands; and helped each other in times of difficulty. War wives banded together and made life, if not pleasant, tolerable.[5]

Women could find a great deal of advice in the press on how to ease the difficulties of traveling. They were told what to pack and "how to live in a trunk."[6] The special problems associated with traveling on crowded trains and busses with young children were widely discussed. Mothers were exhorted to avoid the logistical problems associated with carrying too much luggage, but, at the same time, to bring sufficient diapers, bottles, baby food, and other necessities.[7] While preparing for a long train trip with her two-month-old daughter to join her Army Air Corps husband at his posting in Louisiana, a young Georgia war wife wrote, "I shall bring as little as possible – now, I *will* need the cover for her cradle, won't I?" Four days later, she remarked, "I need more than my two bags for both our things. I may send the coffee maker and bathinette on ahead of me. You have an alarm clock, don't you? Let me know."[8]

Not everyone agreed that service wives should follow their husbands to military bases. Citing the pressures on already overcrowded travel facilities, the Office of War Information urged wives to remain at home. At least some observers described those women who went anyway as "selfish," pointing out that prices were high and conditions near military camps far too crowded. Wives often arrived at bases just as their husbands were about to be shipped overseas. Nevertheless, most wives felt it was important to be with their husbands as long as possible.[9]

The sense of time and space of young war brides living in Hawaii at the time of the Pearl Harbor attack was suddenly and irrevocably disrupted by the events of December 7, 1941. In a December 8 letter to her sister, one young war bride, Fern Steuteville Wilson, vividly described the onset of hostilities on her life and how her sense of personal space within the home had been threatened by the Japanese attack:

> I hope you will excuse me for not writing yesterday. At least I can say that I saw the very beginning of it . . . At 8 A.M. a blast woke us up and Jack said, "The damn Navy is practicing bombing over Hickam [Field] because it's Sunday morning." . . . We jumped out of bed and it was a sensation to see a plane coming out of a dive almost even with the bedroom window . . . Jack yells, "It's the Rising Sun!" I didn't know what he meant, it was 8 A.M. so why shouldn't the sun be rising. Then he said, "It's the Japs!" At that minute my heart started pounding like a trip hammer and kept it up until I woke up this morning.[10]

Over the course of the next four years the dislocations precipitated by the events of December 7 would reverberate in the lives of women throughout the United States. Following a whirlwind courtship, Audrey M. Savell resigned from her job as a librarian at Fort Dix, New Jersey, and traveled across the continent by train to marry her fiancé, a career Navy man stationed at Coronado, California. In March 1945 she accepted a position at the Presidio in San Francisco, where she was appointed chief of training and inspections for the Army 9th Service Command. The exhilaration and trepidation she felt about her new job were the focus of her March 16, 1945, letter to her husband:

> I'm so terribly excited I can hardly hold the pen! This afternoon Mr. Xeno-
> phon Smith from [the Presidio in] San Francisco phoned and wants me to
> take a job up at headquarters, in his office – and what a job! I'm positively
> shattered when I think of the responsibility of it! It will consist equally in
> training new librarians to replace the 24 on this command who are already
> going overseas and more to follow, and travelling all over the Service Com-
> mand giving the libraries a technical inspection. Gad, *me*! I'm thrilled and scared
> all at once, but I just can't see turning it down.[11]

Audrey Savell made one major move during the war years, but other war wives became modern-day "camp followers" as they crisscrossed the country with their service husbands.[12] In a November 1, 1944, letter to her Marine husband, in which she reminisced about their travels in Virginia, North Carolina, and California prior to his shipment to the Pacific theater, Marjorie Killpack of Ogden, Utah, wrote: "Do you remember the broken bed at Mrs. Royens and how damn squeaky it was. Also, the bed we broke down at Mrs. Kelly's in Quantico. Gee, we've sure left a 'trail of broken beds' behind us. Ha! What made me think of it was this one – It's very good inasmuch as it's soft. But is very shaky, and wouldn't stand much working on."[13]

Women separated from their fiancés by wartime exigencies traveled alone to meet future in-laws, and wives made frequent journeys to the homes of their husbands' families. Women also traveled great distances for brief rendezvous with sweethearts and husbands. The lobby of the Saint Francis Hotel in San Francisco and under the clock at New York City's Grand Central Station were two legendary meeting places. Perhaps the most poignant journeys of all were the hurriedly arranged and occasionally clandestine trips to ports of embarkation to say good-bye.[14]

Uprooted war wives faced many new challenges and were sometimes required to adapt to entirely new ways of life. For example, Lilian Selinkoff of Wilmington, Delaware, followed her Army husband to his assignment in the Canal Zone. Her letters to friends in Wilmington included a report of her attendance at a Jewish wedding where the marriage canopy was made of palms and lilies. She also wrote about making borscht from canned spinach and beets and preparing gefilte fish from local fish, such as corbina, ocean perch, and snook. As she said in one letter, "We even serve it to goyim when they come to dinner."[15]

The pressing demands of World War II also resulted in the uprooting of women from "traditional" female roles. With the decline of the rural population of the United States as farmers joined the military or sought more lucrative work in war industries, an estimated three million non-farm women took on farm jobs between 1943 and 1945.[16] Following a train trip through rural Arkansas, Mabel Opal Miller reflected on the changing wartime landscape of rural America. In a September 6, 1944, letter she sent to her Army Air Corps boyfriend, she observed: "I noticed on the farms, mostly the little ones with just a shack for a home, there seems to be no one but the women left to do the work. You see them out taking care of cattle, etc. It makes one proud to see how the women have picked up where the men left off and are keeping the home fires burning."[17]

The landscape of industrial/urban America underwent equally striking changes during the wartime years as the proportion of women in the work force increased from 25% at the beginning of the war to 36% at the war's end.[18] After securing a job at a shipyard, Polly Crow of Louisville, Kentucky, proudly proclaimed to her Army husband: "You are now the husband of a career woman – just call me your little Ship Yard Babe!" She described the "grand and glorious feeling" of opening her own checking account, gas rationing and automobile maintenance, the many "wolves" on the swing shift, and what it was like to join a union. Late in 1944, upon learning that the work of building Landing Ship Tanks (LSTs) at the shipyard would be completed within the next few months, she wrote a letter in which she bemoaned the fact that "my greatly enjoyed working career will come to an end."[19]

While most wartime separations occurred when loved ones were inducted into military service, the events of the war resulted in forced separations of a very different type for Americans of Japanese descent. In 1942 the 120,000 Japanese-Americans living along the West Coast were evacuated to camps located in remote areas of the United States. This relocation process sometimes resulted in painful separations. Sonoko Iwata and her three young children were sent to the Colorado River Relocation Camp near Poston, Arizona, while her husband, Shigezo Iwata, was detained at the Lordsburg, New Mexico, Internment Camp. After writing an appeal to Attorney General Francis Biddle in which she "solemnly affirm[ed]" that her husband had "at all times been loyal to America and had always cooperated with our government," and that to be considered otherwise was "a dishonor which we cannot bear to face," the family was reunited at Poston in July 1943. In letters written to her husband during their sixteen-month separation, Sonoko Iwata described the task of building a new community in the Arizona desert as well as the difficult personal adjustments she faced. Yet in a March 5, 1943, letter, she found the emotional strength to state: "You know, I was thinking today that time marches on and if I'm to keep up, we should bury the past and always look toward what's coming."[20]

Unanticipated avenues for travel and adventure opened up for those women who profited from the opportunities to don military uniforms. When writing to their families, in particular, their mothers, women in uniform made special efforts to describe their new and different circumstances. WAC Private Katherine Trickey of Lewiston, Maine, was stationed at Camp Wheeler, Georgia. When writing to her mother, she often commented on her experiences as a northerner living in the South. On March 6, 1944, she wrote:

> You have heard, undoubtedly, of Georgia as the Peach State. Yesterday, I found out why. Six of us hired a car and drove to Fort Valley to see the peach blossoms. It was the Sunday when they were in full bloom and we had been told it was a sight worth seeing. There are acres of trees. The pink blossoms against a background of a heavenly blue sky was a sight I shall never forget.[21]

Marion Stegeman of Athens, Georgia, was one of approximately a thousand women who received the silver wings of the Women Airforce Service Pilots. Her vivacious letters to her mother and to her fiancé, dated from many cities as she ferried aircraft throughout the United States, recount her joy in flying. In an April 23, 1943, letter to her mother, she wrote:

> The gods must envy me! This is just too, *too,* to be true! (By now you realize I had a good day as regards flying. Nothing is such a gauge to the spirits as how well or how poorly one has flown). . . . I'm far too happy. The law of compensation must be waiting to catch up with me somewhere. Oh, God, how I love it! Honestly, Mother, you haven't *lived* until you get way *up* there— all alone—just you and that big beautiful plane humming under your control.[22]

As a member of the Army Nurse Corps, Marjorie La Palme was sent to England in June 1942, where she worked at a military hospital. Following the D-Day invasion of June 6, 1944, she was transferred to an evacuation hospital that followed the Ninth Army through France, Belgium, Holland, and Germany. During her thirty-nine months of overseas duty, she was often in the front lines of battle. In mid-December 1944 she wrote a graphic letter to her mother in which she described the Battle of the Bulge:

The buzz bombs have stopped for awhile but enemy planes come over and then the ack ack guns start–we see flashes and explosions all along the horizon–we are very close to the fighting.

Everywhere through all these countries we see the havoc of war–piles of bricks and rubble–streets and streets of it–once homes and public buildings, bridges bombed. . . . Not just a few homes but the entire city is gone. . . .

It was a terribly exciting night last night–so much activity all over the place–many enemy planes over head–we could hear them strafing–explosives and mortar fire continually all the night long. . . . The weather is frigid cold and snow is deep. My heart goes out to our poor boys out there in the dark and cold.[23]

After joining the American Red Cross, Rita Pilkey of Dallas, Texas, was sent to China, where she was given the responsibility of establishing Red Cross facilities in Kunming and Luliang. Pilkey penned long letters to her parents which were filled with descriptions of Chinese life, her meetings with Chinese dignitaries, and information about her Red Cross work. In March 1944, shortly after her arrival in China, Pilkey wrote about learning to fire guns in small arms class because, as she noted in another letter, "when you drive any place away from the base you are on, you always take a gun because of the bandits." In November 1944, after being selected to set up the first tent facility at a new base, she told her parents that "I like it here, but I feel honored to be chosen to go there because it is supposed to be the hardest place here."[24]

WAC Private Betty Donahue was stationed in Port Moresby, New Guinea, and Tacloban, Leyte, the Philippines, where she worked as a mail clerk. Upon her arrival in New Guinea in September 1944 she wrote a letter to her family in which she described the "exotic" life she encountered in the South Seas:

Your wandering gal has finally come to rest in her South Sea Island Paradise–I always say it's not exactly as the movies picture it, but considering everything it is very nice. . . . Gad, is it hot here–The perspiration just rolls off you when you just sit in your underwear – Oh, well, I came to do a job and I can do it out as well as the next guy. . . . This is really a very interesting place – coconut palms, grass houses, odd shells on the beach, huge trees with roots that spread for a half a block and natives with red hair and rings thru their noses – really things I never expected to see.[25]

For women who remained at home during World War II, the opportunities for imagined and vicarious travel were widespread. One young war wife from New Athens, Illinois, wrote to her recently departed husband and said, "I know that with every minute you're going farther away from me. I figure that you are somewhere in Texas now, Darling."[26] Isabel Kidder of Durham, New Hampshire, expressed similar sentiments when she commented, "My darling, I call this the first day, for it is the first day in which I do not know where you are. If your ship slipped out into the wideness of ocean last night, to-night, or tomorrow, I shall not know until after the war probably."[27] Indeed, the themes of separation and distance regularly occurred in the letters written by women during World War II.

In their efforts to bridge the miles that separated them from their loved ones, war wives often set aside a special time each evening to write letters to husbands stationed far from home. As one letter writer commented, this was "the best time of each twenty-four hours." From the seclusion of their bedrooms, women recalled past events, included information about the day's activities, discussed the whereabouts of relatives and friends, and even symbolically smoked "the last cigg before cutting the light off" just as they had done before the separation.[28]

Women on the home front listened to radio broadcasts about the war and carefully read newspaper and magazine articles that reported on the activities of United States forces scattered around the world. The columns of well-known journalists, such as Ernie Pyle, Richard C. Hottelet, and E. J. Kahn, Jr., were scrutinized for information concerning the whereabouts of relatives and friends. In a January 31, 1945, letter, Catherine Pike of Esmond, Rhode Island, informed her husband, who was engaged in heavy combat with the Allied forces in Europe, that "I even know where you are exactly by following the news closely." Seven weeks later she wrote, "George, you'd be surprised if you knew how much I know about the war, how much reading I do about it, and how well I can talk about it."[29] Women gleaned additional information about wartime events taking place around the world from servicepersons' letters, radio commentary, newsreels, and movies.

Distant geographical placenames, such as Anzio, Okinawa, Dresden,

Stalingrad, and Yalta, were incorporated into everyday vocabulary. Newspapers and magazines regularly published detailed maps of the various theaters of war. Public buildings, such as schools and post offices, featured war maps on their bulletin boards. Moreover, maps lined the walls of many American homes as armchair strategists marked the advance of Allied forces. The war maps of Keith Frazier Somerville of Cleveland, Mississippi, even spread onto the walls of her bathroom, and she noted in her wartime journal, "Now I have to stand in the tub to follow the African campaigns and we . . . go so far as to conduct guests into the Maproom."[30]

Across the United States women envisioned both the extraordinary and quotidian events encountered by loved ones stationed at "far-flung" fronts. Flora Southwick of Marietta, Ohio, wrote to her husband, who was assigned to the Supreme Headquarters Allied Expeditionary Force in England, while she listened to the D-Day broadcasts from the beaches of Normandy. As a former newspaper reporter for the *Marietta Times,* she used her journalistic acumen to visualize the events of the invasion even though she could not be there:

June 6, 1944

Dearest Darling:

Today we have lived history. I can't even describe my sensations when I turned on the radio this morning. Somehow there is a feeling of relief that things have actually started. . . .

I guess my old newspaper days got the better of me this morning when I was listening to the radio. I fairly ached to be there and see it all with my own eyes. Even the possible loss of one's life seemed a small price to pay for being part of one of the biggest things in history. If a man survives he will always know that he made history. If he does not he went out in a supreme moment and there is something to be said for going that way. . . .

Devotedly, Flora[31]

Service wives often contemplated what combat conditions were like for their husbands. One young war wife wrote, "As I hung out Georgie's wash this A.M. my hands became so cold that I could hardly move them. It made me think about you. Gosh, Honey, how can you shoot when your hands are stiff? I wonder if you'd like me to send you a couple of pairs of gloves? You could wear them when you're not shooting maybe."[32]

As women confronted the harsh realities of war, they could not avoid envisioning the personal tragedies which might and did occur. Josephine Keutman, a fifty-three-year-old widow from the Bronx, New York, wrote an emotional letter after learning that her only son had been listed as missing in action following his failure to return from a bombing mission over Poland:

October 25, 1944

To My Darling (where ever you are, come back to me):

Today is exactly 6 weeks that you went on that fatal mission. Maybe some miracle or gift of God has happened that will enable you to come back to your base or maybe home. God only knows how I am worrying about you so far away from home and maybe being tortured or sick or even wounded. . . .
    While I am writing I am being blinded with tears which are running faster than the pen is writing. . . . I miss you much, my heart is broken.

Love, Mom[33]

The return of loved ones from combat provided still another opportunity for women on the home front to ponder and envision the battlefront experience. Margaret Barrow of West Point, Georgia, wrote a joyous letter when she learned that her Navy son, who had been wounded in battle, had arrived safely in California:

May 14, 1944

Dearest Jody Boy:

Cannot find words to express my joy to know my sweet boy is actually back in the U.S.A. Still have to stop and think at intervals if it is really a fact, or am I dreaming. . . .
    Bet you are confused and mixed up about the "states." All of the boys coming in from the Pacific area seem to be. It must be very primitive and rugged out there. It will seem wonderful to be back in civilization again after you get "adjusted" to we queer beings, the "civilians". . . .

Lovingly, Mother[34]

Of course, thoughts of death and mayhem did not occupy all of women's musings as they contemplated the experiences of loved ones at war. After reading letters from her Army Air Corps husband stationed in England, Marjorie Gaunt of Cranston, Rhode Island, remarked: "You must be getting real British cycling around and dining in tea rooms. Do those places look like you expected them to look? When you write those things, I have a definite picture in mind."[35]

As one might expect, questions relating to fidelity and love sometimes emerged in the minds of service wives who were separated from their husbands. When one Army husband failed to report fully about his furlough in Paris, a city once described as the "silver foxhole," his young war wife, Barbara Wooddall Taylor of Fairburn, Georgia, scolded him with the following "choice" remarks:

> You probably didn't have time to write me while you were in Paris – and for that I don't blame you one bit. Although there was one short paragraph about the trip, I gather you had a *nice* time. What if I should go to the mountains or beach and when I returned say just a few words like you did. You'd probably think the same things I am thinking right now and I would doubt it if you would like it even as much as I. Do I make myself clear ole top? Since we are miles apart with an ocean between us there isn't a helluva lot I can do about it – as you well know. I am glad that you are "rested mentally" – must be a great feeling – wouldn't know for ten months is a long time – and as you have told me, "It's all in your mind, Barbie" – and who knows?? You could be right about it![36]

The coming of peace in August 1945 provided further opportunities for women at home to visualize events taking place around the world. One young war bride wrote an exuberant letter to her soldier husband in Europe and exclaimed: "THE WAR IS OVER. . . . Mother and I were listening to the radio when the news first came on – and we were laughing and crying together. I kept saying, "I want to go to Paris" – meaning, I wanted to go on the air by radio – and sure enough – we did go to Paris – and I felt as if we were there together."

In their correspondence, women of the World War II generation readily acknowledged that both they and their loved ones had been dramatically changed by the events of the war. Writing from the Mississippi Delta at the end of August 1945, Keith Frazier Somerville offered some succinct observations on these changes:

> We have lived with war so long – it almost seems forever! It's even hard to remember a time when we weren't hanging over the radio for "the news." . . . This has been such a horrible war, and so far flung that even we noncombatants, who have suffered not at all, are exhausted emotionally and mentally trying to keep up with it, do our small parts, and try not to worry. We've lived on a tension for so long that it's going to be hard for all of us to relax.[38]

On a more personal level, Edith Speert, a supervisor of a federally funded daycare center in Cleveland, Ohio, wrote a forthright letter to her husband on October 21, 1945, and declared:

> I must admit I'm not exactly the same girl you left – I'm twice as independent as I used to be and to top it off, I sometimes think I've become "hard as nails" . . . Also – more and more I've been living exactly as *I* want to and . . . I do as I damn please. As a whole, I don't think my changes will affect our relationship, but I do think you'll have to remember that there are some slight alterations in me. I'm pretty sure that holds true for you too.

Three weeks later, Speert reiterated her concerns:

> Sweetie, I want to make sure I make myself clear about how I've changed. I want you to know *now* that you are not married to a girl that's interested solely in a home – I shall definitely have to work all my life – I get emotional satisfaction out of working; and I don't doubt that many a night you will cook the supper while I'm at a meeting. Also, dearest – I shall never wash and iron – there are laundries for that! Do you think you'll be able to bear living with me?[39]

The events of World War II also contributed to women's growing geopolitical consciousness. During the final months of the conflict, women's letters were punctuated with astute comments about the complexities of world politics and their hopes and dreams for the postwar world. Following the Russian declaration of war on Japan on August 8, 1945, Kay McReynolds, a senior at the University of Missouri, wrote to her fiancé and announced: "My next to the favorite country is Russia. . . . Isn't it wonderful? It will bring the end of the war sooner, but I'm not one of these optimistic souls who are saying that it may be over in two or three weeks. But, with the atomic bomb, maybe we won't have to lose so many lives in an invasion."[40]

In their victory letters women wrote of the ecstasy and euphoria of peace while acknowledging that the new atomic age had unleashed many enigmatic challenges. Edna Golan of New York City expressed these ideas with exceptional clarity when writing to her Army husband in Europe:

August 9, 1945

My Love:

> Can you feel the brilliant sunshine on this page? And the peace? And hear the splashings of the summer? And the laughter of the children? . . . And the goldenrods, and the lovely bushes and trees all along the edge of the water? . . .

For the events of these last four days give great reason for . . . optimism what with the atomic bomb and the announcement of Russia's declaration of war on Japan. As far as the atomic bomb is concerned, my Darling, I can see where the end of fighting for us might be sooner, but it's a great sacrifice, my Darling, for this really seems to be, the beginning of the end of all civilization. . . .

Your own, Edna[41]

In an August 18, 1945, letter to her future husband, Constance Hope Jones of Kirkwood, Missouri, presented a perceptive analysis of the fragile and transitory nature of the politics of peace:

Now, I suppose President Truman and Congress really have a big job of getting things and people adjusted to peace time ways of hiring and doing! Perhaps the biggest job is yet ahead. Over the radio yesterday . . . I heard the starting of another war! All about how the U.S. was developing new and secret weapons and how we should keep our secrets from the Russians! One was Winston Churchill, another was the head of the Army Air Forces! Talk like that is a betrayal of those who died or were wounded in this war and of those who are working to make it possible for nations to live in peace with each other.[42]

With the misery and anguish of World War II uppermost in their minds, women were inspired to call for a world in which peace would be paramount. In an August 14, 1945, letter to her husband, Rose McClain of Snoqualmie Falls, Washington, spoke for many women and men when she expressed the hope that World War II would mark "the end of war for all time," and "that our children will learn kindness, patience, honesty and the depth of love and trust we have learned, from all of this, without the tragedy of war. That they shall never know hate, selfishness and death from such as this has been."[43]

The geographic horizons of women in the United States were significantly altered and expanded by the events of World War II. As women journeyed to remote areas and encountered new people and ways of life, their view of the world was greatly enhanced. Service wives crisscrossed the continent and women in uniform often traveled to the far corners of the world, while, at the same time, women who remained at home vicariously followed the journeys of loved ones. The changing landscape of rural and urban America enabled women to take on new social and economic roles. Moreover, utilizing their augmented geopolitical knowledge, women were better prepared to confront the challenges presented by the postwar world.

The wartime correspondence of United States women provides unmistakable evidence that World War II had an enormous and far-reaching effect upon women's real and imagined geographies. The war transformed the way women thought about themselves and their world, and the events of that war continue to reverberate in many women's lives.

NOTES

1. Frances Zulauf to Bob Zulauf, July 29, 1944. The letters of Frances Zulauf are part of our archive of more than 30,000 letters written by United States women, representing a socioeconomic and geographic cross section of American life, during World War II. A seventy-reel microfilm edition, *The World War II Letters of United States Women,* is in preparation for publication by Scholarly Resources Inc. We have designed a database application, written in FoxPro, that will enable us to present detailed statistical analyses of the geographical and socioeconomic backgrounds of the letter writers as well as information about a number of other topical categories. A Researchers Edition of the FoxPro database application will accompany the seventy-reel microfilm edition. The database application will facilitate the research efforts of future scholars as they formulate and develop new interpretations of these letters. For additional information on the database application, see Judy Barrett Litoff and David C. Smith, "Understanding the Home Front: World War II Letters of American Women" (paper presented at the Organization of American Historians annual meeting, Louisville, KY, April 1991). A selection of the letters of Frances Zulauf appears in Judy Barrett Litoff and David C. Smith, " 'I Wish that I Could Hide Inside This Letter': World War II Correspondence," *Prologue 24,* (Summer 1992): 103–114, and in Judy Barrett Litoff and David C. Smith, *Since You Went Away: World War Letters from American Women on the Home Front* (New York: Oxford University Press, 1991), 24–31. All letter collections cited in this chapter are part of our archive – the World War II Letters of United States Women.

2. Saidee R. Leach to Douglas Leach, October 23, 1944. A selection of the letters of Saidee R. Leach appears in Litoff and Smith, *Since You Went Away,* 12–13, 183–189.

3. For an examination of the important role of letter writing during World War II, see Judy Barrett Litoff and David C. Smith, " 'Will He Get My Letter?': Popular Portrayals of Mail and Morale during World War II," *Journal of Popular Culture 23* (Spring 1990): 21–43.

4. Vance Packard, "Millions on the Move," *American Magazine,* October 1944, pp. 34–36, 97, has a good map of the migratory routes. See Bertram B. Fowler, "You're Moving July 1st," *Saturday Evening Post,* June 12, 1943, pp. 20–21, 105–106; "Soldiers' Wives Give Up Home and Job for Camp Life with Husbands," *Life,*

October 12, 1942, pp. 56–62; and Constance Bennett, "Blue Star Wife," *Cosmopolitan,* July 1943, pp. 54–55, 65.

5. Elizabeth R. Valentine, "Odyssey of the Army Wife," *New York Times Magazine,* March 5, 1944, p. 14. See also "Island of Navy Wives," *Saturday Evening Post,* September 5, 1942, pp. 26–27, 68–69; Mary Ellen Green and Mark Murphy, "No Mamma's Girls," *Saturday Evening Post,* April 3, 1943, pp. 20–21, 83–84; Vernon Pope, "War Brides," *Saturday Evening Post,* June 12, 1943, pp. 28–29, 84–85; "Navy Wives at Key West," *Life,* June 2, 1943, pp. 58–60; Louise Paine Benjamin, "Safe Conduct: The Dos and Don'ts of Keeping Him Loving You Always," *Ladies' Home Journal,* January 1943, pp. 71, 90; Ann Maulsby, "War Wives: The Four Types," *New York Times Magazine,* May 6, 1945, p. 20.

6. See, for example, "How to Live in a Trunk," *Good Housekeeping,* January 1942, pp. 106–109; Elizabeth Gordon, "The Triumph of Little Things," *House Beautiful,* May 1943, pp. 35, 37, 100–101, 104–105; Christine Holbrook, "You Can't Take It with You," *Better Homes and Gardens,* July 1944, pp. 18–19; Florence Kas and Betty Thompson, "A War Bride Equips Her Kitchen," *Ladies Home Journal,* February 1944, p. 116; and Elizabeth Beveridge, "Cooking in Cramped Quarters," *Woman's Home Companion,* June 1944, pp. 98–99.

7. *If Your Baby Must Travel in Wartime,* Children in Wartime series. no. 6, United States Department of Labor, Children's Bureau Publication no. 307 (Washington, DC: Government Printing Office, [n.d.]); Josephine H. Kenyon, "Traveling with Baby," *Good Housekeeping,* January 1945, pp. 59, 142–143; Gladys Denny Shultz, "If Baby Must Travel," *Better Homes and Gardens,* July 1943, pp. 30, 59–60; and Gladys Denny Shultz, "Hints for Tiny Travelers," *Better Homes and Gardens,* June 1945, pp. 40, 98–99.

8. Barbara Wooddall Taylor to Charles E. Taylor, October 7 and 11, 1943. For an account of the World War II experiences of the Taylors, see Judy Barrett Litoff, David C. Smith, Barbara Wooddall Taylor, and Charles E. Taylor, *Miss You: The World War II Letters of Barbara Wooddall Taylor and Charles E. Taylor* (Athens: University of Georgia Press, 1990).

9. "A Question of Wives," *Magazine War Guide* (Office of War Information), October 1944, pp. 27–29; Leslie B. Hohman, "Don't Follow Your Husband to Camp," *Ladies' Home Journal,* September 1943, pp. 108–109; and Helen B. Sweedy, "I'm Following You," *New York Times Magazine,* October 3, 1943, p. 32.

10. Fern Steuteville Wilson to Mary Steuteville, December 8, 1941.

11. Audrey M. Savell to Carleton Kelvin Savell, March 16, 1945. A selection of the letters of Audrey M. Savell appears in Litoff and Smith, *Since You Went Away,* 166–171.

12. A very good contemporary account of the life of a service wife on the move is Barbara Klaw, *Camp Follower: The Story of a Soldier's Wife* (New York: Random House, 1943). A serialized version of this book appeared in the *Atlantic Monthly* for October, November, and December 1943. A memoir that discusses the dilemmas wives encountered as they followed their husbands to military bases is Virginia Mayberry, "Draftee's Wife: A Memoir of World War II," *Indiana Magazine of History 79* (December 1984): 305–329.

13. Marjorie Reid Killpack to Elliott Killpack, November 1, 1944. A selection of the letters of Marjorie Reid Killpack appears in Litoff and Smith, *Since You Went Away,* 100–102.

14. Numerous examples of this type of travel can be found in Litoff and Smith, *Since You Went Away,* and in Litoff, Smith, Taylor, and Taylor, *Miss You.*

15. Lilian Selinkoff to Mollye Sklut, January 11, March 18, September 28, 1943, in the Mollye Sklut Papers, Historical Society of Delaware, Wilmington, DE.

16. For an examination of the role played by women in the United States agriculture during World War II, see Judy Barrett Litoff and David C. Smith, " 'To the Rescue of the Crops': Women and United States Agriculture during World War II," *Prologue,* (Winter 1993): 346–361.

17. Mabel Opal Miller to Ivan Johnson, September 6, 1944. A selection of the letters of Mabel Opal Miller appears in Litoff and Smith, *Since You Went Away,* 208–212.

18. Two important sources on United States women and war work during World War II are Susan M. Hartmann, "Women's Work and the Female Labor Force," in her *The Home Front and Beyond: American Women in the 1940s* (Boston: Twayne, 1982), 77–100, and D'Ann Campbell, "Making Way for Rosie," in her *Women at War with America: Private Lives in a Patriotic Era* (Cambridge, MA: Harvard University Press, 1984), 101–138.

19. Polly Crow to William Crow, June 12 and 17, November 6 and 9, and December 5, 1944. A selection of the letters of Polly Crow appears in Litoff and Smith, *Since You Went Away,* 146–152.

20. Sonoko U. Iwata to Francis Biddle, July 21, 1942, and Sonoko U. Iwata to Shigezo Iwata, March 5, 1943, in the Iwata Papers, Balch Institute for Ethnic Studies Library, Philadelphia. A selection of the letters of Sonoko Owata appears in Litoff and Smith, *Since You Went Away,* 213–223.

21. Katherine Trickey to Mrs. Harold A. M. Trickey, March 6, 1944.

22. Marion Stegeman to Mrs. H. J. Stegeman, April 24, 1943. A selection of the letters of Marion Stegeman appears in Judy Barrett Litoff and David C. Smith, *We're in This War Too: World War II Letters from American Women in Uniform* (New York: Oxford University Press, 1994), 113–119.

23. Marjorie E. La Palme to Ethel Pendlebury La Palme, December 16, 1944.

24. Rita Pilkey to her parents, March 8, November ?, 1944, in the Rita Pilkey Papers, Blagg-Huey Library, Texas Woman's University, Denton, TX.

25. Betty Donahue to her parents, September 14, 1944.

26. Anna Beadle to Clinton Beadle, February 8, 1943. A selection of the letters of Anna Beadle appears in Litoff and Smith, *Since You Went Away,* 14–15.

27. Isabel Kidder to Maurice Kidder, October 1942. A selection of the letters of Isabel Kidder appears in Litoff and Smith, *Since You Went Away,* 2, 11, 93–100.

28. Barbara Wooddall Taylor to Charles E. Taylor, April 30 and November 12, 1944. For additional discussion of this aspect of letter writing see Litoff, Smith, Taylor, and Taylor, *Miss You,* 143–145.

29. Catherine Pike to George Pike, January 31, Match 22, 11945. A selec-

tion of the letters of Catherine Pike appears in Litoff and Smith, *Since You Went Away,* 82–91.

30. Keith Frazier Somerville, 1943 Journal. On the wartime experiences of Keith Frazier Somerville, see Judy Barrett Litoff and David C. Smith, eds., *Dear Boys: Word War II Letters from a Woman Back Home* (Jackson: University Press of Mississippi, 1991).

31. Flora Gaitree Southwick to Erman D. Southwick, June 6, 1944. A selection of the letters of Flora Gaitree Southwick appears in Litoff and Smith, *Since You Went Away,* 111–118.

32. Catherine Pike to George Pike, November 25, 1944.

33. Josephine Keutman to Charles Keutman, October 25, 1944. A selection of the letters of Josephine Keutman appears in Litoff and Smith, *Since You Went Away,* 258–261.

34. Margaret Barrow to Joseph L. Barrow, May 14, 1944. A selection of the letters of Margaret Barrow appears in Litoff and Smith, *Since You Went Away,* 190–194.

35. Marjorie Gaunt to Rowland Gaunt, February 25, 1944. A selection of the letters of Marjorie Gaunt appears in Litoff and Smith, *Since You Went Away,* 248–252.

36. Barbara Wooddall Taylor to Charles E. Taylor, April 3, 1945. Tom Siler, "Paris: The G.I.'s Silver Foxhole," *Saturday Evening Post,* January 27, 1945, pp. 26–27, 66.

37. Barbara Wooddall Taylor to Charles E. Taylor, August 16, 1945.

38. Keith Frazier Somerville to "Dear Boys," August 31, 1945. This letter is excerpted in Litoff and Smith, *Dear Boys,* 243–245.

39. Edith Speert to Victor Speert, October 21 and November 9, 1945. A selection of the letters of Edith Speert appears in Litoff and Smith, *Since You Went Away,* 152–159.

40. Katherine McReynolds to James McKemy, August 8, 1945. A selection of the letters of Katherine McReynolds appears in Litoff and Smith, *Since You Went Away,* 47–52.

41. Edna Golan to John Golan, August 9, 1945. A selection of the letters of Edna Golan appears in Litoff and Smith, *Since You Went Away,* 65–74.

42. Constance Hope Jones to Donald C. Swartzbaugh, August 18, 1945. This letter is excerpted in Litoff and Smith, *Since You Went Away,* 279–280.

43. Rose McClain to Charles McClain, August 14, 1945. This letter is excerpted in Litoff and Smith, *Since You Went Away,* 273.

II

RETHINKING MAPPING

7

Occupying the Suburban Frontier: Accommodating Difference on Melbourne's Urban Fringe

LOUISE JOHNSON

Australia attained independence from Britain in 1901, but the challenge posed by postcolonialism is yet to fully impact on the geographies written in this country. The form and timing of postcolonial discourse emerges from the particular history and demography of Australia, as the term embraces both a practice of resistance by indigenous Australians and a politics of difference demanded by those from non-Anglo-Celtic backgrounds. Within geography some work has been done with indigenous people – on the quality of urban life, land rights, and control over resource use[1] – and on the charting of ethnicity as a demographic variable,[2] but little has been done to engage theoretically with postcolonial literatures or the struggles undertaken by indigenous and non-Anglo-Celtic Australians.

There are a few exceptions; for example, Fay Gale and Jane Jacobs have addressed both the marginalization of Aboriginality and of black women in geography. In arguing for social scientists to "see women in the landscape," Gale documented some of the limitations and costs incurred as a consequence of the patriarchal assumptions held by researchers, bureaucrats, and lawyers who ignored Aboriginal women's interests in land, ritual, and the sacred.[3] Similarly, Jacobs has unpacked some of the issues surrounding the construction of Aboriginal "identity" – by those in positions of power in the bureauracy, in the judiciary, and in the academy as well as by Aboriginal groups themselves – while also recognizing that women's knowledge of land, ritual, and family history is particular, historically varible, and provides a foundation for their power within their own communities. From such observations, Jacobs argues for the importance of women's memory in the constitution of territories, both for their own groups and for those in authority who arbitrate on land "ownership."[4]

Such a concern with Aboriginal and white landscapes is not confined to geographers. In sociology, history, anthropology, cultural studies, and literary studies, there has been a vibrant generation of, and engagement with, postcolonial literatures.

Thus in 1968, the year after Australia's indigenous population was formally recognized as citizens of their own country, the anthropologist W. E. H. Stanner drew attention to "the great Australian silence." There was, he argued, "a cult of disremembering," "a cult of forgetfulness practised on a national scale," which resulted in Aborigines appearing in Australian history "only as a melancholy footnote." The neglect was too total to be accidental: it was structural, the result of "a view from a window which had been carefuly placed to exclude a whole quadrant of the landscape."[5]

Subsequent historians have moved to open that window and document the violent but also variegated ways by which white settlement moved across this landscape. Thus Charles Rowley and Henry Reynolds initiated a revision of Australian history with their works on Aboriginal-white contact, resistance, and interdependence.[6] Despite its path-breaking nature, their writing joined that by others in history and anthropology in concentrating on somewhat undifferentiated groups called "Aboriginals" and "whites." They also tended to focus on the men in these groups, both in their source materials and in the accounts they wrote.

It was not until the 1980s that feminist anthropologists and historians such as Diane Bell, Ann McGrath, Susan Hunt, and Lyndall Ryan focused on women and gender relations within and between indigenous and white groups, examining the detail of frontier interaction but also documenting the ways in which "Aboriginal" groups were variously constituted in relation to land, resources, belief systems, and gender.[7] Notions of difference within the general groupings thus began to appear.

This body of writing exists alongside, draws from, and is increasingly joined by that coming from the Koorie, Murri, Nyunga, and Nungga people themselves as they begin writing their own stories and more general histories.[8] Thus in their personal explorations of kin, place, resistance, and racism, Faith Bandler, Kevin Gilbert, Ruby Langford, Sally Morgan, Mudrooroo Narogin, Elsie Roughsey, Margaret Tucker, and Ida West bring their own lives to others,[9] while Jackie Huggins joins Marcia Langton and Bobbie Sykes in reconstructing the many pasts of indigenous women.[10]

Huggins, for instance, has researched and written of the ways in which the colonization of Aboriginal people continued well beyond the early frontier days and, through various institutions of containment and regulation, actively perpetuated the process of cultural destruction. She explains how the system of reserves, schools, and missions established in the 19th century tore families apart (as children were forcibly taken from their parents), imposed alien ideologies of hygiene and Christianity, and constructed a labor force for the use of white men and women in their homes and on their farms. She argues that such practices have continued well past the dismantling of these institutions through the regulatory activities of welfare agencies and the police and as a result of the dire consequences of poverty. It is a story differentiated across Australia – as each colony and state set up particular institutions and legal frameworks and as each Aboriginal population negotiated specific responses within their own countries – but also a story of how territory was used as a weapon of colonization. Thus the wrenching of Aboriginal people from their lands, their placement in walled and regulated institutions, and the subsequent containment within police cells, welfare jurisdictions, and Aboriginal Departments shows the many ways in which space has been an active component of ongoing colonization. Women experienced these processes in particular ways. While Huggins remains critical of the utility of the women's liberation movement in understanding the needs of Aboriginal women, she recognizes that their experiences of colonization – especially through the abuse of their bodies; through interventions based on their status as mothers; through their concern for their children, their men, and their communities; and through their exclusion from many of the deliberations about their futures – are quite different from those of Aboriginal men. Constituted as a group through their experiences of colonization and by their own politicization, Huggins recognizes the importance of a colonial patriarchal nation and the politics of spatial containment on Aboriginal women and men.[11]

But postcolonialism in Australia is not solely about the dispossession and agency of its indigenous population; it also embraces the calls by those from non-English-speaking countries for recognition and a voice within a dominant Anglo-Celtic culture. Immigration into Australia, an ongoing process dating back to at least the 18th century, has primarily been a subject of academic and political interest when it has involved people from countries other than Britain, Ireland, and Scotland. In particular, it has been those groups migrating after World War II from a myriad of European, North African, Asian, Latin American, and South American countries who have become the focus of recent scholarly endeavor. Besides arguing for or criticizing a variety of policy positions – ranging from assimilation to integration and most recently multiculturalism – bureaucrats, demographers, political scientists, and sociologists have studied the various groups migrating to Australia, examined their politics, and explored the interconnections of class and ethnicity.[12]

The focus of early work on the male experience has been corrected by texts explicitly examining the intersections of class, ethnicity, and gender while more recent work has begun the process of deconstructing these very categories.[13] Thus in the final chapter of *Intersexions* Jan Pettman reviews the ways in which gender, race, and ethnicity have been conceptualized singly and relationally to argue for:

> (the) need to . . . represent the specificity and variety of women's experiences and social identities, and to locate those experiences and identities within structures of domination and resistance, and within the politics of category and identity-making.[14]

This is the task Pettman pursues in her book-length study, *Living in the Margins: Racism, Sexism and Feminism in Australia*. In this work, addressed primarily to a sociological and women's studies audience, Pettman surveys the contested and highly political use of terms like "Aboriginal" and "migrant" to challenge notions of fixed identity and to offer a future project that is feminist, antiracist, and anticolonialist. She elaborates:

> Central to this project is how to treat difference in theory and practice, and how to talk and work across the category boundaries. It means owning one's own speaking position/s, social interests and politics, and locating multiple and contingent identities and politics within structures and social relations. It means finding a language to interrogate difference, secure home bases and build alliances in a critical engagement.[15]

Coming from literary and cultural studies, Sneja Gunew takes up the challenge posed by immigrants from non-Anglo-Celtic traditions and, along with Paul Carter, offers directions whereby such accounts can be researched and written. Thus, as Chapter 1 of this book noted, Carter constructs "spatial histories" of Australia through a series of historical artifacts – paintings, photographs, documents, and journals – which he interrogates for their ambiguities, divergences, and poetic and linguistic play, to create histories rich in simultaneity, difference, and a cacophany of multiple and unresolved voices. Places too are constructed in these ways. It is a reading and mode of presentation that successfully engages the problems of recognizing "difference" and multiple identities as well as one that recognizes the importance and dynamic nature of space in history.[16]

In a somewhat different but related vein, Sneja Gunew presents "multicultural writing" as an ongoing challenge to the dominance of Anglo-Celtic culture in Australia. Through the creation of bibliographies, anthologies, and specialist libraries, the work of such writers is made visible,[17] while in her critical writings a challenge to the hegemonic Anglo-Celtic culture is made through various textual and political strategies. Thus in "Denaturalizing Cultural Nationalisms: Multicultural Readings of 'Australia,' " a serious retelling of *the* standard and authorized history of Australian literature is juxtaposed with excerpts from those non-Anglo-Celtic women writers who have been denied a place in such a canon.[18] Elsewhere, the notions of center and margin and irreducible differences when applied to Australian migrant women writers are problematized, while sociological categories are also probed for their closures, ambiguity, political effects, and alternatives.[19]

Postcolonial literatures in Australia have therefore been concerned with effacing silences within existing narratives of settlement, with recovering a neglected past, and with making sure that issues of racial exclusion and ethnic difference are articulated. Further, they have also begun to interrogate the whole question of identities and categorization, using a variety of techniques to present alternative ways of researching and presenting material.

How, then, can such work inform a study of something far removed and apparently unrelated to such concerns: a Melbourne housing estate? Some general directions I see emerging from these literatures are:

- A need to recognize that at least 300,000 people inhabited the land mass now called Australia for years prior to British occupation.
- An awareness that colonization occurred in a number of different ways, was uneven regionally, impacted differentially on women and men, and was perpetrated by a variegated "white" population. It also was met with resistance, accommodation, and adaption by a variety of "Aboriginal" populations.
- A recognition that colonization, initiated in 1788 and continued throughout the 19th and 20th centuries, is not something that occurs

at one time or in one place, but is an ongoing process of dispossession, negotiation, transformation, and resistance.

- An awarencess that land seizure and delegitimization of belief systems was accompanied by elaborate justifications, first, in terms of 19th-century ideologies of race and Christianity, and more recently by an intellectual blindness and amnesia in academic discourse purporting to describe and analyze that history.

- There is a debate about the nature of white, ethnic, and "Aboriginal" identity; with the poststructuralist parts of postcolonial opinion arguing for fractured, discursively constructed, and contested identities, and others constructing their political movements upon relatively fixed identities – be they racial or ethnic.

- A need to admit that everyone in Australia is, in some way, implicated in this history. It is therefore necessary to position myself as a white, Australian-born woman of mixed Anglo-Celtic, Spanish, and Burmese descent who has, for most of my life, avoided trying to seriously engage with the colonial past, my own diverse ancestry, with the multitude of ethnicities around me, and with the Koorie populations of New South Wales and Victoria where I have lived.

This chapter is but a first attempt to articulate some aspects of such a personal history and the academic debates now being generated around it. It also represents a move to bring some of these issues directly into my work as a feminist geographer – work which has long been insulated from the hard questions they raise.

How, then, can such ideas inform and transform the study of a topic well within the mainstream of geographical concern: the configuration of Australian cities and their ongoing suburban expansion? In particular, how does the postcolonial critique direct my enquiry into Roxburgh Park, a new suburban estate of 26,000 people being laid out by the Victorian Urban Land Authority on a 600-hectare site 20 kilometers northwest of Melbourne? The directions pursued in the following discussion of this estate are fourfold:

1. My consideration of this or any other urban development must recognize the significance of its prior occupancy and revisit the colonial past to retell some of the histories of initial dispossession of the land involved.

2. The issue is not only one of initial invasion, but of ongoing dislocation and exclusion. It is therefore appropriate to consider the processes whereby colonization was affected over time.

3. How does any suburb construct or reflect Melbourne's population diversity? While not without contestation and subversion, those invoved in planning and marketing Roxburgh Park see this estate as *different* primarily in terms of the income of its inhabitants, lot sizes, service provision, and ecology. Ethnic, racial, or linguistic variations in the targeted population are either obliterated or subsumed in such a construction.

4. In the process of constituting a somewhat homogeneous suburban population, *identity* is actively constructed in *place* terms. The newly built locality and its "community" are consciously designed as the focal point of individual and group meaning. Identity thereby becomes fixed and tied to locality, the home, and the life-cycle stage. Other variables are factored out, but of course remain and rupture the best laid plans of those in control of this new colonization.

These four elements of *prior occupancy, ongoing dispossession, the marketing of difference,* and *construction of community identity* can be rendered symbolically through a series of maps. The interrogation of these representations will structure the following discussion.

WHOSE *TERRA NULLIUS?*

Traveling as a scientific observer with the British explorer Captain James Cook, the botanist Joseph Banks observed in 1770 that there were "very few inhabitants" on the eastern coast of Australia and, further, "we may have liberty to conjecture however that [it is] totaly uninhabited."[20] The notion of an empty continent ripe for British settlement was contradicted soon after by the first sightings of and ongoing contacts with the indigenous population. Subsequently the concept of *terra nullius* was modified to embrace not only the occupancy of land but its *appropriate* use. Thus in the *Sydney Gazette* of 1824 it was argued:

Any doubt, therefore, as to the lawfulness of our assuming the possession of this Island, must arise from the opinion that it was the *property* of its original inhabitants. Such opinion, however, would be incorrect; for the very notion of property did not exist among them. . . . Each tribe wandered about wheresoever inclination prompted, without ever supposing that anyone place belonged to it more than to another. There were the *inhabitants,* but not the proprietors of the land. This country then was to be regarded as an unappropriated remnant of common property; and, in taking possession of it, we did not invade another's right, for we only claimed that which was unclaimed by any.[21]

Despite the convenience of such notions for those wishing to occupy and use the lands of southeastern Australia, it was far from universally accepted and the contested interpretation of *terra nullius* impacted on the tract of land 14 miles northwest of the first permanent settlement in the Port Phillip colony.

MAP
OF
Port Phillip
from
The Survey of Mr Wedge

FIGURE 7.1. *Terra Nullius,* Map of Port Phillip from the 1836 survey of Mr. Wedge. (From I. W. Symonds, Bulla Bulla: An Illustrated History of the Shire of Bulla *Melbourne: Spectrum Publications, 1985, p. 61).*

In the years prior to British occupation, the land now called Roxburgh Park was but a small part of the tribal territory occupied by the Woiwurrung, Jajowrong or Wurundjeri tribes.[22] The tribe numbered about 200, according to the anthropologist A. W. Howitt writing in 1904, and its territory stretched from the junction of the Maribynong and Yarra rivers to Mount Macedon, thence to the Dandenongs and back.[23] A subarea between Koroit Creek, the Maribynong, and Sunbury – including what is now Roxburgh Park – was, according to the historical research conducted for the Urban Land Authority, inhabited by a family clan of about 20 people.[24] These tribal boundaries, drawn differently by a number of white observers, across time for a range of purposes, using various techniques, enclosed Koorie groups of divergent names and number. Who occupied this site prior to European occupation is, therefore, a contentious issue in the anthropological and historical literature. Solely for convenience, I will refer to the Korrie group who occupied the Roxburgh Park site as "the Wurundjeri."

The territory's tussocky grasslands, swamps, and water courses were surveyed by the British explorer William Hovell in 1824. It also fell within the region traversed by William Fawkner as he ventured from Tasmania in search of more pasture and was ultimately "ceded" to the Port Phillip Association in the "Batman Treaty" of June 6, 1835. The very existence of such a "treaty" raised a number of dilemmas. For it recognized prior occupancy and gave some legitimacy to indigenous land rights, while also contravening official policy on land settlement.[25]

In a plea to the British government to sanction his treaty, John Batman wrote:

> My object has not been possession and expulsion, or what is worse, extermination, but possession and civilisation – and the reservation of the annual tribute to those who are the real owners of the soil will afford evidence of the sincerity of my professions in wishing to protect and civilise these tribes of benighted but intelligent people [26]

In this document and the exchange of trinkets for land which underlay it, the notion of *terra nullius* was denied by both the assertion of British sovereignty and the assigning of common law property rights to the indigenous occupants. The denial of the treaty's legitimacy in terms of usual practice did nothing to undermine the contradiction it represented between practice and British law. The existence of native title has only been belatedly recognized in the 1992 ruling in favor of a group of Murray Island people in the Mabo case.[27] However, when it came to mapping the Port

Phillip area in 1836, the surveyor Mr. Wedge was of the opinion that such title and those who held it did not exist. His map (see Figure 7.1) affirms the fantasy of *terra nullius* with its record of European settlement sites and "natural" features of importance. As noted in Chapter 1 of this book, such a map readily reveals the imperial gaze. But this map and the politics encircling its creation also registers – if only by the absences and white spaces on the drawn surface – the contradictions of, and resistances to, the colonization process. Engagement with these contradictions shaped the process of ongoing dispossession at Roxburgh Park.

ONGOING DISPOSSESSION

In the first census taken of Port Phillip in September 1838, three years after the first British settlement, the number of indigenous inhabitants was not known or sought. Instead, it was recorded that there were 3,511 (white) people, 3,080 of them male; 310,946 sheep; 13,272 head of cattle; and 524 horses.[28] Priority was given to land occupation and the generation of wealth from it. In this quest, the recognition of prior occupancy under common law right was rare, as land was either squatted on under license or surveyed and sold for the sum of £1 an acre – in that area within 25 miles of Melbourne known as the "Settled District." Some of the occupants of the area whose names appear on the parish map included George Sinclair Brodie, a pastoralist from Tasmania who subsequently worked in Melbourne as a land auctioneer, and William Pomeroy Greene.[29] Formerly of the Royal Navy, Greene chose his officer entitlement of 640 acres on the Moonee Ponds Creek. He arrived with full retinue consisting of a wife and seven children, a governess, a butler, a carpenter, a groom, a cook, a housemaid, a nurse, and two young men friends. Anne Greene took over the management of the property following her husband's death in 1845 and turned it into a model farm and a center of upper-class rural social life, complete with balls and steeplechases.[30] Her very name contradicts the predominantly male or often sexless, initialized pattern of occupancy recorded on the squatter's map (see Figure 7.2).

Of the Wurundjeri, the young Mary Greene was to record: "When we first took over our abode at Woodlands, a tribe of Aborigines used to camp on the creek which ran through our property."[31] Others had different experiences. For the Greenes joined men such as William Jackson and John Aitken who literally marked themselves on the landscape as they lent their names, respectively, to a creek and to one of the higher peaks in the district (see Figure 7.2). The son of a Scottish farmer, John

FIGURE 7.2. Ongoing dispossession. Squatter and freehold occupancy. (From R. Spreadborough and H. Anderson, *Victorian Squatters*. Ascot Vale Red Rooster Press: 1983, appendix, settled districts.)

Aitken was a sheep breeder in Tasmania before seeking more grazing lands across Bass Strait. His boat ran aground and his party, along with a large flock of sheep, had to be driven ashore and thence to the land north of Melbourne. In this operation he was assisted by about 80 "natives." In relating this story, Allan Gross, a local historian, notes that as a consequence, Aitken made a policy then and later of conciliating Aborigines, mainly by giving them rations.[32]

A somewhat different impression is given by another local historian, Ian Symonds, who quotes Aitken's account of April 14, 1838:

> I was attacked by 40 native blacks at my station. . . . They came to me armed with spears and guns. . . . They cocked their guns as we went up to them. When I took hold of the gun the black named De Villiers or Warra Worrock attempted to strike me with a tomahawk.[33]

The reasons why such an attack occurred and the retribution that followed are not mentioned by Symonds, whose story ends with the above quotation.

The notion of "conciliation" was one that had some currency at the time and led to the creation of four "Aboriginal Protectorates" in the Port Phillip colony in 1839. Seen as a way to smooth the occupancy of the district, Protectorates joined with Christian missions and schools as key ways in which the "Aboriginal population" of the colony was to be constituted, "civilized," and contained. Adjacent to Roxburgh Park were two of these institutions: the North West Aboriginal Protectorate was ruled from 1839 to 1840 from Jackson's Creek, and a Baptist mission school existed at Merri Creek from 1846 to 1851 (see Figure 7.2 for the location of the creeks). Both generated vectors of power that defined, regulated, and were challenged by the Koories in their charge. They represent disruptive elements in the smooth operation of the grid lines of white occupancy registered on the parish and squatter's maps.

The extension of British sovereignty and citizenship rights over the native population was accompanied by a recognition that their containment in space and pacification was necessary for the securing of white property values, while their education was also deemed essential so that they could assume the mantle of British citizenship. Thus in a letter from the governor of New South Wales (then including the Port Phillip District) to the colonial officer Lord Glenelg, Sir George Arthur wrote in 1837:

> Conciliatory measures . . . ought, therefore, be adopted from the very first. . . .
> From what has happened within the last four years in Van Dieman's Land,

Your Lordship has the proof of the extraordinary effect of personal security upon the value of land; for no sooner was that country relieved from the dreadful outrages of the Aborigines . . . then land, almost suddenly, rose in value from 50 to 100 percent at least![34]

Two years later the colony was divided into four "Aboriginal Protectorates." A temporary administrative center of the North West Protectorate was established by Edward Stone Parker at Jackson's Creek. His brief was to:

attach himself as closely and as constantly as possible to the aboriginal tribes . . . attending them in their movements . . . until they can be induced to assume more settled habits . . . teach and encourage them to engage in the cultivation of their grounds, in building suitable habitations . . . watch over (their) rights and interests (and) defend them . . . from any encroachment on their property and from acts of cruelty, oppression or injustice; and . . . faithfully represent their wants, wishes or grievances . . . promote, with conscientious and unremitting assiduity . . . the moral and religious improvement of the natives . . . by teaching, recommending and exemplifying the obligation of the Christian Sabbath and by persuading them to yield in cheerful submission to the salutory restraints and moral discipline of the Christian religion, which . . . is the surest instrument of effecting the *real* civilization and of ameliorating the temporal condition of barbarous tribes.[35]

In addition, the protectors were expected to learn native languages, compile a population census, and be responsible for the distribution of rations. Parker proceeded to conduct his duties at Jackson's Creek and later further north on the Loddon River, but he quickly realized the ambivalence of his brief. While charged with protecting native rights to land and ensuring their protection under British law, he constantly encountered the theft and occupancy of that land and violence toward native women and men. In particular, he noted the violence toward Koorie women – though he saw this as a result of female seductiveness rather that a product of white male racism and aggression – and tended to see such interaction as part of a general problem of colonization without compensation. Thus he wrote in his report of April 1840:

I cannot persuade the younger females to resist the importunities of the white man, while I am unable to offer a counter-inducement in the shape of food, clothing or shelter. I cannot draw away the men from the stations while they can obtain more liberal supplies than I can furnish, by pandering to the lusts of those who occupy them. The results of the viscious intercourse – disease, jealousy, brutal quarrels . . . – are rendering the condition of the native more deplorable, and the property of the colonists more insecure.[36]

From which Parker generally observes and concludes:

> The entire country of the Waworang and Witowrong tribes . . . is now sold
> or occupied by squatters. . . . Appointed to . . . protect them from encroach-
> ments on their property . . . I deem it my duty respectfully but firmly to as-
> sert the right of the Aborigines to the soil and its indigenous productions until
> suitable compensation be made.[37]

The contradictions facing those administering the protectorates – of
guarding indigenous rights to land and safeguarding their bodies in the
face of a settlement policy and set of practices that denied these rights –
did not befall those solely committed to the Christian education of the
native population. Rather, a different set of problems arose as these efforts were met with indifference, selective utilization, and active denial.

Parker had been a Wesleyan minister and schoolmaster in Britain pri-
or to his posting to Port Phillip and took to the task of bringing Christianity to his charges with enthusiasm, helped directly by his wife. The
number of pupils tended to be small, while attendance was related to the
provision of foodstuffs. Some children in 1842 refused to attend their school
with the ultimatum: "No damper, no school."[38] Parker wrote with dis-
may of how the children would be taken away with no notice by their
kin and would not appear again for weeks.

Despite the selective use and active resistance to schooling by the native population, the idea of educating them persisted and was to receive
a boost in 1846 by the creation of a Baptist boarding school at Merri Creek
(see Figure 7.2). Overseen by Edward Peacock, initially the school was
regarded by the colonists as successful, with 20 pupils in its first year who
read, sung hymns, and displayed their handwriting and needlework to
250 townspeople in November 1846.[39] The boys were schooled in car-
pentry and gardening, the girls in food preparation. While the boys ex-
celled in literacy and numeracy, commentators were content to note the
excellence of the girls in sewing. Success was measured by the numbers
attending, the Christian principles that imbued the curriculum, and the
British pattern of gendered skills that were instilled. However, despite these
achievements, in December 1847 tribal elders came and took the children
into the mountains. As the minutes of the school committee noted in February 1848: "(over the last couple of months) the old Aborigines have
separately induced, or compelled, several of the (children) to leave the
school."[40] The ongoing problem of mass desertion meant that the school
was ultimately closed in 1851, with the experiment in formally schooling the native population in Christian ways declared futile by most of
those whose opinions were recorded.[41]

The mission school and the protectorate present disruptions to the neat grid lines of colonial occupancy registered on the parish map (see Figure 7.2). Unmarked on this map, they serve as absent traces on the European landscape. But their presence is asserted by the debates and correspondences that have been retrieved and on the embodied male and female subjects with whom they dealt. Through these documents and accounts, a picture emerges of an area occupied by force and stealth, as the gaze of British explorers was replaced by those men – joined by a number of women – who brought their sheep and land tenure system to the area. As a consequence, the emptiness of the first maps charting *terra nullius* (see Figure 7.1) was replaced by the lines of occupancy (see Figure 7.2). Further, though, these grid lines in turn obscure the ongoing processes of regulation, dispossession, containment, and resistance that made this region a site of ongoing conflict from 1835 to 1851.

The negotiation of racial differences and the imposition of British gender stereotypes therefore constituted this area, though the power imbalance in such a contest was ultimately registered on the parish and squatters maps (see Figure 7.2). This was to provide the framework for the Urban Land Authority in its acquisition of Lots 1 and 14 in the Parish of Yuroke on which they are presently building "Melbourne's newest and most exciting suburb of Roxburgh Park" (see hatched area on Figure 7.2).

ROXBURGH PARK: MELBOURNE'S NEWEST AND MOST EXCITING SUBURB

From 1835 to 1845 the block of land that now comprises Roxburgh Park was officially unoccupied, in that within the straight lines that delimited its boundaries there were no legal European settlers. The land was, up until 1848, *terra nullius,* though it was part of Wurundjeri territory and fell within the boundaries of the North West Aboriginal Protectorate and the Merri Creek Baptist mission. In 1848 the southern portion of the site was purchased by a Scottish family of sheep breeders, the Camerons. They held the property until 1888 when it was chosen by what Michael Cannon describes as "land boomers" for speculative subdivision into a new suburb called "Hopetoun."[42] Complete with plans for roads, city tramline, public buildings, services, and recreational facilities, according to historian Miles Lewis, "the whole elaborate puff [was] in the realms of fantasy. *Even today the area seems a remote one for suburban living.*"[43] With the 1893 depression, this scheme collapsed and the property was acquired by the flour miller and politician Thomas Brunton, after which it was used by a variety of owners for sheep, cattle, and horse grazing until purchased in 1950 by the Moonee Valley Racing Club. They sold it to the Urban Land Authority (ULA) in 1988.

Established as a statutory authority in 1973, the brief of the ULA is to maintain a reasonable supply of affordable land for housing, by acquiring, developing, and selling large tracts. Since 1973 the ULA has disposed of between one-tenth and one-fifth of all urban land in Victoria, and in 1990 it handled "more than half of all new development land in Melbourne, thus making it the state's largest and most influential land developer."[44]

The site for Roxburgh Park is on the edge – or frontier – of the city, in one of Melbourne's four growth corridors. Because of the city's expansion to the southeast, this northwest region has remained relatively close to the city center and therefore was an attractive prospect for subdivision. However, suburban development in this sector had been blocked by large institutional owners – the Moonee Valley Racing Club and the Commonwealth Government – and by a number of small holders. They were all to ultimately sell to the ULA because of its financial power (for the racing club), its public-sector location (for the Commonwealth), and as a consequence of its compulsory acquisition powers, which were applied to dislodge the remaining small land holders. State power was therefore variously mobilized to assemble a large parcel of land that could then be comprehensively developed. This possibility – of state-sponsored, coordinated planning across 600 hectares on the fringe of a large metropolis – meant that it was *different* from other suburban subdivisions, which, for the project manager, Bryce Moore, made it "Melbourne's newest and most exciting suburb."[45]

If colonization involves the exercise of superior, state-sanctioned force – be it military, financial, or legal – in the acquisition of land, which is then commercially developed and organized in such a way to constitute specific populations, then this phase in the history of the site involves a continuation of the colonization process. However, unlike the 19th-century colonizations, this occupation did not involve the imposition of a foreign sovereignty, nor was it driven by nationalist, Christian, or racialist ideologies. But, having acquired the area through the exercise of bureaucratic and financial power, the ULA has proceeded to mold it physically and socially. The whole process represents a more discreet, less violent but nevertheless potent exercise of state authority.

Administration of the site by the ULA has involved a series of discourses that embrace elements – echoing the past – of containment, regulation, and appropriate habitation. These planning, design, marketing, and population regulations, comprise four interrelated elements: affordability; ecological sustainability; comprehensive, coordinated, and adequate servicing; and the creation of a community.

Affordability is created through the very means by which the land was acquired – through the use of state resources and powers that have never involved compensation to the original Wurundjeri owners – by the economies of scale in service provision, and by the intensification of land subdivision, so that up to 15 dwellings per hectare are built. These small building blocks are linked to the ideal of ecological sustainability through the subsequent design of houses on "Smart Blocks." The ULA is intensively promoting blocks of land of between 450 and 600 square meters, on which the house is positioned so as to maximize privacy and minimize energy use and loss. This derives from the placement of the house relative to the best aspect, by its virtual attachment to the neighboring house through a south-facing wall, placement of windows along the north and east, and courtyard orientation. This is occurring in a city where 80% of houses are free standing on 600 or more square meters of land and therefore represents a big change in the nature of suburban housing. Incentives offered to purchasers to agree to such an arrangement are great – ranging from financial to regulatory to moral ones. For smaller house blocks are cheaper and houses built in "smart" ways incur lower energy bills. There is added pressure on buyers to be "smart" (rather than dumb!), having been exposed to the many virtues of this way of building at one of the ULA-sponsored "Welcome Home" workshops for all new purchasers, and by having the uplifting, well-publicised and model "Green Home" on the estate.[46] Any house plan also has to be approved by the ULA before local government authorities view it. To receive ULA sanction, a plan has to conform to a bewildering array of set-back, color-scheme, and building-material requirements and will be treated more sympathetically if a "smart" design has been adopted.

The ecological design and affordability of Roxburgh Park does indeed make it different from other new suburban developments. But the designs may also challenge other established social relations. Many studies have shown the importance of outside space to the male occupant of the suburban house. It is here that he assumes a degree of responsibility, engages in domestic labor, and can conduct the ongoing physical maintenance of the dwelling. Such private open space has also long been seen as vital to the play needs of young children and their necessary scrutiny by the housebound mother. It is therefore both ironic and perhaps deeply challenging to existing domestic divisions of labor that the most obvious feature of the "Smart Blocks" is the reduction in size of the privately owned backyard, a shift to public open space provision, and the relative increase in scale of the house itelf on the block. One therefore has to ask who these blocks and new designs are "smart" for: is it the male occupant who sees his traditional domain of work reduced or the woman whose childcare responsibilities are made more difficult and public, while her interior space and associated housework is increased?[47]

In Australia, new suburbs are notorious for being poorly serviced. As a consequence, the intention is to have Roxburgh Park fully serviced in physical terms before house blocks are sold and to introduce social services in stages. Planning for these elements is comprehensive, conducted by a team representing the ULA, local councils, and state government departments responsible for public transport, community services, education, housing, sport, recreation, and health. Their 120-page *Community Plan* sets down the nature of the services required, and links their provision to allocated sites and the projected population of each neighborhood (see Figure 7.3).[48] Many services for women have been incorporated into general planning for children, retailing, health, leisure, and community centers, while those services required by non-English speaking residents have been deferred, pending further knowledge of the population attracted to the area. However, the conceptualization of these services and such deferral are both problematical and a potential source of disruption.

When it comes to services for women, these are viewed very much in terms of women's domestic and childcare responsibilities. While commendable for encompassing many of the demands long articulated by women, there is also a model family implicit in such provisions. In these families there is no domestic violence, family breakdown, or abuse – only shopping, minor health problems, and free time for recreation. It is therefore an idealized vision of womanhood and the family that is being constituted through the service inventory. Those services that may be required by non-English speakers or the disabled are left undetailed – supposedly awaiting the articulation of their demands. However, such a voice will be difficult to hear above the homogenous community that is being constituted.

But even with non-group-specific services, such as the electrification of the railway linking Roxburgh Park to Melbourne and the construction of schools on the estate, in a political climate where railways and schools are being closed and social services drastically curtailed, there has to be some skepticism that all the promised and planned infrastructure will be delivered. Having created high expectations, though, ULA's nondelivery of such support may become a source of future local agitation and political disquiet.

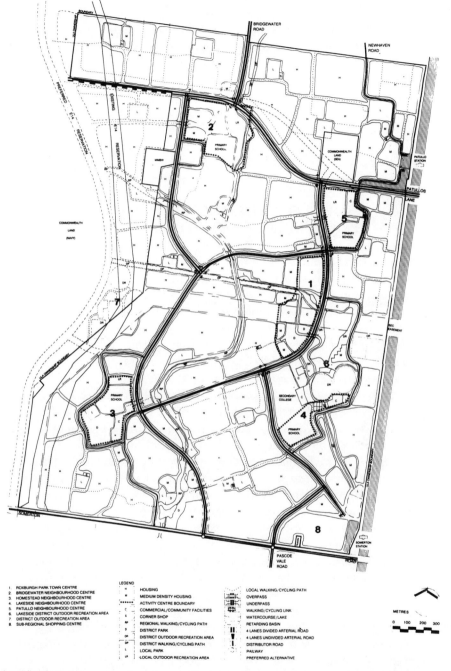

FIGURE 7.3. Roxburgh Park, "Melbourne's newest and most exciting suburb." (Local structure plan provided by the Urban Land Authority, Melbourne, 1993.)

Roxburgh Park is therefore projected to be a different suburb because of its affordability, ecological sensitivity, and service provision. These elements of difference owe more to planning imperatives and marketing techniques than they do to postcolonial critiques. Dimensions of social differentiation apart from class are acknowledged in the planning of Roxburgh Park, but this recognition occurs in ways that surpresses and subsumes the critique mounted by those outside of dominant Anglo-Celtic planning discourses. This is most apparent when the fourth distinguishing element of Roxburgh Park is examined: the creation of community.

IDENTITY THROUGH COMMUNITY: PLACE MAKING AT ROXBURGH PARK

The planning and marketing rhetorics surrounding Roxburgh Park have a remarkable consistency, as the agents involved in this process are all variously incorporated into the ULA teams. As a result, press reports, promotional material, and interviews with the project manager and the community development officer all produced similar descriptions and analyses.[49] In these representations a consistent feature is the importance of "building a community." What such a notion means can be gleaned in part from the *Local Structure Plan* of the estate.

In the *Local Structure Plan* Koorie occupancy is briefly noted in the historical overview of the site – though not recorded in the neat table that summarizes (white) ownership – and also recognized in the section on "Vegetation" as causing significant landscape modification.[50] No Wurundjeri names appear on the main streets or neighborhood centers – though those of pioneer families, such as the Camerons and Patullos, certainly do (see Figure 7.3). Any suggestion that Koories may wish to reoccupy the site or the housing being constructed upon it was met by stunned silence and then dismissal by the community development officer.[51] This place is to be colonized anew, not returned in some way to its prior occupants.

In this document, when describing the changing demographic contexts in which they planned Roxburgh Park, the ULA concentrated on household size, income variation, and family forms. Other components of population diversity explicitly mentioned – ethnicity and disability – were acknowledged as forming a part of the future population for whom services would have to be provided once details were known. Women's needs are not addressed directly in this document, though they are referred to obliquely by observations on the loneliness experienced by residents in neighboring estates, as well as by a recognition that childcare and maternal health services need to be provided at an early stage. Women's interests are therefore addressed primarily through their roles as mothers and domestic workers in heterosexual family units. Cheerful submission to the statutory restraints and moral discipline of the suburb here echo those of earlier colonizations.

In projecting the population that might be attracted to Roxburgh Park, the ULA suggested that there would be a relatively high level of cultural and ethnic diversity. This conclusion was based on the population profile of neighboring suburbs – one of which, Meadow Heights, is also a ULA development and has a 70% Turkish and Vietnamese population – that would serve to attract those of similar backgound, its affordable housing, its public housing component (10%), its accessibility to public transport, its new services, the nearby location of "significant 'blue collar' employment opportunities," and its identity as "the next stage in the outward migration of residents . . . from the western and north-western suburbs."[52] In this evaluation, ethnic diversity is linked to class location, sectoral and chain migration, and service accessibility. The planning response to such an expected influx was deferred and placed in the hands of the community development officer.

However, to date, such expectations have proven incorrect in that a ULA survey of 300 purchasers has revealed that 65% were Australian-born and 98.5% were English speaking.[53] Why this should be the case elicits incredulity and comments on the mysteries of such things from the developers, but it also invites observations on the nature of the promotional advertising for the estate – which relies on the heterosexual family unit described above – in suburban and tabloid newspapers and on popular radio stations with a young English-speaking audience. The blocks of land were also more expensive than those offered in adjacent suburbs and, I would argue, were targeted to a culturally homogenous population. For the suburban houses were to be differentiated only in terms of their affordability and ecological design, not in other ways, while the operation of the suburb itself around the neighborhood and community centers assumed and guided the generation of a culturally-specific, Anglo-Celtic ideal of a place-based identity.

Confirmation of such a view was offered at the May 15, 1993, land ballot. For here, as the predominantly Anglo-Celtic, heterosexual, young couples gathered to secure their building blocks, an extended family of seven Sikh Indians requested, first, to be able to bid on behalf of an absent brother, and second, to have a medical clinic in one of their houses. Although politely listened to, the Sikhs' desires – arising perhaps from kinship relations and cultural needs – could not be accommodated at Roxburgh

Park. They were told about rules that allowed only those present to bid for land and that dictated that all service-type activity would have to be located in the neighborhood or town centers. The rigidity of zoning and ULA regulations – as well as their cultural specificity – were thus exposed. In so doing, "community" was disrupted, and ultimaltely those who did not fit left the room and did not participate further in the land ballot. It is, then, a community defined by Ango-Celtic norms and culturally ex-clusive planning regulations.

In its early planning, the ULA had concluded that a mix of hous-ing densities and lot sizes, comprehensive servicing, and the creation of a community would address the issue of population diversity. Population differences were to be explicitly dealt with through physical planning (Figure 7.3).

Thus the *Local Structure Plan* envisages the creation of 6,000 strong neigh-borhoods focused on an activity center that will, in turn, relate to a town center serving all 26,000 residents. These centers are the planned social hubs of the suburb and in them are to be located all the retail, health, leisure, and other services; their siting adjacent to recreational areas and linkages with bikepaths and walkways will ensure their utility and via-bility. Through such carefully placed centers – neatly organized in a hier-archy of floor areas – a community will be constituted. It is a community to be built by the women who are anticipated to be its main users. It is also a community built by propinquity, where identity is constituted and ultimately fixed in place. Other social variables are deemed to be either expressed by the initial choice of such a place – such as life-cycle stage and economic position – or are neatly subsumed by such considerations and the many opportunities for social mixing in the town centers. Differenti-ation, then, is to be limited and is planned to occur primarily through neigh-borhood. Those who do not accept the rules of the estate are either screened out during the land-purchasing process (as happened at the May 15 bal-lot) or remain to disrupt the planned course of community creation.

To speed such a process of neighborhood and community formation along, one of the first appointments in the planning process was of a "com-munity development officer" whose task was initially to liase with adja-cent areas, to gauge what was missing and what had worked in these ethnically diverse areas, and then to put those who purchased house blocks at Roxburgh Park in contact with each other – through the "Welcome Home" workshops – and with the services they may require. In the suc-cess of this task lies the construction of a community through unity of purpose, sociability, and place. It is also an inherently unstable task. For such a process may indeed work, so that neighbors will come to cooperate with each other and demand the delivery of promised services in a united and effective way. Or alternatively, other identities may emerge to disrupt the neat plan, through, for example, unities around gender, age, disabilities, or ethnicity, that have not been anticipated. The regulation and fixing of identities around the neighborhood and community will, therefore, create tensions and resistances as this colonization of the suburban frontier generates further contradictions.

CONCLUSION

Postcolonial literatures in Australia–with their concern to retrieve an indigenous past, to document ongoing dispossession, and to recognize the importance of racial and ethnic difference–have directed my attention to four dimensions in this examination of Roxburgh Park. They have impelled the consideration of suburbanization as a process of ongoing colonization–of land and of difference–as well as the means by which particular identities are constituted. Thus in the initial mapping of the Port Phillip region, the presence of large tracts of "empty" land belied its prior occupancy, while the neat lines of parish subdivision both confirmed a dominant set of power relations and obscured the dynamic processes of exclusion, containment, resistance, and regulation that constituted them.

More recently, the process of suburbanization has produced a different sort of colonization as "difference" was taken, not from the literatures of postcolonialism, but from marketing and planning. As a consequence, while Roxburgh Park will indeed be different in its cost, ecological sustainability, and services, it has not yet admitted population diversity. The result is a place in which ethnic differences and the particular needs of women are subsumed by the techniques of place making and homogenization. Difference is accommodated through the constitution of *a* suburban identity in this colonization.

NOTES

1. Work by geographers with and on Aboriginal Australians include: David Dukakis Smith, "Aboriginal Underdevelopment in Australia," *Antipode 13,* No. 1 (1981): 35–44; Fay Gale, ed., *Women's Role in Aboriginal Society* (Canberra, Australia: Australian Institute of Aboriginal Studies, 1978); and Fay Gale, ed., *We Are Bosses Ourselves: The Status and Role of Aboriginal Women Today* (Canberra, Australia: Australian Institute of Aboriginal Studies, 1983); Richard Howitt and John Connell, eds., *Mining and Indigenous Peoples in Australasia* (Sydney: Sydney University

Press/Oxford University Press, 1991); Jane M. Jacobs, " 'Women Talking Up Big': Aboriginal Women as Cultural Custodians, a South Australian Example," in *Women's Rites and Sites*. P. Brock, ed. (Sydney: Allen and Unwin, 1989), 76–98; Elspeth A. Young and E. K. Fisk, *Tribal Communities in Rural Areas* (Canberra, Australia: Development Studies Centre, 1981); and Elspeth Young, "Hunter-Gatherer Concepts of Land and Its Ownership in Remote Australia and North America," in *Inventing Places: Studies in Cultural Geography*, K. Anderson and F. Gale, eds. (Melbourne: Longman Cheshire, 1992), 255–272.

2. Geographers who use ethnicity mainly as a demographic variable include Ian Burnley, "Italian Settlement in Sydney," *Australian Geographical Studies 19*, no. 2 (1981): 177–194, and Graeme Hugo, *Atlas of the Australian People* (Melbourne: Bureau of Immigration Research, 1991).

3. Fay Gale, "Seeing Women in the Landscape: Alternative Views of the World Around Us," in *Women, Social Science and Public Policy*, J. Goodnow and C. Pateman, eds. (Sydney: Allen and Unwin, 1985), 56–66.

4. Jane M. Jacobs, "The Construction of Identity" in *Past and Present: The Construction of Aborigines*, J. Beckett, ed. (Canberra, Australia: Australian Institute of Aboriginal Studies [AIAS], 1988); Jane M. Jacobs, " 'Shake 'im This Country': The Mapping of the Aboriginal Sacred in Australia – The Case of Coronation Hill," in *Constructions of Race, Place, and Nation*, P. Jackson and J. Penrose, ed. (London: University College London Press): 100–118; and Jacobs, " 'Women Talking Up Big.' "

5. W. E. H. Stanner, *After the Dreaming: Black and White Australians—An Anthropologist's View* (Sydney: Boyer Lecture Series, ABC Radio, 1968), 18–29. I am grateful to Jan Critchett for drawing my attention to this quotation; see her *The Aboriginal Past, Contemporary Perspectives* (Geelong, Australia: Deakin University, 1992), 29.

6. Henry Reynolds, *Aborigines and Settlers: The Australian Experience 1788–1939* (Stanmore, Australia: Cassell, 1972), *Frontier, Aborigines, Settlers and Land* (Sydney: Allen and Unwin, 1990), and *With the White People* (Ringwood, Australia: Penguin, 1990); C. D. Rowley *The Destruction of Aboriginal Society* (Harmondsworth, U.K.: Penguin, 1970) and *Outcasts in White Australia* (Canberra, Australia: Australian National University Press, 1971).

7. Diane Bell, *Daughters of the Dreaming* (Melbourne: McPhee Gribble, 1983); Susan Hunt, *Spinifex Fairies: Women in North West Australia, 1860–1900* (Nedlands, Australia: University of Western Australia Press, 1986); Ann McGrath *''Born in the Cattle'': Aborigines in Cattle Country* (Sydney: Allen and Unwin, 1987); Lyndall Ryan, *The Aboriginal Tasmanians* (Saint Lucia, Australia: University of Queensland Press, 1981).

8. The word "Aborigine" was used in early British correspondence, as were specific tribal names. Referring to collectivities of indigenous people – of which there are at least 200 tribal groups – Eve Fesl argues for the use of the "Names we use to describe ourselves" which includes the Koorie for those inhabiting southeastern Australia; See Eve Fesl, "How the English Language Is Used to Put Koories Down, Deny Us Our Rights and Is Employed as a Political Tool Against Us" (Melbourne: n.p., 1989).

9. Faith Bandler, *Turning the Tide* (Canberra, Australia: Australian Institute of Aboriginal Studies, 1989); Kevin Gilbert, *Living Black* (Melbourne: Allan Lane/Penguin: 1977); Ruby Langford, *Don't Take Your Love to Town* (Ringwood, Australia: Penguin, 1988); Sally Morgan, *My Place* (Fremantle, Australia: Fremantle Arts Centre Press, 1987); Mudrooroo Narogin, *Writing From the Fringe* (Melbourne: Hyland House, 1990); Elsie Roughsey, *An Aboriginal Mother Speaks of the Old and the New* (Fitzroy, Australia: McPhee Gribble, 1984); Margaret Tucker, *If Everyone Cared: An Autobiography of Margaret Tucker, MBE,* (London: Grosvenor, 1983); Ida West, *Pride against Prejudice: Reminiscences of a Tasmanian Aborigine* (Canberra, Australia: Australian Institute of Aboriginal Studies, 1984).

10. Jackie Huggins, " 'Firing On in the Mind': Aboriginal Women Domestic Servants in the Inter War Years," *Hecate 13,* no. 2 (1987): 5–23; Jackie Huggins with Thom Blake, "Protection or Persecution? Gender Relations in the Era of Racial Segregation," in *Gender Relations in Australia: Domination and Negotiation,* K. Saunders and R. Evans, eds. (Sydney: Harcourt Brace Jovanovich, 1992), 42–58; Marcia Langton, "The Getting of Power," *Australian Feminist Studies 6* (1988): 1–5, and *Being Black: Aboriginal Cultures in "Settled" Australia* (Canberra, Australia: Australia Insitute of Aboriginal Studies, 1988); Bobbie Sykes, "Blacks in the Public Sphere," *Hecate 17* (1991): 51–53, and *Black Majority* (Melbourne: Hudson, 1989).

11. Huggins and Blake, "Protection or Persecution," and Jackie Huggins, "A Contemporary View of Aboriginal Women's Relationship to the White Women's Movement," in *A Woman's Place in Australia* Louise C. Johnson (Deakin University Course HUA 813, Geelong, Australia: Deakin University Press), 16–26.

12. Official evaluations of Australia's immigration policy include: Australian Population and Immigration Council, *Immigration Policies and Australia's Population: A Green Paper* (Canberra, Australia: Australian Government Publishing Service, 1977) and *Multiculturalisn for All Australians: Our Developing Nationhood* (Canberra, Australia: Australian Government Publishing Service, 1982). Academic studies include L. Barzini, *The Italians* (Ringwood, Australia: Penguin, 1965); R. Bird and T. Birrell, *An Issue of People* (Melbourne: Longman Cheshire, 1981); Gill Bottomley, *After the Odyssey: A Study of Greek Australians* (Saint Lucia, Australia: University of Queensland Press, 1979); Ian Burnely, Sol Encel, and G. McCall, *Immigration and Ethnicity in the 1980s* (Melbourne: Longman Cheshire, 1985); Steven Castles, Mary Kalantzis, B. Cope, and Mike Morrissey, *Mistaken Identity: Multiculturalism and the Demise of Nationalism in Australia* (Sydney: Pluto Press, 1988); Jock Collins, *Migrant Hands in a Distant Land* (Sydney: Pluto Press, 1988); Marie de Lepervanche, *Indians in a White Australia* (Sydney: Allen and Unwin, 1984); James Jupp, B. York, and A. McRobbie, *The Political Participation of Ethnic Minorities in Australia* (Canberra, Australia: Australian Government Publishing Service, 1989); Jeannie Martin and Sol Encel, *The Ethnic Dimension* (Sydney: Allen and Unwin, 1981); Des Storer, *"But I wouldn't want my wife to work here." A Study of Migrant Women in Melbourne Industry* (Melbourne: Centre for Urban Research and Action, 1976); N. Viviani, *The Long Journey: Vietnamese Migration and Settlement in Australia* (Sydney: Allen and Unwin, 1984); Gill Bottomley and Marie de Lepervanche, eds., *Ethnicity, Class and Gender in Australia* (Sydney: Allen and Unwin, 1984); Gill Bottomley, Marie de

Lepervanche, and Jeannie Martin, eds., *Intesexions. Gender/Class/Culture/Ethnicity* (North Sydney: Allen and Unwin, 1991); Jan Pettman, *Living in the Margins. Racism, Sexism and Feminism in Australia,* (North Sydney: Allen and Unwin, 1992).

13. Such as Bottomley and Lepervanche, *Ethnicity, Class, and Gender,* and Bottomley, Lepervanche, and Martin, eds., *Intesexions.*

14. Pettman, "Racism, Sexism and Sociology," in *Intesexions,* Botomley, Lepervanche, and Martin, eds., 202.

15. Pettman, *Living in the Margins,* 158.

16. Paul Carter, *The Road to Botany Bay: An Essay in Spatial History* (London: Faber and Faber, 1987) and *Living in a New Country. History, Travelling and Language* (London: Faber and Faber, 1992).

17. Sneja Gunew and Jan Mahyuddin, *A Bibliography of Australian Multicultural Writers* (Geelong, Australia: Centre for Studies in Literary Education, Humanities, Deakin University, 1992); Sneja Gunew and Kateryna O. Longley, eds., *Striking Chords: Multicultural Literary Interpretations,* Sneja Gunew and Jan Mahyuddin, eds., *Beyond the Echo: Multicultural Women's Writing* (Saint Lucia, Australia: University of Queensland Press, 1988).

18. Sneja Gunew, "Denaturalizing cultural nationalisms: Multicultural readings of 'Australia,'" in *Nation and Narration,* Homi Bhabha, ed. (London: Routledge, 1990), 99–120.

19. Sneja Gunew, "Migrant Women's Writers: Who's on Whose Margins?," *Meanjin 42,* no. 1 (1983): 16–26, and "Authenticity and the Writing Cure," in *Grafts: Feminist Cultural Criticism* Sue Sheridan, ed. (London: Verso, 1988), 111–123; and Sneja Gunew, "Feminism and the Politics of Irreducible Differences: Multiculturalism/Ethnicity/Race," in *Feminism and the Politics of Difference,* S. Gunew and A. Yeatman, eds., (St. Leonards, Australia: Allen and Unwin, 1993), 1–19.

20. Joseph Banks, *The Endeavour Journal of Joseph Banks, 1768–1771, vol. 2,* John Beaglehole, ed. (Sydney: The Trustees of the Public Library of New South Wales and Angus and Robertson, 1962), 122.

21. "Sydney Gazette," quoted in Henry Reynolds, *Frontier, Aborigines, Settlers and Land* (Sydney: Allen and Unwin, 1987), 167–168.

22. The spellings of tribal names and the boundaries of their territories vary enormously. These three are taken from the Urban Land Authority, *Local Structure Plan* (Melbourne: Urban Land Authority, 1990); A. W. Howitt, *The Native Tribes of South East Australia* (London: Macmillan, 1904); and I. W. Symonds, *Bulla Bulla: An Illustrated History of the Shire of Bulla* (Melbourne: Spectrum, 1985). For convenience I will use *Wurundjeri* as the name and spelling of the tribal group occupying the Roxburgh Park area and will defer any resolution of the boundary issue. I am grateful for the research assistance of Mariastella Pulvirenti in uncovering material on the tribal groups in this area.

23. Howitt, *Native Tribes.*

24. Urban Land Authority, *Local Structure Plan,* 4.1.

25. Shirley Wiencke, *When the Wattle Blooms Again: The Life and Times of William Barak, Last Chief of the Yarra Yarra Tribe* (Woon Gallock, Australia: S. W. Wiencke, 1984), 4.

26. Wiencke, *When the Wattle Blooms Again*, 11.

27. C. S. Mason, Biennan, Deare, Dawson, Touhey, Gaudron, and S. S. McHugh, *Ruling in the High Court of Australia: Eeddie Mabo and Ors vs the State of Queensland*, (Canberra), 89.

28. Wiencke, *When the Wattle Blooms Again*, 28.

29. R. N. Billis and A. S. Kenyon, *Pastoral Pioneers of Port Phillip* (Melbourne, Australia: Stockland Press, 1974).

30. Symonds, *Bulla Bulla*, 35–41.

31. Ibid., 38.

32. Allan Gross, *History of the Shire of Bulla, 1862–1962* (Sunbury, Australia: Shire Council, 1962), 2.

33. Symonds, *Bulla Bulla*, 16.

34. Sir George Arthur to Lord Glenelg, July 22, 1837, letter in the *Historical Records of Australia, Vol. 2A: The Aborigines of Port Phillip, 1835–1839* (Melbourne: Victorian Government Printing Office, 1982), 26–27.

35. Sir George Arthur, Memo to Applicants for Assistant Protectors, *Historical Records of Australia*, Vol. 2A, 32–33.

36. Parker to Robinson, April 1840, "Being the Report for the Period September 1839 to February 1840, " *Historical Records of Australia*, Vol. 2B, 695.

37. Ibid., 692–693.

38. Quoted in Ian MacFarlane, comp., *Victorian Aboriginals, 1835–1901. A Resource Guide to the Holdings of the Public Record Office* (Victoria, Australia: Public Records Office, 1984), 43.

39. M. F. Christie, *Aboriginals in Colonial Victoria, 1835–1886* (Sydney, Australia: Sidney University Press, 1979), 141.

40. Ramsey, February 4, 1848, Forwarding a copy of the Minutes of Proceedings of the Aboriginal Mission Committees, Merri Creek, Victorian Historical Records Office, transfer No. 1959/3, Series No. 11, 1847–1851.

41. Christie, *Aboriginals in Colonial Victoria*, 144.

42. Michael Cannon, *The Land Boomers* (Melbourne: Nelson, 1976).

43. Miles Lewis, *"Roxburgh Park," Somerton, former "Ruthvenfield,"* Working Paper prepared for the Urban Land Authority, Roxburgh Park *Local Structure Plan* (September 1989), p. 15; emphasis added.

44. J. Brian McLoughlin, *Shaping Melbourne's Future? Town Planning, the State and Civil Society* (Cambridge, U.K.: Cambridge University Press, 1992), 125.

45. Mr. Bryce Moore, project manager, Roxburgh Park, interviewed March 2, 1993.

46. Ben Mitchell, "Home of the Future," *Sunday Age,* March 28, 1993, p. 11.

47. Work on the sexual division of labor in and around the home includes: Duncan Iremonger ed., *Households Work: Productive Activities, Women and Income in the Household Economy* (Sydney, Australia: Allen and Unwin, 1989). I am grateful to Kathy Mee, of the University of Sydney, for the insight on the consequences of reducing outside space for men's work in the home.

48. Roxburgh Park, *Community Plan*, December 1991 (Melbourne: Urban Land Authority).

49. Moore, interview; Monica Sadju, community development officer, interviewed March 2, 1993; Tim Garaham, "Roxburgh Park – An Ambitious ULA Project," *Melbourne Age,* October 16, 1991, p. 41.

50. Urban Land Authority, *Local Structure Plan,* 52–53.

51. Sadju, interview.

52. Urban Land Authority, *Local Structure Plan,* 30–31.

53. Roxburgh Park Survey Analysis, Response to Lot Purchase Surveys, June 1993. I wish to thank Bryce Moore for supplying this information.

8

Earth Honoring: Western Desires and Indigenous Knowledges[1]

JANE M. JACOBS

With each sign that gives language its shape lies a
stereotype of which I/i am both the manipulator and the
manipulated.[2]

Recent developments in environmentalism and feminism have intensified
Western desires to affiliate with indigenous people and to call upon their
knowledges and experiences. In settler Australia, alliances have developed
between feminists, environmentalists, and Aborigines seeking to have their
interests in land recognized. Within the Australian setting, environmentalists have presumed accordance between their interests and those
of Aboriginal Australians seeking land rights. Similarly, many non-
Aboriginal women's groups have presumed that the land struggles of
Aboriginal women resonate with their struggles against patriarchy. As
the case of settler Australia testifies, such alliances do not escape the politics
of colonialism and patriarchy. In particular, there are specific problems
arising from the essentialized notions of Aboriginality and woman that
underpin radical environmentalisms and feminisms. Yet to read these
alliances only in terms of the reiteration of a politics of Western, masculinist
supremacy neglects the positive engagement indigenous women may make
with such "sympathizers" in their efforts to verify and amplify their
struggles for land rights.

This chapter begins with a critical examination of the colonial and patriarchal potentials of recent radical environmentalisms and feminisms. The analysis then turns to the Australian setting, where I establish a historical context by overviewing the ways settler discourses have gendered both the Australian landscape and Aboriginal knowledges of that landscape. I next examine the recent history of political alliances between environmentalists and women's groups and Aborigines. In the final part of the chapter I focus on a specific example of one such political alliance, which formed around the struggle by the Arrernte people of central Australia to stop the flooding of women's sacred sites for the purpose of creating a recreational lake/flood mitigation dam for the residents of Alice Springs.[3] This case provides a specific example through which the troubled intersection of environmentalism, feminism, and indigenous rights can be explored.

My analysis of this particular political alliance requires some explanation. In moving from the political terrain of environmentalisms and feminisms to an analysis of practical political alliances, I move into an ethically uncertain realm of describing Aboriginal political discourse and action. In part, my reading of this political alliance focuses on environmentalist and feminist affiliations with the Aboriginal cause. As such, my concern is with non-Aboriginal depictions of Aboriginal interests and the logic of non-Aboriginal expressions of sympathy for the Arrernte struggle. That is, Arrernte discourses are presented in terms of the ways in which they appear within and are spoken about in white settler discourses and thereby in relation to the power structures of colonialist Australia.[4] This maneuver may appear politically correct because it is social constructionist in its emphasis. However, such approaches are not released from certain difficulties that continue to sustain colonialist power relations. Even in the presence of an empowered voice of the "other," the move to social constructionism has the potential to more complexly and deeply reinscribe colonialist constructions and thereby rerender the "other" passive.

Moreover, such perspectives presume that there is a clear distinction between Arrernte and non-Arrernte discourses/Aboriginal and non-Aboriginal discourses, and that there is a line beyond which I (and others) as a non-Aboriginal, a non-Arrernte, cannot step. I believe there are such lines. But I also believe that the politics of difference in contemporary settler nations like Australia exist in an interdiscursive political space, which is neither solely Aboriginal nor non-Aboriginal. Nor is this space singularly a domain of hybrid identity, for essentialist positions are present both as strategic and internally held realities. My concern in this chapter is with this political interspace. And in my efforts to examine this space I not only draw upon non-Aboriginal discourses but also take the "risk" of making contextualized readings of Aboriginal statements and political actions.

NEW ENVIRONMENTALISMS, FEMINISMS, AND INDIGENOUS KNOWLEDGES

Recent elaborations in Western environmental and feminist thought have heightened interest in "non-Western" peoples and peoples of color in the West. In environmentalism this is most clearly expressed within certain strands of Deep Ecology. For feminism, reconciling issues of gender difference with racial difference has been a major challenge and is variously expressed. On the one hand, there has been an embellishment of the concept of universal patriarchy by "adding" the experiences of Third World women and women of color. In a more radical position, similar to Deep Ecology, ecofeminists turn to "non-Western" women to provide guidance for an alternative society. Radical environmentalism and environmental feminism both provide a relevant insight into the racial and neocolonial implications of this attention to "non-Western" peoples.

Environmentalism has long depended upon Western rational thought, and in particular upon scientific thought, to argue its case against the ongoing exploitation of the environment. In this sense it may be interpreted as having depended upon masculinist knowledges in order to challenge exploitative, masculinist, and colonialist approaches to the environment.[5] In recent years other forms of knowledge have become more central to environmental philosophy and politics. In particular, there has been a conscious insertion of critical "otherness" into environmentalist thinking by means of ecocentric and ecofeminist perspectives.[6] Deriving from this movement has been a turn to "women's knowledges" and to "indigenous knowledges," which are seized upon as providing cultural models for a modernity that might construct itself not around masculinist anthropocentrism, but through a decentered subjectivity–a part of, and at one with, nature. The spiritualism and holistic visions of indigenous peoples readily accords with more radical strands of environmentalism.

Let me turn first to ecocentric environmentalism, or Deep Ecology. Ecocentric environmentalism recognizes a moral value in the nonhuman world and stresses the interconnectedness of the living and the nonliving, the human and the nonhuman.[7] Ecocentrism argues against centering human interests (anthropocentrism) and instead locates nonhuman interests as central to decision making. This is a radical subjectivity, a "transper-

sonality" that advocates the development of a wider sense of self to include all beings and all things.[8]

Knudston and Suzuki's *Wisdom of the Elders* provides a popular advocacy of such radical subjectivity and explicitly turns to "Native peoples" and
their intellectual and experiential insights for guidance into "proper human relationships with the natural world."[9] For Suzuki, the turn to indigenous wisdoms is a specific response to the failure of scientific wisdom.
The struggle of indigenous peoples to protect their land has automatic
accordance with the objectives of his own environmentalism:

> If biodiversity and ecosystem integrity are critical to salvaging some of the
> skin of life on earth, then every successful fight to protect the land of indigenous
> peoples is a victory for all of humanity and other living things.[10]

The diverse cultures that carry the indigenous knowledges Knudston and
Suzuki honor are drawn together under the generic descriptor "the First
People of the world"; these are people with a lineage to precolonial and
premodern times. Under the generic label of "First People," cultural diversity is transgressed by a "shared primary ecological perspective," thereby
emptying these groups of the specificities of their histories and geographies. The First People are located within a global chronology, which begins with them and ends with an environmentally sound "us." At the
hands of Knudson and Suzuki, indigenous knowledges are drawn into
more contemporaneous global discourses of environmentalism that seek
the preservation of the planet.

James Lovelock's christening of the earth as "Gaia," after the "wide-
bosomed" earth goddess of Greek mythology, explicitly genders this "total planetary being."[11] The feminized "planet Gaia" is shown "undis-
guised love, respect and awe." It is "embraced" as "Mother Earth," guardian
of the extended human/nonhuman family. Deep Ecology centers a specific
familial organization which, within Western thought and practice, has
long been confined to a feminized domain. The ecocentric perspective struggles to free itself from patriarchal assumptions about sexual difference.
Indigenous peoples are seen to be specially placed to understand the
feminized planet. It is not surprising that Burger has provided Gaia followers with a much needed "atlas" of "First People" – a spatial guide to
those "indispensable partners" in the movement towards a "sustainable
future on our precious planet."[12] The atlas maps indigenous peoples as
the surface custodians of the feminized planet. Marked on the map, the
"West" captures the geography of ecological knowledge. Such mappings
of ecological knowledge banks may well be part of the serious and urgent

quest for planetary survival; but they are just as likely to circulate, as they do in *Body Shop* marketing, as part of the paraphernalia of global green consumerism – take home souvenirs for the environmentally aware shopper.

Ecofeminism shares with transpersonal ecocentrism a relational image of nature, but ecofeminism stresses the historic and symbolic association of women with nature.[13] Ecofeminists embrace the woman/nature association as a source of empowerment and the basis of a critique of patriarchal domination and the exploitation of both women and nature. Eckersley argues that this is a project that explicitly exposes and celebrates that which was once regarded as "other" by masculinist visions and consistently reclaims the "undervalued nurturing characteristics of women."[14] Ecofeminism engages positively with essentialist understandings of the feminine. Some ecofeminists build upon the "body-based" assumption that woman's reproductive self predisposes her to being a caregiver, which extends to the nurture of nature. Other ecofeminisms build upon the "culture-based" assumption that women and nature share the experience of patriarchal oppression and exploitation.[15]

Janet Biehl argues that ecofeminism takes male characterizations of women and turns them into an "ideology that roots women outside of Western culture altogether."[16] For example, Spretnak suggests that women have a unique biological disposition that provides them with an ecologically sympathetic sense of "boundarylessness," allowing them to know all others, natural and cultural.[17] Thus formed, ecofeminism can turn to nonhierarchical pre-Christian cultures and earth-based traditional cultures for validation and inspiration.[18] Biehl refers to this as "the Neolithic mystique."[19]

The reclaiming of traditions takes a variety of forms in contemporary ecofeminist writings and practices. Celtic and Neolithic cultures are a popular source of guidance for many Western ecofeminist retrievals, particularly if they are documented as matrilineal or matriarchal and were based around a specifically female deity. Increasingly, however, it is not to the past that ecofeminists turn but to contemporary non-Western cultures. This shift is consistent with, but not identical to, wider trends within feminism that attempt to address the experiences of Third World women and women of color. In countries with colonial histories it is often local indigenous cultures that give guidance. Mellor provides a detailed account of the ways in which matrilineal clan societies of North America have provided environmentalists with a regular and locally relevant inspiration.[20] For example, in Carolyn Merchant's ecohistorical account of development in New England, Native Americans are both victims of colonialism and custodians of knowledges which provide clues for future ecosocieties.[21] Similarly, Rogers argues that the "experiences of women from societies with remaining links to matrilineal traditions may prove instructive to feminists from industrialised countries who wish to explore a better relationship with the land."[22]

It should not be presumed that the cultures of Third World women and women of color are only passively appropriated into Western ecofeminist positions. Maori writer Ngahuia Te Awekotuku provides direct testimony concerning the need for the environmentalist project to look to other cultures.[23] Similarly, Vandana Shiva's ecofeminist account of colonialist exploitation of women and nature combines an unusual attention to historical processes with a visionary prescription for the universal adoption of the "transgendered creative force . . . Prakrita," in order to combat Western gendered objectifications of nature.[24]

Ecofeminist perspectives draw much criticism, not least from other feminists. In the first instance, there is consistent criticism of the way in which the identification of women with nature "speciously biologizes the personality traits that patricentric society assigns to women."[25] As Shiva's work shows, even when the women/nature/nurture concept is supplemented by an acknowledgment of its socially constructed form and historical specificity, it remains a central theme in ecofeminist political visions. Biehl argues that this raises important ethical questions about a feminist ecological movement that builds upon an essentialist "falsehood" of "woman," the refutation of which has been a key theme in feminist writings since Simone de Beauvoir. Others have criticized ecofeminist retrievals of clan and Neolithic societies for being romanticized reconstructions that neglect evidence of patriarchal domination and environmental exploitation.[26]

The attention to other cultures contained within ecofeminism has the appearance of a feminism sensitive to difference. Radical feminism may presume a history of Western patriarchy, but more spiritually derived versions often neglect imperial histories and the impact they have had on racialized and colonized groups. Concepts of interconnectedness can stop short of incorporating the uneven histories of global capitalism.[27] Breaking down the boundaries within ourselves and between ourselves may be a necessary step on the path to global survival but this path travels across a terrain marked by inequality.[28] The recourse to an original femininity does not necessarily transcend such uneven geographies and Judith Butler argues that such nostalgia leads to exclusionary rather than inclusionary practices.[29]

It is from women of color that the most trenchant criticisms of such feminisms of difference and particularly the ecofeminist desire for indigenous knowledges has come. Winona LaDuke argues that some New Age environmentalisms have "commodified" indigenous cultures:

> What is happening is that our culture is taken out of context and certain parts of it are sold or just extracted. It's like mining. . . . Certain things are taken out and certain people are practicing those things in their own ways, and to me, that's appropriation of our culture. It's the same thing as expropriating our wild rice or our land. And it is one of the last things we have. It is our culture.[30]

After a colonial history of subjugation and exploitation, these women are rightly suspicious of the West's new fascination with difference. Western feminisms of difference are placing new pressures upon indigenous women and women of color. Audre Lorde criticizes this process:

> Now we hear that it is the task of black and third world women to educate white women, in the face of tremendous resistance, as to our existence, our differences, our relative roles in our joint survival. This is a diversion of energies and a tragic repetition of racist patriarchal thought.[31]

Ecocentric and ecofeminist environmentalisms are coalitional political formations under a guise of celebrated difference. It should not be presumed that such cross-cultural extensions of ecocentric and ecofeminist environmentalisms can divest themselves of colonialist trappings. These eco-driven reclamation processes are unsettlingly similar to earlier forms of colonialist appropriations, such as the museum practices of imperial science, and retain the potential for reinscribing patriarchal and colonialist constructs and practices.[32] Ecofeminist and ecocentric positions depend upon unifying modes of subjectivity, such as women with nature or Western and premodern/non-Western cultures. At one level they seem to celebrate difference, but at another level they obliterate difference through reductionist concepts of "oneness."[33] In such environmentalisms and feminisms, "otherness" becomes an "imaginary space" for "uniting subjectivities" in Western universalist objectives.[34]

There is of course a significant gap between these philosophical positions and the everyday political practices of environmentalists and feminists in, say, Australia. Not all environmentalists consciously follow an ecocentric or ecofeminist philosophical position. And certainly most active conservationists and feminists would be shocked to consider their well-meaning support of Aboriginal land issues to be colonialist or patriarchal. This question of consciousness does not seem to concern ecocentric and ecofeminist philosophers. Hay argues that "ecocentrism is an unarticulated impulse common to most environmentalists."[35] Carolyn Merchant claims the environmental action of minority women worldwide as part of the ecofeminist movement: "They might not call themselves ecofeminists, but that is what they are doing."[36] The relationship between political practices and a consciousness of particular philosophical positions is problematic when attempting to trace connections between the politics of such positionings and everyday political practices. Such linkages may be faintly marked. But in the coalitional politics of environmentalists, feminists, and Aboriginal rights in Australia there is the possibility of seeing more clearly the interweaving of these broader positions and their political effects.

SHE LAND/HE SACRED: LAND, GENDER, AND INDIGENOUS PEOPLE IN SETTLER AUSTRALIA

Kay Schaffer argues that in the early history of masculinist settler Australia a woman's presence was registered through metaphors of landscape. Drawing on Irigaray's notion of woman as "the scene" of rival exchanges between men, Schaffer argues that Australian colonization was of a land "imagined, through metaphor, as the body of a woman." Schaffer continues:

> For centuries Australia existed as an empty space on the map of the world, as a body of desire. Man, as the agent of history, confronted raw nature, as a vast and empty Other, and named it his Australia Felix. The land has taken on the attributes of masculine desire. This desire acts as a generative force in the narratives of exploration and settlement.[37]

Schaffer makes explicit the link between masculine (man, empire, civilization) and the subduing of the feminine (woman, earth, nature) in the settlement of Australia. The colonizing of Australia is enacted through patriarchal constructions of masculinity and femininity in which the land and women were collapsed into a single category.

If the land "Australia" was feminized in the name of colonization and exploitation, then the indigenous inhabitants of the land were in many renditions conveniently consigned to that feminized nature. The declaration of Australia as *terra nullius* discursively emptied the nation. This emptying was an act of desire challenged by the realities of active Aboriginal resistance or merely a persistent Aboriginal presence. Early depictions of

Aboriginal Australians often placed them as part of a feminized nature: sometimes passive, sometimes capricious or wild, but always to be invaded and possessed. Lattas argues, in relation to Australian art, that the land and the Aborigines are simultaneously aestheticized and spiritualized, with Aborigines always depicted as being "in harmony" with the land. The feminized land, the pacified native, were to be dominated, exploited, possessed.[38] As historians Butcher and Turnbull suggest, the settler's perspectives did not provide the basis for "an ecologically-sound understanding of the land."[39] Aboriginal knowledges, they argue, were undervalued and the Aborigines themselves considered simply a nuisance to be Europeanized or eliminated.

Aborigines were not eliminated nor were they ever to become "European." Those in the more remote parts of settler Australia, who maintained tradition-oriented ways of life, came under the anthropological gaze. Early anthropological accounts of "traditional" Aboriginal society were translated through the lens of Western patriarchy. There was a lack of acknowledgment of, or a denigration of, women's "business," that is, the spiritual and ritual knowledges and practices managed by women. Male anthropologists either ignored the business of women or were denied access to it in accordance with the gender-specific restrictions of Aboriginal society. The spiritual knowledge and ritual practices of men were often assumed to provide for the entire community. Women were viewed as "profane," participating in "small-time" rituals and magic unconnected to the more important issues of land and social harmony.[40]

It was only when female anthropologists began entering the profession in Australia that an ethnography of Aboriginal women's business began to emerge.[41] Diane Bell's landmark ethnography of the Kaytej and Warlpiri women of central Australia provided the first detailed study of an empowered and autonomous women's spiritual and ritual life. *Daughters of the Dreaming* shook the foundations of masculinist readings of Aboriginal society. Bell challenged the view of Aboriginal women as "feeders and breeders" servicing the loftier and more spiritual men. Bell's ethnography was crucial in asserting that Aboriginal women had important land-based traditions and were equally important as the men in maintaining the land. Bell writes:

> Aboriginal women ensure that harmonious relations between people and land will be maintained and that the land will continue to "come up green." They perform exclusively female rituals, yawulyu, for the country. . . . There are other ceremonies which men and women perform together. . . . A central responsibility of women is to nurture both people and land.[42]

Bell's ethnography helped redefine the parameters of legitimate claims to land. Women's sites were as important as those of men, they were as "sacred" as those of men. The Dreaming may have contained songlines depicting male violence against women, but in practice women had much autonomy and power over the management of social relations. Bell's reinterpretation of gender roles and relations in traditional central Australian communities was to prove crucial in land claim controversies throughout the 1980s. It is a reinterpretation that also changed the nature of alliances between Aboriginal women and non-Aboriginal women. The shared experience of the violence of patriarchy was optimistically underwrit by a relic separatist environmentalist possibility contained in Kayetj social organization.

Almost a decade later, the centrality of women's business to Aboriginal culture was reaffirmed in Deborah Bird Rose's land-based history of the Yarralin people of Victoria River, in Western Australia. She explains that in Yarralin culture geographical areas are "defined in relation to gender" and are "imbued with the essence and secrets of femaleness or maleness."[43] In Rose's account women and the feminized earth play a pivotal role:

> Men throughout the Victoria River District, recognise that much of their secret ritual and Law ultimately derive from women Dreamings, just as all life originates in mother earth, and as they themselves are born of women.[44]

In Rose's view, "When Yarralin people speak of mother Earth they speak to a similar understanding" to that of Lovelock's Gaia.[45] For the Yarralin, "Dreaming and ecology intersect constantly." But Rose's collapsing of Yarralin women's Dreaming into Western concepts of the "Earth Mother" has not gone without comment. Swaine, for example, goes so far as to suggest that the notion of Mother Earth uncovered in Rose's ethnography is a "reinvention," or more precisely, an elaboration, of indigenous concepts through Christian and ecological thought.[46] Swaine's critique rests uncomfortably on a notion of cultural hybridization and is ghosted by the problematic idea of a pristine authentic, that which really is (or was) Aboriginal, and which has been subsequently "contaminated."

According to Rose, Yarralin accord with contemporary environmentalism not only through the concept of Mother Earth. They also share the radical decentering of self and the "boundarylessness" associated with ecocentric/ecofeminist positions:

> Boundaries between species are immutable; they are not, however, impenetrable. Clever people and clever animals can change their shape, disguising them-

selves as other species and learning to communicate with them. This is what it means to be clever–to be able to cross boundaries.[47]

In Rose's account, the Dreaming is embellished to become the "Dreaming ecology . . . a political economy of intersubjectivity embedded in a system that has no centre." Concomitant with this heightened intersubjectivity comes a fundamental wholeness in which "there is no Other . . . there is only Us." In her final chapter Rose explicitly links her account of Yarralin life to holistic ecovisions. It is here that the prescriptive role Yarralin life holds for global survival is articulated. Citing Carolyn Merchant, Rose reiterates the ecofeminist view that modernity is secular and that the lack of spiritual understanding has "killed Nature." The stories of the Yarralin are offered by Rose as "possibilities" for finding answers to the "difficult questions" raised by the damage being wrought upon the "holistic Earth."[48]

Diane Bell and Deborah Bird Rose confirm a significant shift in anthropological and academic understandings of Aboriginal knowledges of the land, a shift in which women's business and environmentalist and feminist projects are at one. In their attention to difference, these ethnographies displace ideas of universal patriarchy, but retain and embellish essentialized notions of women as nurturers of nature. While these ethnographies are attempting to reinstate the status of women in non-Aboriginal understandings of Aboriginal society (and in so doing, to write new maps of geography), they are also part of a Western feminist/environmentalist project in which Aboriginal gender and land relations serve a non-Aboriginal revisionary political agenda.

COALITIONAL POLITICS IN AUSTRALIA

Australian environmentalists have long seen Aboriginal Australians as the original conservationists. Sackett has noted the predominance of Aboriginal motifs and music as backdrop to populist "wilderness" presentations in the media, as well as the abundance of literature on Aboriginal Australia in conservation shops.[49] The philosophical alliance between environmentalism and Aboriginal views of the land have begun to gain expression in political action and social formations. In the early 1980s a group of people of both non-Aboriginal and Aboriginal background gathered in eastern Australia to celebrate a dawn ceremony "to renew the life force of the dominant hill in the locality." The event was heralded as "the beginning of the renewing of the Dreaming," and was the first of many such ceremonies by "Renewal People" or "Dreamers" (as they call themselves) at "places of power" in the eastern parts of Australia.[50] One "Dreamer" acknowledged that the efforts were "fumbling and hesitant" but that guidance could be found in "our own Aboriginal Earth tradition." Newton's examination of the counterculture movement in eastern Australia shows how it consciously embraced Aboriginality.[51] The 1983 Nimbin Lifestyle Festival in rural Australia held workshops on establishing dialogues with Aboriginal communities. At the event a non-Aboriginal women's group promoted Aboriginal women's knowledges, holding seminars on their land-based culture and on traditional birthing methods. Festival profits went to local Aboriginal groups and the event closed with a collective dance choreographed in a spiral to represent the Rainbow Serpent, a common Aboriginal Dreaming figure. Such events may be seen as fringe activities, but the concern with indigenous knowledges is now considered an important part of mainstream environmental politics. The national Ecopolitics Conference in Australia has in recent years regularly designated sessions concerned with "First Peoples."

In a recent publication Robert Lawlor provides transpersonal environmentalism with a treatise for survival. *Voices of the First Day* is a more spiritual version of *The Wisdom of the Elders,* developed explicitly through Australian Aboriginal culture. Lawlor is concerned with what he describes as the "terminal crisis in the life cycle of the planet." The "spiritual guide" for recovery is "the oldest known human culture . . . Australian Aborigines." He invites the reader to enter into an Earth Dreaming, guided by Aboriginal Dreamings.[52] Lawlor has little sense of a need for boundary between Aboriginal knowledges and his New Age quest for the ecospiritual recovery of the planet. His publisher's preface attests to the way in which this volume conflates difference and denies history in the quest for ecospiritual rebirth:

> The Dreaming has no religious, racial, or cultural boundaries, no governments or social castes. . . . Perception and Dreamtime are the two worlds of all Aboriginal people.[53]

Lawlor is only one of a number of ecospiritual revisionists who have turned to the Aboriginal Dreaming for inspiration and guidance. Matthew Fox, founder of a "creation spirituality" movement, calls for a "wilderness Dreamtime":

> Spirituality must begin with the land. This is basic to the entire Aboriginal consciousness. It is also basic to the environmental survival not just of our species but all the species with whom we share this planet.[54]

As in Lawlor, boundaries of difference are breached in this quest. Fox suggests that ecospiritualists call upon "Australian Aboriginal peoples not only outside you but *in* you." One of Fox's fellow travelers suggests that we must "reclaim" Aboriginal sacred sites and Dreamings and think of the Aboriginal Dreaming "as our root and foundations as Australians."[55] Ecospiritualists evoke the possibility of an ultimate invasive colonial moment in which all Australians are able to claim an Aboriginality by way of an appropriated and reimagined Wilderness Dreaming. In his analysis of Lawlor's text, Thomas notes the presence of a New Age primitivism that constructs Aboriginality as culturally stable and ahistorical.[56] Within the ecological discourse of Lawlor and other environmentalists, primitivist essentialism adjudicates on what is authentically Aboriginal, problematizing the place of Aboriginal communities that are no longer "traditional" on this road to ecological salvation.

In such practices Aborigines become both "an otherness and an origin" in settler Australia's desire for ecological sensitivity.[57] Lattas argues that the ecospiritual alienation from the land that underpins environmentalism in Australia is part of a more pervasive and officially sanctioned discourse regarding the ecologically sound nation. Possessing Aboriginal knowledge is not only the final step in securing the Australian eco-nation, but also in a process of colonization, in which settler Australians can move from the status of aliens to that of indigenes.[58]

The land rights process has consolidated Aboriginal and environmentalist alliances. Many significant tracts of land are returned to Aborigines under land rights provisions *only* if they are then re-leased to National Park authorities. In other parts of Australia, Aborigines are *only* able to claim Unalienated Crown Land or designated National Parks.[59] While this does extend Aboriginal claims to land, it also confines Aboriginal use of the land to ecologically sanctioned options.[60] Under such legal confines, Aboriginal coalitions with environmentalists are as much a strategic necessity as they are a possible recognition of shared environmental objectives.

Indeed, not all Aborigines accept the idea that conservation is compatible with Aboriginal interests. The Aboriginal politician Michael Mansell complained when conservationists failed to seek Aboriginal approval to defend the Franklin River in Tasmania from damming and charged environmental activists with invading Aboriginal land.[61] In the conflict over a road being built through the World Heritage Listed Daintree Forest in northern Australia, Aborigines and environmentalist were far from sharing a "wilderness dreaming." While environmentalists spoke of how important the area was to local Aborigines, the very same Aborigines argued for the construction of the road to their poorly serviced and barely accessible settlement.[62] As Lee Sackett suggests, the view of Aborigines as the first conservationists is often based on a partial, romanticized, and racist understanding of traditional Aboriginal associations with the land and the political action Aborigines may wish to take in relation to that land.[63]

Many environmentalists feel women are specially placed to pursue the goal of the econation. The assumption that women are "natural" caregivers, not only of the immediate family but of the planet, permeates at a policy level in Australian environmentalism. In recent years the Australian government has been outlining a program for ecologically sustainable development. The National Women's Consultative Council, in calling for women to contribute to the consultation program, said this:

> Women are life givers. It is no accident they have led on environmental issues at all levels . . . locally and globally. Women's concern is rooted in concern for the health and well being of our families and communities.[64]

The executive director of Australia's most mainstream conservation lobby group, the Australian Conservation Foundation, holds an equally essentialist position, arguing that "women are more concerned about the environment than men" and that they alone in their role as nurturers have the capacity to "sow the seeds for new attitudes and practices."[65] Certainly, the women's movement in Australia and elsewhere gained new strength through coalitions with the environmental and peace movements.[66]

The joining of the women's movement with environmentalism coincided with a growing alliance between women's right activists and Aboriginal women.[67] This vision of a cooperative ecodevelopment between Aborigines (particularly women) and environmentally sound settler Australians (particularly women) is advocated by some Aboriginal spokespeople. Burnam Burnam argues that

> it will be the female peace-keeping energy which will save the planet from destruction by old males. Females make up three-quarters of the Green movement. . . . And it is Aboriginal women who possess an indisputable connection with our mother the Earth. Her spiritual strength, born out of tradition, is also acquired from male abuse, mainly sexual.[68]

Yet coalitions between Aboriginal and non-Aboriginal women have been sporadic and at times troubled.[69] The source of this conflict was non-Aboriginal women (and indeed some Aboriginal women) seeking to make rape within Aboriginal society (that is, rape of Aboriginal women by Aboriginal men) a general political issue for the women's movement.[70] The women's movement saw such violence as evidence of the workings of patriarchy within another cultural setting, whereas Aboriginal women opposed the politization of rape in this manner arguing it set female solidarity ahead of racial solidarity. For Aboriginal women, colonization had meant an ongoing battle to protect the family, most starkly from government policies to forcibly remove children who were known to have non-Aboriginal parentage. The appropriation of the issue of rape within Aboriginal society into the political agenda of the women's movement was seen as yet another non-Aboriginal invasion into the Aboriginal family.[71] Such rifts point toward the limits of coalitional politics and suggest that these limits are grounded in the historical specificities of colonialism.

In the final part of this chapter I want to examine a recent development controversy in remote Central Australia, in which Aboriginal women, conservationists, and feminists came together in a loose political coalition. I want to explore this coalition in the context of the critique of radical environmentalisms covered in the early part of the chapter. I think it is important to consider such political formations, for they reveal complexities and ambiguities that are often conveniently avoided when one's analytical field is confined to easy target texts such as Robert Lawlor's ecospiritualism or more extreme ecofeminist prescriptions against which charges of "appropriation" are easily laid. Examining such a political alliance problematizes the notion of "appropriation," which as Meaghan Morris notes, has become "the model verb of all and any action" setting "predation" as "the universal rule of cultural exchange."[72]

EARTH DREAMINGS:
THE ARRERNTE LAND STRUGGLE

Since the early 1960s the Northern Territory government has been considering building a dam in the vicinity of landlocked Alice Springs, in central Australia. The dam was intended to offer both recreation amenities and flood mitigation for the occasions when the usually dry Todd River rages. In 1983 the Northern Territory government announced that a site on the Todd River north of the town and near the Old Telegraph Station had been selected as the most suitable dam location. The site is part of a historic reserve that incorporates the remains of the first European telegraph station and government outpost to be built in the area.

There was strong opposition to the proposed dam site from local Aborigines. As early as 1979 they had alerted the Aboriginal Land Council for the area of the presence of sacred sites in the proposed dam location. A special committee, the Welatye Therre Defence Committee, was established to assist in organizing support for the protection of the site.

The most dramatic form of protest came in April 1983, when the traditional Aboriginal owners of that area, the Arrernte people, reoccupied the site. To the Arrernte people, it is the site of the "Two Women Dreaming" songline, which traverses Australia from south to north. According to an Arrernte press release, the main site in the area is "Welatye Therre" (Two Breasts), a place where "women have danced and sung for thousands of years to assert and strengthen their unique relationship with the country."[73]

Some 50 Arrernte men and women remained camped at the site for six months. An Aboriginal government official and leader, Charles Perkins, set up office at the site for a week in order to draw national media attention to the concerns of his Arrernte people.[74] Women's ceremonies were held at the site, during which Arrernte women were joined by other central Australian Aboriginal women, to reaffirm the significance of the country.[75] Aboriginal opposition was largely unsupported by the local non-Aboriginal population. Two prodevelopment petitions received by the government about the proposed dam contained over 5,000 signatures, accounting for some 75% of the local urban voting population.[76] To resolve the conflict, the federal government called for an inquiry.

The Northern Territory government were not insensitive to the likelihood of Aboriginal sites being present in the proposed dam area. The authors of early feasibility studies had consulted with the relevant Aboriginal Lands Council, but had reported that there appeared to be no Aboriginal opposition to the flooding of known sacred sites in the area. But the confusion over Aboriginal approval of the proposal to flood the sites simply reenacted the anthropological practice of men's knowledges being privileged over that of women's. This gender bias had been carried into the emerging government structures to accommodate Aboriginal interests in the land: and early consultations were primarily "by men and with men."[77] The official inquiry into the dam deadlock guaranteed that future consultations about Aboriginal interests in the area acknowledged the rights of women. The Aboriginal Sacred Sites Protection Authority (ASSPA) arranged for female anthropologists to consult with local Aboriginal women. The importance of the area to women was recorded and the site, Welatye Therre, was placed on official registers of sites of significance to Aboriginal peoples.[78] Although both men and women know about the site, the responsibility for speaking for that country rested with the women.

The protection of Welatye Therre required details of its secret and sacred content to be revealed, at the very least to the official site-recording agents. Elsewhere I have discussed the political and cultural implications of such transferrals of knowledge.[79] Within established land rights mechanisms "traditional" land-based knowledge has become a key means of verifying the legitimacy of land claims. However, the passing over of such knowledge to government agents has the potential to undermine Aboriginal self-determination and particularly to enhance non-Aboriginal powers of arbitration over the "authenticity" of Aboriginal claims, seriously disadvantaging those Aborigines who cannot or will not bring "traditional" proofs of evidence to bear on land claims.

In the case of Welatye Therre, the Arrernte agreed to disclose information to the official site recording authorities on the condition such information was not widely circulated. This request was adhered to. But as the likelihood of the dam proceeding grew, it was the Arrernte themselves who reluctantly decided to make known that which should be unknowable to non-Aborigines. This caused considerable anxiety among the Arrernte, for such disclosures transgress important rules of secrecy surrounding such sites.[80] It is this process of disclosure and the political alliances that emerged around this disclosure that I want to concentrate on in the last part of this chapter.

The Arrernte women's opposition to the dam proposal was organized through the Welatye Therre Defence Committee. This group made public the Arrernte struggle throughout Australia and overseas, by means of press releases, pamphlets, a newsletter, and a video which specifically targeted conservation and women's groups. The Arrernte deliberately allowed selected members of the press to see and photograph the site. Reports by the chosen journalists were sensationally explicit about the content of the site. In one report a group of Arrernte women are pictured "cradling" sacred stones stored at the site. The report opens with this provocative evocation of the site's significance:

> The dry Todd River bed in Alice Springs conceals an ancient secret story of violence and rape. Only Aboriginal eyes which know the Dreaming can read and understand the story, laid out in rocky outcrops in the river bank.[81]

The narrative flirts with the knowability of the sacred content of this site. Simultaneously, readers are being told a story and being told it is a story they cannot know. The report continues, taking us into the explicit realms of the unknowable. I am not going to quote this section of the 1983 press report. This detail was released into the public domain under the specific pressures of development, not the conditions of the production of this chapter. My concern rests not with the explicit detail of the site (beyond the media designation of it as a "rape site"), but with the knowability of the site, especially how non-Aboriginal interests come to know of it and demonstrate support for its protection.

While journalists were strategically led to view certain aspects of the site, the Arrernte still engaged in strategic nondisclosure, for there were "other stones" nearby, that journalists were told of but not permitted to see. It was the presence of *these* ritual objects that was of paramount importance to the Arrernte women. A non-Aboriginal spokesperson suggested that if these objects were removed or flooded over, then sickness and death would occur among the elders.[82] Another warned that "if they go ahead and build the dam here it will be no good for all the women in Australia."[83]

Arrernte women were not insensitive to the resonance of their struggle with those of women elsewhere. Speaking of the sacred objects stored at the site, one Arrernte woman said:

> They are a vital part of being a women. Like you've got women's liberation, for hundred of years we've had ceremonies which control our conduct, how we behave and act and how we control our sexual lives. . . . They give spiritual and emotional health to Aboriginal women.[84]

The Welatye Therre Defence Committee campaign was successful: statements of support and donations poured in from across the country. It was indeed becoming an issue for all women. Support and donations were received from Women's Action Against Global Violence, the Feminist Antinuclear Group, Women's Health Centres (Adelaide and Sydney), the Feminist Bookshop (Sydney), a Sydney women's refuge, Women for Life, and the Women's International League for Peace and Freedom.[85] The Arrernte women were keen to advertise this wider support for their cause: a broadsheet was released that listed and quoted many non-Aboriginal supporters.

Welatye Therre resonated with existing forms of feminism in a variety of ways. The disclosed content of this site hints at a premodern patriarchal violence against women. Designated as a "rape site," it acts as an embodiment of the most violent act of male oppression. Under the pressure of development this violence is disclosed and threatens to be reenacted through the dam construction as rape of the landscape. Pushed into the public sphere, the content of the site is opened to the gaze of all women (and men) and can be collectively claimed as a symbolic site of the violence of patriarchy. The site entered a discourse of universal patriarchal oppression. The Arrernte sites became proof of women as "archetypal victims," spanning all time and all cultures.[86]

The violence this site and these women now faced reiterates the specific violence of colonialism.[87] This site and the struggle around its protection were absorbed as symbolic markers into a feminism that was struggling to come to grips with the concept of "double oppression"; women's and black oppression added together.[88] Aboriginal women had ensured that the Australian women's movement was aware of the sexual as well as the racial violence of colonization.[89] In this adjustment the Aboriginal "other" was included as a "variegated amplification . . . of . . . global phallocentrism."[90]

The alliances formed between women's groups and the Arrernte women may well be an example of a colonizing, self-aggrandizing feminism. But Welatye Therre is also a site whose violent content operates to provide guidance: it is a pedagogical site that teaches Aboriginal women and men about appropriate behaviors, in short, how to avoid the violence of patriarchy and how to care for the land. It calls into question a totalizing feminism and provides the type of template desired by ecofeminist visions. Yet even within this less totalizing conjuncture with feminism, it is difficult for the Arrernte struggle to remain untouched by the force of feminism.

Environmentalists too found that the concerns of the Arrernte women resonated with their own concerns. Statements of support were received from Greenpeace, Friends of the Earth, and other, more local, environmentalist groups. Extracts from some of the statements of support reveal how the political alliances around Welatye Therre were closely linked to an ecocentric/ecofeminist retrieval of indigenous wisdom. The Canberra-based Friends of the Earth wrote:

> The proposed Alice Springs dam will destroy a sacred site of great significance. It is a site where, for thousands of years, Aboriginal women have performed ceremonies to strengthen their special relationship with the land. . . . Aboriginal culture['s] ecological sensibility is exemplary. The Aboriginal relationship to the land, spanning 40,000 years of judicious ecological management, puts to shame 200 years of European pillage.[91]

The London-based Aboriginal Support Group made clear their sense of saving this site as part of a global indigenous knowledges project:

> We have all come to admire and respect the deep feeling Aboriginal people hold for their land and feel that we in Europe and people all over the world have much to learn from you in caring for the earth and its people whoever they are.[92]

Under the pressure of development, the Arrernte excessively express the nature of their Dreaming site: disclose it beyond unusual limits of disclosure and warn of an effect beyond the geography of their local land interests. This is not to say the women exaggerated the possible outcome of site destruction or invented the site. It is to say that this site has an amplified presence under the conditions of modernity, it is spoken (and not spoken) within the global geography not only of development but also of non-Aboriginal political agendas. In the modern discursive constitution of Welatye Therre the site's significance was amplified by the ways in which its specific characteristics as a women's site, a site of violence against women, and a site belonging to "indigenous nurturers" of the land intersected with non-Aboriginal environmentalisms and feminisms. Arrernte women's business, and its very localized expression in the sacred site of Welatye Therre, was being globalized through its intersection with planetary environmentalisms and feminisms.

The alliance between the Arrernte women and feminist and environmentalist groups is more complex than a process of appropriation of indigenous knowledges. For a start, the idea of appropriation is at the very least complicated by the issue of Arrernte women's agency: their strategic, albeit pressured, engagement with more universalist conservation and feminist agendas. But I think the complication of this alliance lies in something that is neither purely domination nor purely strategic agency. Nor does it reside satisfactorily in an explanation that presumes hybridization, that Aboriginal women's business is no longer "purely traditional." The importance of this alliance is that it maps a discursive interspace typical of race relations in settler countries like Australia.[93] It is that space formed out of a constant interplay of dominant constructions of Aboriginality and Aboriginal self definitions. The political alliances that formed around Welatye Therre may evidence some form of "enunciative appropriation." But the power dynamic of this process has a political ambiguity, suggesting that it is "neither displaced identity, nor colonialist invasion, but a process that takes place in both," a struggle to "fix the terms of reference."[94]

The political problem of "fixing the terms of reference" for the Aboriginal sacred is well illustrated by later developments in the ongoing efforts of the Northern Territory government to build a dam near Alice Springs. In the early stages of the controversy the disclosure of the content and effect of the Welatye Therre site was done reluctantly and strategically by the Arrernte. Some five years later the proposals for a dam reemerged. A new location was considered, but it too encroached on land with sacred sites with "sexual significance" relating to the Two Women Dreaming (as well as a men's Dreaming).[95] The Arrernte women seemed to take a more cautious approach to widespread disclosure in this second round of negotiations.

One Arrernte woman explained this caution to the second board of inquiry established to arbitrate on the deadlock:

Only the Traditional owners used to hear these stories that their grandparents told them. Now they are going to hear this story all over the place. This dam has made the story really come out into the open; the story that used to be really secret. Now other tribes are going to hear about it . . . now everybody is going to learn, and the white people as well are going to learn about it. The country story that used to be hidden. It was like that for . . . Welatye Atherra. Now they know about that place all over the world, about the Dreaming as well. . . . We are giving away all our secrets now, and it will be heard all over the world, if there is a protest against building the dam. We'll have to give away our secrets again.[96]

A newspaper report on the second dam proposal evokes the Aboriginal interest in the land not by disclosing secrets that would not normally be disclosed, but by focusing on the impact of desecration and on secrecy itself. The *Age* newspaper reports:

The sickness affects women, in ways that are so secret that only the half dozen older women who are its custodians are allowed to know the full dreaming story of the site and the implications of its destruction. . . . Aboriginal women will not discuss the site with men, and they will speak about it to a woman for publication only in generalities.[97]

While the detail of the site remained more carefully guarded in this second round of the controversy, the effect of damaging the site was again clearly put. Destruction of the site, an Arrernte spokeswoman is quoted as saying, would "bring a curse on all women. . . . Not just Aboriginal or local women, but all Australian women."[98]

So far I have argued that detailed disclosure of the sacred content of sites assisted in the process of amplification of significance in a political interspace between Aboriginal land rights and its sympathizers. But part of the presentation of this women's Dreaming arises not out of a detailed elaboration of its content and geography, but instead out of quite the opposite; it is, in a Lacanian sense, the lack of representation. In the first stage of the dam controversy the explicit disclosure of the content of the site was accompanied by an act of nondisclosure: journalists were told some things but were also told there were other things they could not see and could not know. In the second part of the controversy even fewer details of the sites to be affected by development were disclosed. This hardened line on nondisclosure and the explicit statements by the Arrernte about the anxiety of disclosure had two effects. For nonsympathizers, the unknowability of the sacred opened the way for discrediting Arrernte claims. But for non-Aboriginal sympathizers the secrecy of the Arrernte sacred worked to intensify allegiance and, under the political force of this alliance, to finally ensure that the proposed dam did not proceed.

Secrecy around a sacred site is not simply a strategic measure: it accords with Aboriginal law. But within settler Australia secrecy has a strategic effect beyond the limits of Aboriginal society. Secrecy hints at an unknowable dimension of the women's concern for the Dreaming.[99] It is this unrepresentability that in a paradoxical sense authenticates the women's Dreaming for sympathizers and positively amplifies the significance of sites. It is under conditions of secrecy and partial disclosure that Welatye Therre becomes known. It becomes a sublime object, an embodiment of the lack in non-Aboriginal gender and environment relations. It is the "half-seen" status of the women's sites that ensures their role in fulfilling the desires of contemporary sympathizers. Trinh argues that when noncolored feminists embrace "the other" they seek the "unspoiled," an "image of the real native – the truly different." She adds that "the less accessible the product . . . the greater the desire to acquire and protect it."[100] In the case of Welatye Therre the globalization of this local geography of the sacred was as much driven by the nostalgic desires of environmentalisms and feminisms as it was by the forces of development. And nondisclosure had a strategic effect with sympathizers by not only intensifying the authenticity of Aboriginal claims in their eyes but also by presenting the Aboriginal sacred as a lacuna that could be filled with their own political aspirations.

CONCLUSION

This chapter has attempted to understand the logic of Western environmentalist and feminist affiliations with "non-Western" peoples. My analysis of the ecocentric and ecofeminist perspectives uncovered their colonialist and patriarchal subtexts, borne of a rearticulated desire of the West to possess indigenous knowledges held within a primitivist stereotype of the environmentally "valid" and "useful" indigene. It has been commonplace for postcolonial critiques to attack essentialisms like those in the primitivist or womanist subtexts of ecocentric and ecofeminist positions. Part of the presumption of this critique is that these essentialist idealizations are the constructions of colonial and neocolonial formations and may work to contain indigenous identities within a nonexistent premodern identity. Within this discursive terrain, charges of appropriation are easily laid. It is possible to presume that "predation" does indeed remain the dominant power dynamic of cultural exchange in settler states and that this is only negative in its effect, reenacting an ongoing process of invasion of Aboriginal knowledges and determining of Aboriginal identity.

Yet the Arrernte struggle unsettles this reading. The political alliances around their sacred sites do sustain the dynamic of appropriation, particularly in the sense that Aboriginal culture serves universalist environmentalist and feminist agendas. Yet the issue of secrecy and nondisclosure provides a key to an important complexity in the way "appropriation" needs to be understood. Under the conditions of secrecy the desires of non-Aboriginal sympathizers to support Aboriginal rights did not diminish, but intensified. Secrecy may enhance desires of sympathizers, providing an unknowable space into which their imaginative desires about Aboriginality are projected. When one outcome of non-Aboriginal imaginative projections (such as the nostalgias of environmentalism and ecofeminism) is a political alliance that desires and does not discredit secrecy and assists in the acknowledgment of Aboriginal rights, then narrow adjudications of "predatory appropriation" are problematized. They are not, however, eliminated. The disclosure of Arrernte business happened under the force of modernity. This includes the familiar pressures of development. It also includes the political imperative of harnessing the force of antidevelopment sympathizers. The sites were saved through such an alliance, but the politics of the alliance resonates with less sympathetic moments in the history of settler Australia.

It is the ambiguity of these sites, their ability to slip into and out of the universal issues of patriarchy and environmentalism, as well as an elusive premodern ecosensibility, which made them the loci of broader political coalitions. These sites contained a memory of universal oppression and exploitation as well as an unknowable hope of an alternative world. These sites became objects of desire for those who seek ecological salvation in the wisdom of the elders.

NOTES

1. Part of the title of this chapter is taken from a recent book that defines "a new male sexuality" through a reconsideration of the relationship between masculinity and environmental ecology; see Robert Lawlor, *Earth Honouring: The New Male Sexuality* (Newtown, Australia: Millennium Books, 1990).

2. Trinh T. Minh-ha, *Woman, Native, Other* (Bloomington: Indiana University Press, 1989), 52.

3. This has been a long-running dispute that reached final resolution only in 1992. My account focuses mainly on the early stages of the dispute in 1983–1984 when there was concern for the site known as Welatye Therre.

4. Patrick Wolfe, "On Being Woken Up: The Dreamtime in Anthropology and in Australian Settler Culture," *Comparative Studies in Society and History* 33, no. 2 (1991): 197–224, esp. 198.

5. See, for example. Andree Collard, *Rape of the Wild: Man's Violence against Animals and the Earth* (Bloomington: Indiana University Press, 1989): Maria Mies, *Patriarchy and Accumulation* (London: Zed Books, 1989); Vandana Shiva, *Staying Alive: Women, Ecology and Development* (London: Zed Books, 1989); Susan Griffin, *Women and Nature: The Roaring Inside Her* (New York: Harper and Row, 1978); Carolyn Merchant, *The Death of Nature: Women, Ecology, and the Scientific Revolution* (San Francisco: Harper and Row, 1980), *Ecological Revolutions: Nature, Gender and Science in New England* (Chapel Hill: University of North Carolina Press, 1989), and *Radical Ecology: The Search for a Livable World* (New York: Routledge, 1992).

6. Robyn Eckersley, *Environmentalism and Political Theory: Towards an Ecocentric Approach* (London: UCL Press, 1992), 67.

7. See, for example, Arne Naess, "The Shallow and the Deep, Long-Range Ecology Movement, a Summary," *Inquiry 16* (1989): 95–100; Alan R. Drengson, *Beyond Environmental Crisis: From Technocrat to Planetary Person* (New York: Peter Lang, 1989); William R. Catton, Jr., and Riley E. Dunlap, "A New Ecological Paradigm for Post-Exuberant Sociology," *American Behavioural Scientist 24* (1980): 15–47; Warwick Fox, *Toward a Transpersonal Ecology: Developing New Foundations for Environmentalism* (Boston: Shambhala, 1990); and Mary Mellor, *Breaking the Boundaries: Towards a Feminist Green Socialism* (London: Virago Press, 1992).

8. See Eckersley, *Environmentalism and Political Theory;* Fox, *Toward a Transpersonal Ecology;* and Freya Mathews, *The Ecological Self* (London: Routledge, 1992).

9. Peter Knudston and David Suzuki, *Wisdom of the Elders* (Toronto: Allen and Unwin, 1992), xiii–xiv.

10. David Suzuki, "A Personal Foreword: The Value of Native Ecologies," in Knudston and Suzuki, *Wisdom of the Elders,* xxi–xxxv, esp. xxxiv.

11. Knudston and Suzuki, *Wisdom of the Elders,* 46.

12. Julian Burger, *The Gaia Atlas of First Peoples* (Ringwood, Australia: Penguin Books, 1990), 6.

13. See Griffin, *Women and Nature;* Merchant, *The Death of Nature;* and Irene Diamond and Gloria Orenstien, eds., *Reweaving the World: The Emergence of Ecofeminism* (San Francisco: Sierra Club Books, 1990).

14. Eckersley, *Environmentalism and Political Theory,* 64.

15. Mellor, *Breaking the Boundaries,* 51.

16. Janet Biehl, *Finding Our Way: Rethinking Ecofeminist Politics* (Montreal: Black Rose Books, 1991), 15.

17. Charlene Spretnak, *The Politics of Women's Spirituality: Essays on the Rise of Spiritual Power within the Feminist Movement* (Garden City, NY: Anchor, 1982).

18. Eckersley, *Environmentalism and Political Theory,* 64.

19. Biehl, *Finding Our Way.* As a recent example, see Diamond and Orenstien, *Reweaving the World.*

20. Mellor, *Breaking the Boundaries,* 119.

21. Merchant, *Ecological Revolutions.*

22. Barbara Rogers, "The Power to Feed Ourselves: Women and Land Rights," in *Reclaim the Earth: Women Speak Out for Life on Earth,* Leonie Caldecott and Stephanie Leland, eds. (London: Women's Press, 1983), 101–106, esp. 103.

23. Ngahhuia, Te Awekotuku, "He wahine, he whenua: Maoir Women and the Environment," in *Reclaim the Earth,* Caldecott and Leland eds., 136–140.

24. Vandana Shiva, *Staying Alive: Women, Ecology and Development* (London: Zed Books, 1989).

25. Biehl, *Finding Our Way,* 15.

26. Mellow, *Breaking the Boundaries;* Biehl, *Finding Our Way.*

27. George Bradford, *How Deep is Deep Ecology?* (Hadley, MA: Times Change Press, 1989).

28. Mellor, *Breaking Boundaries,* 47.

29. Judith Butler, *Gender Trouble,* (London: Routledge, 1990), esp. 35.

30. Winona LaDuke, "Racism, Environmentalism and the New Age," *Green Left Notes 4* (1990): 15–34, esp. 32.

31. Audre Lorde, "The Master's Tools Will Never Dismantle the Master's House," in *This Bridge Called My Back: Writings by Radical Women of Color,* Cherrie Morraga and Gloria Anzaldua, eds. (Watertown, MA: Persphone Press, 1981), 98–101, esp. 100.

32. Rogers, "The Power to Feed Ourselves," 101–106, esp. 101; Te Awekotuku, "He wahine, he whenua," 136–140.

33. Biehl, *Finding Our Way,* 130.

34. Andrew Lattas, "Aborigines and Contemporary Australian Nationalism: Primordiality and the Cultural Politics of Otherness," in *Writing Australian Culture: Text, Society and National Identity,* Julie Marcus, ed. (Special issue *Social Analysis: Journal of Cultural and Social Practice 27:* 50–69, esp. 58).

35. P. R. Hay, "The Environmental Movement: Romanticism Reborn?," *Island Magazine 14*(1981): 10–17, esp. 13.

36. Merchant, cited in Virginia Westbury, "Ecofeminism Australia," *Bulletin,* July 2, 1991, pp. 89–91, esp. 90.

37. Kay Schaffer, *Women and the Bush: Forces of Desire in the Australian Cultural Tradition* (Cambridge, U.K.: Cambridge University Press, 1988), esp. 22, 77, and 79.

38. Lattas, "Aborigines and Contemporary Australian Nationalism," 50–69, esp. 58.

39. Brian Butcher and David Turnbull, "Aborigines, Europeans and the Environment," in *A Most Valuable Acquisition: A People's History of Australia since 1788,* Verity Burgmann and Jenny Lee, eds. (Melbourne: McPhee Gribble/Penguin, 1988), 13–28, esp. 28.

40. Adolphus P. Elkin, "Introduction," in *Aboriginal Woman: Sacred and Profane,* Phyllis Kaberry, ed. (London: Routledge, 1989).

41. See Diane Bell, *Daughters of the Dreaming* (Sydney: McPhee Gribble/Allen and Unwin, 1983); Annette Hamilton, "A Complex Strategical Situation: Gender and Power in Aboriginal Australia," in *Australian Women: Feminist Perspectives,* Norma Grieve and Patricia Grimshaw, eds. (Melbourne: Oxford University Press, 1981), 69–85; Jane M. Jacobs, " 'Women Talking Up Big': Aboriginal Women as Cultural Custodians," in *Women Rites and Sites: Aboriginal Women's Cultural Knowledge,* Peggy Brock, ed. (Sydney: Allen and Unwin, 1989), 76–98.

42. Bell, *Daughters of the Dreaming,* 36–37.

43. Deborah Bird Rose, *Dingo Makes Us Human: Life and Land in an Australian Aboriginal Culture* (Cambridge, U.K.: Cambridge University Press, 1992), 51.

44. Ibid.

45. Ibid., 218.

46. Tony Swaine, "The Mother Earth Conspiracy: An Australian Episode," *Numen 38* (1992): 3–26.

47. Rose, *Dingo Makes Us Human,* 90.

48. Ibid., 90, 220, 232, 235.

49. Lee Sackett, "Promoting Primitivism: Conservationist Depictions of Aboriginal Australians," *Australian Journal of Anthrpology 2,* no. 2 (1991): 233–246, esp. 235.

50. Chris Framer, "Some People Say the Earth Is Still Dreaming," *Habitat Australia 12,* no 2 (1984): 32.

51. Janice Newton, "Aborigines, Tribes and the Counterculture," *Social Analysis 25* (1988): 53–71.

52. Robert Lawlor, *Voices of the First Day: Awakenings in the Aboriginal Dreamtime* (Rochester, VT: Inner Traditions, 1991), esp. 9.

53. Ehud Sperling, "Preface," in Lawlor, *Voices of the First Day,* xii–xvi, esp. xvi.

54. Matthew Fox, "Creation Spirituality and the Dreaming," in *Creation, Spirituality and the Dreaming,* Matthew Fox, ed., (Newton, Australia: Milennium Books, 1991), 1–20, esp. 7.

55. Elizabeth Cain, "To Sacred Origins–Through Symbol and Story," in *Creation, Spirituality and the Dreaming,* Fox, ed., 73–86, esp. 78.

56. Nicholas Thomas, *Colonialism's Culture* (Cambridge, U.K.: Polity Press, 1993).

57. Lattas, "Aborigines and Contemporary Australian Nationalism," 58, 63.

58. *Advertiser,* May 23, 1989, quoted in Lattas, "Aborigines and Contemporary Australian Nationalism," 52.

59. See Tim Rowse, "Hosts and Guests at Uluru," *Meanjin 51,* no. 2 (1992): 265–276; Tony Birch, " 'Nothing has changed': the Making and Unmaking of Koori Culture," *Meanjin 51,* no. 2 (1992): 229–246; L. M. Baker and Mutitjulu Community, " Comparing Two Views of the Landscape: Aboriginal Traditional Ecological Knowledge and Modern Scientific Knowledge," *Rangeland Journal 14,* no. 2 (1992): 174–189; Jim Birkhead, Terry DeLacy, and Laurajane Smith, eds., *Aboriginal Involvement in Parks and Protected Areas* (Canberra, Australia: Aboriginal Studies Press, 1992).

60. See Laura Beacroft, "Conservation: Accommodating Aboriginal Interests or the New Competitor," *Aboriginal Law Bulletin 26* (1987) 3–4; and Philip Toyne and Ross Johnston, "Reconciliation, or the New Dispossession?," *Habitat 19,* no. 3 (1991): 8–10.

61. Michael Mansell, "Comrades or Trespassers on Aboriginal Land," in *The Rest of the World is Watching,* Cassandra Pybus and Richard Flanagan, eds. (Melbourne, Australia: Sun Books, 1990), 101–106, esp. 103.

62. Chris Anderson, "Aborigines and Conservationism: The Daintree-Bloomfield Road," *Australian Journal of Social Issues 24* (1989): 214–227.

63. Sackett, "Promoting Primitivism."

64. National Women's Consultative Committee, *What on Earth Can a Woman Do?* (Canberra, Australia: National Women's Consultative Committee, 1991), 4.

65. Patricia Caswell, "Women and Ecologically Sustainable Development," *Australian Women's Book Review 4,* no. 4 (1992), 15–17, esp. 15.

66. Curthoys, "Doing It for Themselves," 426. Curthoys notes that one of the inputs to the 1980s women's movement in Australia was a visit by the ecofeminist Mary Daly.

67. Fay Gale, ed., *We Are Bosses Ourselves* (Canberra, Australia: Australian Institute of Aboriginal Studies, 1983); Jan Larbalestier, "The 1980 Women and Labour Conference. Feminism as Myth: Aboriginal Women and the Feminist Encounter," *Refractory Girl,* nos. 20–21 (1980): 31–39.

68. Burnam Burnam, "Aboriginal Australia and the Green Movement, " in *Green Politics in Australia,* D. Hutton, ed, (Melbourne: Agnus and Robertson, 1987); 91–104, esp. 92.

69. Anne Curthoys, "Doing It for Themselves: The Women's Movement since 1970," in *Gender Relations in Australia: Domination and Negotiation,* Kay Saunders and Raymond Evans, eds. (Sydney, Australia: Harcourt Brace Jovanovich, 1992); 425–447, esp. 444.

70. Diane Bell and Topsy Napurrla Nelson, "Speaking about Rape Is Everyone's Business," *Women's Studies International Forum 12,* no. 4 (1989): 403–416. For a summary of the debate, see Jan Larbalestier, "The Politics of Representation: Aboriginal Women and Feminism," *Anthropological Forum, 6,* no. 2(1990): 143–157.

71. Heather Goodall and Jackie Huggins, "Aboriginal Women are Everywhere: Contemporary Struggles," *Gender Relations in Australia,* Kay Saunders and Raymond Evans, eds. (Sydney: Harcourt Brace Jovanovick, 1992), 398–424, esp. 401–402; Jackie Huggins, "Black women and Women's Liberation," *Hecate 13,* no. 11 (1987): 5–23.

72. Meaghan Morris, *Pirates Fiancee: Feminism Reading Postmodernism.* (London: Verso, 1988), esp. 267.

73. Welatye Therre Defence Committee, *Voices from Mparntwe,* newsletter. (Alice Springs, Australia: Welatye Therre Defence Committee, 1983).

74. *Australian,* May 14–15, 1983.

75. Justice Hal Wootton, *Significant Aboriginal Sites in Area of Proposed Junction Waterhole Dam. Alice Springs,* Report to the Minister for Aboriginal Affairs (Canberra, Australia: Aboriginal and Torres Strait Islander Commission, 1992), esp. 25–26.

76. Robert Lloyd, Fay Gale, and Minna Sitzler, *Report Alice Springs Recreation Lake,* vol. 1, (Alice Springs, Australia: Board of Inquiry into Alice Springs Recreation Lake, 1984), 15.

77. Diane Bell, "Sacred Sites: The Politics of Protection," in *Aborigines, Land and Land Rights,* Nicholas Peterson and Marcia Langton, eds. (Canberra: Australian Institute of Aboriginal Studies, 1983), 278–293, esp. 284.

78. Lloyd, Gale, and Sitzler, *Report,* 34.

79. Jane M. Jacobs, "Politics and the Cultural Landscape: The Case of Aborigi-

nal Land Rights," *Australian Geographical Studies 26* (1988): 249–263, and "The Construction of Identity," in *Past and Present: The Construction of Aboriginality,* J. R. Beckett, ed. (Canberra, Australia Studies Press, 1988), 31–44.

80. Lloyd, Gale, and Sitzler, *Report.*

81. *Age,* April 22, 1983.

82. *Sydney Morning Herald,* July 21, 1984, p. 23.

83. Rosie Ferber, quoted in Welatye Therre Defence Committee, *Voices from Mparntwe,* n.p.

84. Welatye Therre Defence Committee, *Voices from Mparntwe,* n.p., cited in *Sun,* May 9, 1983, p. 13.

85. Lloyd, Gale, and Sitzler, *Report,* 7–8: Welatye Therre Defence Committee, *Voices from Mparntwe.*

86. Chandra Talpade Mohanty, "Under Western Eyes: Femininst Scholarship and Colonialist Discourses," in *Third World Women and the Politics of Feminism,* Chandra Talpade Mohanty, Ann Russo, and Lourdes Torres eds. (Bloomington: Indiana University Press, 1991), 51–79, esp. 58 and 71.

87. Jenny Sharpe, "The Unspeakable Limits of Rape: Colonial Violence and Counterinsurgency," *Genders 10* (1991): 25–46; Roberta Sykes, "Black Women in Australia," in *The Other Half: Women in Australian Society,* Jan Mercer, ed. (Melbourne: Penguin, 1975), 313–321; Raymond Evans, " 'Don't You Remember Black Alice, Sam Holt?' Aboriginal Women in Queensland History," *Hecate 8,* no. 2 (1982): 7–21.

88. Curthoys, "Doing It for Themselves," 443.

89. Goodall and Huggins, "Aboriginal Women Are Everywhere," 398–424.

90. Butler, *Gender Trouble,* 13.

91. Ian Watson, Friends of the Earth, letter to editor, *NT News,* May 25, 1983, p. 19.

92. Aborigonal Support Group, cited in Welatye Therre Defence Committee, *Voices from Mparntwe.*

93. What postcolonialist writers like Homi Bhabha and Edward Said might call the "third space." See Homi Bhabha, "Introduction: Narrating the Nation," in *Nation and Narration,* Homi Bhabha, ed. (London: Routledge, 1990), 1–7; and "Postcolonial Authority and Postmodern Guilt," in *Cultural Studies,* Lawrence Grossberg, Cary Nelson, and Paul Treichler, eds. (New York: Routledge, 1992), 56–68; and Edward Said, "Yeats and Decolonization," in *Nationalism, Colonialism and Literature,* Terry Eagleton, Frederick Jameson, and Edward Said, eds. (Minneapolis: University of Minnesota Press, 1990), 69–95.

94. Meaghan Morris, *The Pirate's Fiancée: Feminism Reading Postmodernism* (London: Verso, 1990), 259.

95. Rosemary West, "Damning the River," *Age,* March 20, 1992, p. 9.

96. Cited in Wootton, *Significant Aboriginal Sites,* 74.

97. West, "Damning the River," 9.

98. Ibid.

99. Slavoj Zizeck, *The Sublime Object of Ideology* (London: Verso, 1989), 203.

100. Trinh, *Woman, Native, Other,* 88.

9

White Women Researching/ Representing ''Others'': From Antiapartheid to Postcolonialism?

JENNIFER ROBINSON

Mapping and placing "others" has been central to the project of apartheid: an archcolonial enterprise, currently in transition and, it is hoped, soon to be superseded by a new, postapartheid political structure. Like all postcolonial situations, though, the traces of the past remain: in the social order itself and in the subjects who forge and transform these contexts. In this chapter I am concerned with these traces of colonial interactions, which mark South Africa as an important context in which to reflect upon mapping and remapping others. The focus here is on a very specific set of interactions; those between researchers and the researched. Arguably, of course, there are many other more important contexts within which the mapping of "others" occurs – and this volume has explored some of them. Historically in South Africa missionaries, administrators, politicians, popular representatives, and travelers have all played significant roles in scripting both the landscape and the people living in this region.[1] My aim here is to link current feminist concerns with representing others and the (im)possiblities of researching and writing about "others" with earlier examples of researchers who set out to explore the worlds of others within an apartheid context. Through the analysis of the positionality of these researchers and the strategies they adopted in textually constructing others, I hope to reflect upon some of the possibilities for developing a more appropriate postcolonial/postapartheid methodology.

In South Africa the task of building a postcolonial methodology and disrupting hegemonic maps of representation has a certain political immediacy, but has also been a longstanding concern of antiapartheid academics and activists. The paths that we in this place have followed through the issues that have concerned the other authors in this book have an air of familiarity about them, but they are most definitely placed. The dynamics of resistance, oppression, state control and invasion of the research process; the currency of a protracted and ever uglier (internal) colonialism; and now the "negotiated revolution" of the 1990s[2] – all have set a backdrop for, and have profoundly influenced, the trajectory of research work and debates about representation and methodology.

However, while I hope that the following discussion of mapping others within the apartheid and postapartheid contexts places familiar debates about representation within an important and different setting, I will also be exploring these issues in a clearly socially "located" way. As a white woman academic trained in a relatively privileged educational environment here and abroad, from an ordinary white middle-class background, I speak from a specific set of social and disciplinary locations. I also trained at a time when most liberal and progressive academics in this country were strongly influenced by notions of "action" research and the empowerment of the poor, and when many were involved in "advocacy"-type interventions in urban, economic, and antiapartheid struggles. Most of us were convinced of the need for politically partisan research, representing the needs and interests of the poor and the racially oppressed. A whole generation of white women feminists, for example, spent most of their time researching poor African women in order to fulfill the demands for politically relevant work, and in an attempt to put their not-inconsiderable skills and resources at the service of these oppressed and underresourced communities.

The intersection of international debates about representation with this particular research environment has been particularly confusing. Accused of never studying white women and of constantly appropriating the experiences of black women for their own personal gain, white feminist researchers in South Africa have some grounds for feeling "misunderstood." But clearly the mappings of African women's experiences that have been generated in the 1980s spurt of predominantly white feminist writings in South Africa must have been implicated in the particular social positioning of the authors, as well as in the methodological and theoretical assumptions that underpinned this "politically accountable" research.[3]

I plan to explore, first, the contours of the arguments that have been emerging between white feminist academics and black academics and researchers (including – in South African "racialized" terminology – African and Indian or Coloured women), as well as black (and white) women activists. These debates I refer to also have a spatialization that is relevant: they have taken place in texts, but also in angry confrontations at conferences, sedate luncheons, in personal exchanges and upset discussions late into the night, at editorial meetings, and in practical discussions in research, activist, and political contexts. The placing of this discussion in a text authored by me loses much in the translation.

The second part of the chapter, at least partly in response to these debates and in search of a way forward, will look more closely at the (white) woman researcher. Here my interest in the work of the other authors in this collection will be apparent. The disruptive effect of the mappings of white women travel writers within the colonial discourse about the "other" makes fascinating reading. My concern is that this is also very much a reading of an "other": the historically distant, other white woman. And in some ways this does not necessarily connect very directly with an exploration of our own subjectivity, representations, and locatedness. This is not a plea for endless self-examination, but simply for us to place ourselves and our own project of research and mapping of others more clearly within the scope of our questions about representation.[4]

Here my explorations have led me in two directions. The first is an encounter with some "other" women academics, from the history and past of my own place and institution. I discuss the work of three women, primarily that of Hilda Kuper, and, more in passing, that of Mabel Palmer and Fatima Meer. All three of these women have written about the "Indian" community in Natal and Durban and all of them have worked at my own university. The connections with my own work and locatedness are therefore very close and, I hope, interesting in terms of linking the deconstructions of earlier mappings with the debates and concerns about social location and representation in the present. The second direction my explorations of these topics took me in was a rather precocious "experiment" to "do" some ethnographic work in a community different from my own. I wished to confront my own experiences in this kind of work – which I have never embarked upon before except in a very textualized sense – with the debates in the literature and in my vicinity. I will briefly explore some of my reflections on these efforts in the final section of this chapter, which considers the possibilities for generating postcolonial mappings in a research setting. My comments on the potential for a postcolonial methodology are in many ways an expression of hope rather than of certitude, as I am in the middle of the fieldwork experiences on which such comments are based; the hard analysis of this experience remains to be conducted. But the weaving of the issues of mapping and representing others within the South African context which I offer in this chapter, I feel, adds some important dimensions to debates that are usually located within other places.

ANGRY ENCOUNTERS: BLACK WOMEN IN THE ACADEMY SPEAK BACK

Angry, defensive, upset, irritated, dissatisfied, disempowered, neglected, commodified, silenced, othered, objectified, distorted. . . . "people denied and discounted each other's realities": such were the responses to and assessments of the first Women and Gender in Southern Africa Conference held in January 1991.[5] The issues cited as being of concern included that the conference had been organized by a group of mostly white academic women; that those who attended the conference were also mostly white academic women; and that those who gave most of the papers were white academic women. Although activist and grassroots women's organizations had been invited to participate in all aspects of the programming and presentations, the conference, in both its content and its form, excluded and marginalized women without an intellectual background. Also at issue were the images of black women which were being drawn upon by the conference organizers and in the papers being presented. The conference logo (see Figure 9.1), for example, has been criticized as portraying "a tiny-headed, naked and burdened Other, 'present' only as object for scrutiny by the self-defining, theorising subject."[6] Indeed, the logo was chosen for its local and historical significance, for it is the only surviving representation in local San paintings of women; it portrays a woman heading off to gather food with her digging implement and container to collect sustenance for the community.[7] With this display of the different potential meanings of feminist symbols for different discursive and socially located communities, the debate over the logo in many ways symbolizes the contrasting and emotionally charged positions taken by an "old guard" of committed feminist academics (mostly white) and a new wave of articulate and critical black writers.

The debate about representation, long pursued in other countries, emerged in South Africa in the face of a long tradition of nonracial politi-

FIGURE 9.1. Logo from the Conference on Women and Gender in Durban, South Africa, 1991.

cal organizing, and left most conference participants feeling confused and emotionally distressed. Personally, I felt very silenced by the debate, which was characterized by strong references to the political and academic authenticity granted to the voices of black academic women and feminist activists. Since the conference, though, the voices have multiplied and women from a variety of backgrounds have responded to and debated the issues involved here. My own silence has ended in a disruptive deviation from my usual research efforts, and a lot of thinking and discussion about the concerns of women researchers from a wide variety of backgrounds.

Among the respondents, Lewis – a black women academic from the University of the Western Cape – makes a strong argument that white women academics writing about black women have been constructing black women as objects in a racialized discourse.[8] She does not offer us any detailed textual support for these arguments in her paper,[9] but in its broadest outline, her complaint that left feminist writers in South Africa have textually constructed black women as subjects in ways that distort the experiences of many black women is probably quite accurate. And this may well have to do with the inescapable fact that white women write out of a very different life experience from black women. Whether this means that white women have in fact straightforwardly set white Western feminist norms and experiences as the basis for their interpretation of black women – as Lewis suggests[10] – needs to be demonstrated. This is particularly necessary in the South African context because in the decades of antiapartheid work, a strong sense of the very different life situations of black and white women infused both feminist writing and feminist activism. From the first forays into feminist theorizing – for example, in Bozzoli's notion of a "patchwork quilt of patriarchies," or Beall's discussion of the different colonial patriarchal systems affecting white, Indian, and African women in Natal[11] – South Africa's stark apartheid social structure has foisted upon us an awareness of difference.

Elsewhere, in an unpublished conference paper, Lewis constructs a neat and plausible account of the way in which feminist writers have assessed black women's political activity – which has often centered around the mobilization of women in gendered roles such as "mother," "wife," or "sister" – on the basis of the goals of western feminist politics.[12] Rather than criticizing black women for their absence of "feminist consciousness," she argues that we should explore these women's self-perceptions and consider how, even within "these disempowering statuses (mother, wife, sister) . . . women often developed new roles of authority and strength."[13] However, Lewis is critical of similar "womanist" arguments made by African-American women writers, in this case because they ignore gender oppression. But she does insist on the need to avoid imposing Western political agendas on the "context-bound" experiences of particular women. This intervention by Lewis marks an important, if preliminary,[14] step along the road of deconstructing our previous understandings of gender relations and feminist politics in South Africa.

Lewis clearly presents some important challenges for white feminist academics. She charges that their response to black women's criticisms has been to reconstitute the criticizing black subject – as middle class, alienated and disgruntled – rather than to explore the implications of this previously silent subject's criticisms of their writing and practices. The task, then, is for us (both black and white women) to probe our positionality with ruthless honesty, to acknowledge the implications of this positionality for our writings, and to build, with sensitivity, "affinities" among women whose life experiences are very different.[15] It is inappropriate for white or privileged women to seek authority in the political imperatives of feminism, women's "interests," or nonracialism, as Hassim and Walker and Horn have attempted to do,[16] for these imperatives discursively constrain and once again externally shape the stories we can tell about women. It is, however, equally inappropriate for the black woman researcher or subject to claim an unambiguous authenticity and privileged insider knowledge by virtue of her own life experiences.[17] While I will explore this rather controversial point further below, Lewis herself forecloses this ambitious alternative route as she writes:

I do not present a case for a "correct position," nor do I claim the legitimacy of a particular set of experiences as a basis for a single authentic interpretation of "women and gender"; rather, my concern is with how hegemonising discourse needs to be replaced with what Ong has referred to as "leads for recognising a mutuality of discourse in our encounter with (other) women." . . . Feminists in South Africa need to thrash out these issues instead of dismissing ideas that do not fit into their paradigms as signs of others' false consciousness.[18]

In the light of such reasoning, Lewis most appropriately wonders about the "politics underlying many white feminists' defensiveness" in the light of black women's criticisms.[19] Apart from the confusion resulting from the strong sense of political responsibility involved in the choice of black women as research subjects in the past, I feel that this defensiveness is at least partly because the various dimensions of the debate have not been separated out in a useful way. We have conflated issues of institutional marginalization (the representation of black women within the academy and gender studies circles) with concerns about representing the "other" and authenticity in research, and confused these further with the appropriate emotional responses to the debates that different women have experienced.

On this last point, being "talked about" has caused a great deal of hurt and indignation among black women (academics).[20] These feelings are indeed important and in many ways are at the very core of the representation debate. But it is women within the academy who are themselves engaged in such activities – talking and writing about others – who are responding with feelings on behalf of those who are being talked about, who are seldom based in the academy. Are we perhaps picking up our own anxieties about (mis)representation as we respond in these angry ways?; our own fears that the process in which we as academics are all involved has its necessarily messy and abusive dimensions: that like modernity, it is both progressive and destructive? Are we perhaps putting emotions and words in the mouths of the subjects of research which are not necessarily there, but which are more clearly in our own hearts and minds?[21]

Whatever the source(s) and implications of these emotional responses, the central issue in the debate is obviously the controversy surrounding the representation of "others," which lies at the heart of all research. In this regard, black women researchers talking about black women subjects also have to confront the problems of representing the other which white women confront. Precisely because of the black woman researcher's dual location in the academy (or within particular disciplinary or discursive "grids") and as an "insider" in her community, she must also face the

problems of translation inherent in writing about experiences, in select-
ing and re-presenting those experiences, and in being unable to "know"
the truth of the subjects involved in her study, being able only to negotiate the meanings and interpretations surrounding the individual or the
actions she is concerned with. In fact, except in her very own neighborhood, the suggestion that any given black researcher has privileged access
to knowledge about people because they are black links straight back into
the kinds of complaints that black women have been making about white
women reducing black women's experiences to a universalizing stereotype. For outside of your own language group, culture, and local social
arrangements, clearly, skin color aside, you are an outsider.

However, as Collins argues,[22] the black woman in the academy, as
an "outsider within," brings an important disruptive element into particular disciplinary and institutional situations. And the productive South
African debate about difference was sparked and given an intensity it would
not otherwise have had without the significant contributions of black wom-
en researchers. The political implications of such inputs have also been
profound, offering disruptive perspectives on immediate political proposals,
such as that for a women's ministry in a postapartheid government. In
this light, white women researchers need to look more closely at their
emotional responses to the difference debate, and take up the challenges
offered to their previously hegemonic, modernist readings of women's experiences. The research agendas in this respect seem clear: to examine from
a critical perspective the effect of positionality and discursive location upon
feminist writings in South Africa to date; to explore the complex issues
surrounding representation, "truth," and method in feminist research; and
to examine our own positionalities and social locations in and through
the research we do. And the institutional importance of redressing the
kinds of apartheid-induced imbalances between the numbers of white versus
black researchers and teachers has been strongly reaffirmed. The rest of
this chapter addresses these urgent research agendas in a preliminary way,
examining the role of positionality and subjectivity in shaping some writings by South African women researchers about men and women of Indian origin, and exploring some methodological points relevant to a
contemporary project concerned with a similar topic.

WHITE WOMEN/INDIAN SUBJECTS

Europeans in Natal, by refusing to know anything of the Indians who live
amongst them, actually cut themselves off from many interesting and worth-

while experiences. The number of dignified and distinguished looking elderly Indian men is noticeable. The young Indian girls are often lovely and admirably graceful in their brightly coloured saris. Many of the younger men are educated and intelligent. A natural human interest in the culture and customs of Mohammedans and Hindus would break down the barriers of race hostility and substitute a friendly attitude to fellow human beings. But these are only dreams. In fact the clouds of race prejudice are darker than ever. Neither side knows the other, and it is the fixed policy of the Government to restrict their opportunities of meeting.[23]

Despite the strenuous efforts made to separate races in the name of apartheid in South Africa – as criticized by Palmer in the above quotation – the ideal of separate and noninteracting, clearly defined racial groupings, although visually evident and physically effective in all sorts of ways, is somewhat misleading as a characterization of South African society. For the numerous interactions and mutually constitutive negotiations of identity between the rulers and the ruled are as significant in understanding South African history as they are in other colonial contexts. Rulers and ruled interacted to name and shape cultures and identitites in complex ways. Goldin, for example, has written about the ways in which Coloured political organizations were as involved in making and shaping the identity of the Coloured people over time, as was the apartheid state.[24] Ironically, in their desire to overcome the apparent barriers between different race groups, enlightened academics, such as Mabel Palmer and Hilda Kuper, whose work I will be discussing here, fed into the (colonial/apartheid) process of constructing communities and racial identities. At the same time as they helped to create clear, separate identities for disparate social groupings, however, they also engaged in the (always) negotiated process in which both observers and the observed construct these images. Indeed, the apparent fact of separateness (apartheid) within the South African context has hidden from view those engagements that lie at the heart of the processes constituting and transforming the social order which are crucial to understanding both the past and the present in this country. And as scholars of South African history are increasingly realizing, this involves the complex negotiation and transformation of subjectivities, and not simply a conflictual clashing of opposing, self-contained subjects (such as capital and labor, administrators and "natives").[25]

In this section I wish to explore the process of engagement between researchers studying the Indian community in Natal and the subjects of their research.[26] How were these researchers involved in the construction of subjects and how did their own location and subjectivity shape the accounts they developed? Hilda Kuper, especially, was not unaware of a

number of these issues and processes, and I hope that pointing to the contradictions at the heart of both the research process and the textualization
of others in the work of these women will enable me to lay some foundations for a postcolonial, postapartheid research methodology. The role
of the subjects of the studies in this process of the construction of identity
is harder to grasp without detailed historical research, but this role also
emerges from time to time in the texts I have chosen to analyze, which
are primarily concerned with the Indian community in Natal.

A significant proportion of the population in Natal, a province of South
Africa, and especially of the Durban metropolitan area, the second largest
metropolitan area in the country, trace their origins to India. Most people's families began their settlement in the region as indentured laborers,
working in extremely arduous and impoverished conditions primarily on
the sugar estates. But some Indian people arrived as "passenger Indians":
they were usually wealthier, with no obligations to work, paying their
own passage, and forming the nucleus of a successful merchant class in
the cities and rural areas of Natal and the Transvaal. Indentured laborers
could remain in the country once their indentures were complete, but a
heavy tax on "free" Indians led many to renew their five-year indenture,
sometimes several times. Confined to the margins of colonial life, people
of Indian origin in South Africa have experienced generations of discrimination at the hands of the colonial government, local governments, and
the white population. Prior to the policy of apartheid in which segregation of race groups was rigorously enforced (with arguably the most serious consequences for the Indian group, especially in terms of residential
segregation and loss of property), the government had been intent on repatri-
ating Indian people to India. A long history of resistance and accommodation in response to this policy ended, then, with the granting of a definite
claim to citizenship, albeit a citizenship that was different from, and inferior to, that accorded to whites by the same state.[27]

Indian people in South Africa, and especially in Natal, have been written
about a lot. South Africans of Indian origin have been inscribed textually
in the documents of the state, in the words and actions of "coolie agents"
and "protectors of Indian Immigrants" (appointed by the state in a minimal
attempt to redress the serious abuses of the rights of indentured laborers
that were taking place in the colony), in the writings of white liberals
and Indian activists who exposed the political and socioeconomic conditions of Indian life in South Africa at different times, and in the texts of
observers, academics and anthropologists, both white and, increasingly,
Indian. It is with these latter texts that I am concerned here, since my
project is not so much to look at the ways in which "Indianness" in general

has been constructed, textually and nontextually, but to look at the process of mapping others in which academic researchers particularly have been involved.[28] The women researchers I have chosen to focus upon here are very different from each other. They were all, however, strong and independent, extremely capable academic women. In some ways their personal lives offer an emotional and inspirational image for contemporary women researchers. But my primary purpose in engaging with their work is unlikely to display them in a favorable light, as we explore the ways in which they were involved in naming and placing those they were studying.

Mabel Palmer, a formidably energetic woman, with a Fabian Socialist political background in the United Kingdom, spent most of her adult life working at the University of Natal and other educational institutions to foster the development of tertiary education for Indian and African people in Natal. Her biographers paint a picture of her as an independent-minded, tremendously energetic, generous, and inspiring organizer and thinker.[29] Her correspondence reveals her to be as much at home in discussing national policy and educational development as she was in sharing recipes, discussing the daily routines of household pets, gardening, and housekeeping. If students letters received by her in her old age are anything to go by, she was a truly inspirational educator, loved by her students, remembered long after they had moved on in the world, and described as a "mother" to them. However, her relations with her charges were not always so gentle and harmonious. Indeed, as Shula Marks's touching account of her correspondence with a young African girl from the Transkei, Lily Moya, indicates, she was often tetchy, could be brutally honest, and frequently displayed an ignorance of the conditions of life of the poor and of people in different cultural situations.[30] Her lens of interpretation was often firmly Eurocentric.

In her writing about Indian people in Natal, this interpretive context pops up in the midst of what is an otherwise bland historical account of the political and economic history of Indian people in the country. Mabel Palmer's contact with Indian people took place in the context first of her educational work (where her ambivalent but generous relationship with students and associated members of the public would have shaped the impressions she developed) and second through her association with the liberal groupings interested in fostering contact between Europeans and other race groups (Indians and Africans) and opposing discriminatory legislation, such as segregation and repatriation. As Mesthrie has noted, these groupings did not have much political impact, working mostly among the wealthy, but their contribution in terms of social welfare projects was often long-lasting and quite significant.[31]

Palmer's considerations in terms of her interactions with Indian people were governed by a positive view of Westernization and the benefi-
cial role that white liberals could play in assisting with Indian advancement
in these terms. She writes, "The Indians, when properly led and trained,
are quite as capable as any other race of developing modern methods for
tackling social problems."[32] She also deployed a number of (albeit pater-
nalistic) stereotypes in her asides on "the Indians" (see the quotation at
the beginning of this section). She writes, for example, that "the open
discourtesy shown to Indians in shops and offices must be most galling
to these sensitive people,"[33] Nonetheless, she herself objects to the stereotypes of Indians offered by other white people: "For them the Indian is
typified by the ragged untidy vegetable 'Sammy' who calls at the back
door with his baskets . . . and whenever proposals are made for any sort
of collaboration with the Indians, this is the figure with whom they imagine they are called upon to associate."[34]

Faced with the "different" subject she is writing about, she builds us
a picture of the suffering, exotic and noble "other" – but then she works
hard, in a most personal and sometimes obviously angry tone, to exercise
a measure of control over the nature and activities of this other by reclothing
him/her in Western, liberal values, ambitions, and tactics. Her process of
mapping "the Indian people" attempts to fix the process of interaction,
of knowing, and the transformations that result from complex colonial
encounters within her own terms. Tetchy, indeed, she chastizes Indian
politicians for their policies of noncooperation and strategies of passive
resistance. Seeing these as impractical, she suggests they should adopt more
measured, rational, Western political techniques which, in her opinion,
would enable them to win more of their demands. The subject, however,
substantially resisted this definition and the trajectory of Indian politics
has been interesting, complex, certainly syncretic, but uncontrolled by the
mapping Palmer and others wished to impose.

Mabel Palmer, of course, was no anthropologist (hers was a political
history of the Indian people) and the distance of her analysis from the
life experiences of Indian people and the relatively taken-for-granted (liberal)
ways in which she interpreted this community, are not surprising. Hilda
Kuper, however, who wrote *Indian People in Natal,* published in 1960, was
an anthropologist of international standing: she published a seminal and
widely acknowledged study of the Swazi people in 1947. Before exploring something of Kuper's interpretations of the Indian community in Natal,
it will be useful to consider this earlier work on the Swazi people as well
as Kuper's methodological reflections on this work.

I have found two aspects of Hilda Kuper's writings especially useful in thinking about issues of representation. First, her methodological considerations and second, her "nonacademic" writings: a novel, play and short stories, which provide a wonderful counterpoint to the professional anthropological writing for which she is much better known. Her play, *Inhliziyo Ngumthakathi* (1970; A Witch in My Heart, or literally, The Heart Is a Witch) describes a rural Swazi family, and the emotional stresses of polygamous marriage customs, jealousy, the trials of withcraft (which, in her assessment, makes people afraid of their closest kin), and the emerging relationship between rural life and growing urban areas in the region. At a time when descriptive, empiricist anthropological work was the norm, her exploration in this play of the emotional world of her subjects stands out as somewhat unusual, although her own anthropological texts do reproduce this empiricist tradition. After spending almost four years living in Swaziland, among various communities (although usually hosted by chiefs and important people), she obviously felt that she had observed and heard enough about the complex inner emotional worlds of men and women to formalize a play, attempting to capture these feelings. She writes:

> An anthropologist who has lived closely with people in a foreign land is confronted with the very difficult problem of how to present her data. To communicate with her colleagues she must fit her material, expressed in a world of different symbols, into the compartments acceptable in the discipline. She is expected to write in scientific journals and monographs, aware of problems of social rather than personal relationships. No matter how deeply her experiences and reflections in the "field" change her perceptions and enrich her personal life, she must strive to be "objective" by the standards of her colleagues in the craft. The writer of fiction, on the other hand, is allowed greater freedom of expression and imagination. She is expected to personalize general experiences, is permitted to develop her own style and eccentricities. . . . She need not explicitly distinguish between ideas and emotions and may deliberately use the ambiguity of words to extend the reader's perception. . . . She is entitled to ecstasy. . . . The drama, the novel, the poem and the monograph complement one another, each presenting a different facet of the whirling worlds around and within the self."[35]

While today we have a strong sense that all these aspects of the world and the self are within the domain of intellectual enquiry and interpretation, Hilda Kuper resolved the duality of her emotional and professional responses and responsibilities in her research context in two quite different media. At first it seems like an unfortunate split, a dichotomy, a disjuncture. But clearly the two are strongly interconnected. Her anthropological observations certainly underlie her fictional account of

Swazi society, and as we will notice below, her "objective" data-driven account of the Swazi people was juxtaposed – but not interwoven – with her personal and emotional experiences in the field. But more significantly, we can also notice that her own subjectivity is crucially involved as reference and observation point for the construction of both sorts of tales: anthropological and fictional. Indeed, the fictional account is, following her own observations quoted above, an intensely personal one – located in her personal feelings and subjectivity. Thus while her anthropological studies mark the boundaries of difference with cultural practices and appearances that vary from the experiences of a clearly located Western observer and audience, her "emotional" study (the play) can also be read as a Western concern with the tragedy of the destruction of romantic love in the face of hurtful and irrational traditional practices, such as the divination of witches.

In her introduction to the play she notes that in Swazi marriage, "the emotions of the individual are relatively unimportant" – a clearly Western-centric observation.[36] Max Gluckman, who wrote in the foreword to this play, observes that "no anthropologist has baulked at the fact that to live in a situation where the agony of misfortune, illness or death, is aggravated by the fear that you may have suffered because of the evil machinations of someone close to you . . . is miserable and agonising. . . . Whatever the miseries of industrialisation, it has liberated us, and will liberate Africans, from adding to our misfortunes the fear that they are caused by the alleged occult powers of those we love."[37] While Hilda Kuper herself does not make this observation explicitly, she notes that the male protagonist, on learning that his most loved wife was the witch who caused his child by another wife to die, leaves his now gravelike household, banishing himself to the city, to which she argues "he is escaping, . . . [but] he is not emancipated."[38] Her assessment, then, that romantic love and involvement in industrialization (leaving for Johannesburg) could emancipate the Swazi from these destructive aspects of their society suggests a concurrence with Gluckman's Eurocentric account of witchcraft.

In her methodological reflections on her anthropological work in Swaziland, Kuper embarks upon a self-exploration of her "location" as a researcher and writer that seems extraordinarily ahead of its times. Here, the picture I have been drawing of the unself-consciously Eurocentric author is somewhat disrupted. She places herself in her association with the chief of the Swazi people (Sobhuza II) who, "is interested in anthropology; . . . has read a number of books on the subject, subscribes to anthropological journals, enjoys descriptions of the customs of other people, and is proud of his own."[39] While observing that her friendship with Sobhuza affected her ability to disclose certain privileged pieces of information gleaned while doing her research, she does not pursue the implications of this association in terms of her more routine research activities, or in terms of the broader effects that her textual construction of the Swazi culture based on information gleaned from informants with significant political purpose and power must have had. But her location while doing fieldwork was more extensively explored. She spent much of her time in the capital living in "the most Westernised house in the village – a square brick room with a wooden door about six feet high, glass windows, and a partition dividing the room into two sections. In it were a few leather chairs – the only chairs in the capital and used mainly for European guests."[40] Wherever she visited, in fact, she was accomodated in the chief's homestead, and she was acutely aware of the ways in which both this physical location and her social location (as white, outsider, woman) affected the "data" she collected. As she comments, "On entering any community a new arrival is automatically assigned a 'place.' "[41]

She writes of the effects of these "placings" upon her investigations:

> Despite the open friendship of Sobhuza, the dominant attitude towards me, especially the attitude of the semi-educated Swazi, was fear and suspicion; they were afraid that I was a spy – a European who had ingratiated her way into the confidence of the rulers in order to betray them later. I was *mabalana,* a scribe; in my right hand I held the most dangerous of all spears, the pen, and in my left an impenetrable shield, my notebook. . . . As a woman once said, pityingly, "we deceive you like anything because you are white." I established intimate contact with a limited circle of people, and these I used as my main informants. The rest of the community were actors in the situations that are the laboratory experiments of the anthropologist.[42]

Being married or unmarried, a woman or a man, speaking Swazi, learning common local activities (grinding grain, brewing beer, dancing, singing) – various fixed and contingent social "locations" – all affected the nature of the information that Kuper collected. She was also powerfully aware of the mutual learnings involved in these "located" interactions. She influenced "the lives of natives" in various ways – including a trip with school-chilren to the Empire Exhibition in Johannesburg where "they gazed with wonder on a new world,"[43] and she was clearly personally affected by her fieldwork experience (as the introduction to her play indicates). She nonethelesss observed that "complete identification with the Swazi was neither possible nor, from the point of view of obtaining a comprehensive picture of Swazi life, desirable or necessary."[44] While aware of the transformative effects of the social interactions entailed in the research process, her primary focus remained upon the construction of a manuscript, the "facts of which" she hoped would reflect as well as possible the reality of the Swazi people. She acknowledges that her own interpretation of the facts in terms of her position as a sociologist had an important influence upon the final document. She organized her account of the Swazi society around the key concept of "rank," for example. She also described something of the effect that the processes of synthesizing information and writing had upon her text. She concluded these methodological reflections with the comment,

> Anthropologists in most parts of the world are no longer describing the lives of illiterates, unable to speak for themselves or to judge the books to which they contribute the living substance.[45]

One could speculate that her association with Sobhuza and other "educated Swazi," while clearly shaping and politically locating (prejudicing?) her analysis, may well have encouraged her in a process of constructing the Swazi that was more reflexive and more negotiated than many of the accounts produced by her contemporaries. And yet while she explored and at times pressed against the constraints of the inescapable influence of her locatedness upon the textual interpretation she offered of the Swazi people, she retained a firm belief in the value and validity of the data she had collected. Thus although Kuper's reflections on her research practices – and her exploration in her fictional writings of aspects of society not generally acknowledged to be "facts" – seem to offer us some important signposts beyond a colonial appropriation and construction of subjects, they fail to affect the substance of her writings and research. These disruptive questionings need to be brought more directly into the purview of the text if we are to embark upon a methodology more sympathetic to the idiom of postcoloniality.

But if Kuper's location in Western society and in anthropological discourse was important in shaping her constructions of the Swazi people, mapping and placing the Indian community in Natal – her next substantial ethnographic project – was also not possible without significant interruptions of her own positionality. Hilda Kuper, of course, found this project methodologically problematic, as with her earlier Swazi study, but she did not seek to question its overall purpose and integrity. In the introduction to her book on the Indian population of Natal, she explains her reasons for embarking on the project:

> My field work was slanted towards the family, its structure and values, by my association with the Family Research Unit of the Institute of Family and

Community Health whose Director, Professor Sidney Kark, was carrying out a series of studies in growth and development in different racial groups in South Africa. He and his team of colleagues realised the necessity of anthropological knowledge in dealing with people of varied culture, and while material was already available on Africans and Europeans, there was little on the South African Indian apart from economic or historical studies and political reports. " 'The Indian' was 'a problem,' not a person."[46]

Anthropology, then, could be useful in providing information for state and quasi-state institutions, such as health authorities, to intervene more effectively in the management of different population groups. The exercise was the source of some methodological concern to Hilda Kuper. Language and communication were initial problems, but translation was only found to be necessary with a few older informants. The complexity of "the South African Indian" population in terms of religion and language necessitated a focus on only one group, the Hindu (thus Muslim and Christian Indians were excluded), who are also internally differentiated in terms of religion and language. As she herself comments in the concluding chapter to this book, "It is by reaction to an externally imposed identity that there are 'Indian South Africans.' "[46a] And yet her text contributes substantially to the constitution of just such an identity, through her mapping of cultural, religious, and linguistic boundaries, which make "Indian people" identifiable, observable, able to be interviewed, described, and even tabulated. It is the differences from other South Africans that are explored and documented. However, with the lenses of a social scientist concerned with processes of assimilation of minority groups, Kuper had first expected that because most Indian South African people had been born in South Africa, "their ancestral way of life would be of little importance."[47] But, while she found that "the social system of India, particularly caste and village organisation, had been replaced by the social system of their immediate South African milieu with its class structure and competitive individual economy, . . . many of the more personal values were extraneous and distinct from the values of the dominant white group."[48] These complexities are noted in the text (e.g., when she discusses the emergence of an elite grouping of Indian people grounded in an intersection of caste, economic position, and political activities), but the project of the book itself, and the structure of the text, is overwhelmingly concerned with documenting, and making, difference.

The view in such an endeavor is necessarily one from the outside, as is evident when she writes about the "vivid saris" that mark Durban as a place of Indian people, the "mosques and temples [which] break the line of colonial architecture with minarets and domes adorned with statues of the Hindu pantheon" (see Figure 9.2), "oriental" goods in the "Indian market," "as well as more familiar goods which themselves become unfamiliar in the excited atmosphere of oriental bargaining."[49] Durban, then, is mapped as a landscape of exotica, referenced against the "colonial" or "white" dominant images and society. Importantly, these cultural markers of difference are significantly gendered – the saris worn by women, the food cooked by women. And it is not only in these physical artifacts, but also in the production of different social meanings that "Indians" are inscribed as different, and specifically different from some Western or white experience as is shown in her comment that "an Englishman's home is his castle, an Indian's home is his shrine."[50]

Although implicated in the process of constituting the other in this self-referential way, Kuper was herself concerned about the consequences of such an activity within the tense South African political context of the 1950s. She writes, "Their position in the country is so insecure that some of them expressed anxiety at a book which discussed their way of life as being in any way different from that of white South Africans. Others

FIGURE 9.2. Indian-owned buildings in Durban, South Africa. (From H. Kuper, *Indian People in Natal.* Pietermaritzburg, South Africa: University of Natal Press, 1960, p. 44.)

were eager that the material be presented in such a way as to show the richness of *traditional* Indian culture as a contribution to the culture of all South Africans."[51] The tension, of course, concerned the consequences of difference in an apartheid system: the price was segregation, loss of property, access to facilities, social circles, prestige, and so forth. Alternatively, for many years Indian South Africans had been precariously resident in the country, and were eager to reinforce their claims to citizenship: hence the desire to present themselves as South African in the first instance, and to show that Indian culture had made a positive contribution to South African culture. Tensions of this sort, between the values of a separatist (ethnic) identity and a national (South African) identity, remain today, albeit for very different reasons. But it was texts such as that offered by Kuper which facilitated or at least fed into the construction of a wider definition of "the Indian population" in the face of a considerable diversity of social, economic, religious, and cultural groupings: something that even the grotesque creativity of apartheid racial legislation struggled to do.[52]

The role of such "objective" texts in constituting subjects is thrown into relief when we look at the incorporation of Kuper's sociological/anthropological enterprise in another text that also constituted the Indian people as an entity, mapping an other. The example I am struck by here is Fatima Meer's important work, *A Portrait of Indian South Africans,* which still invites considerable interest.[53] She offers us a fascinating view of Indian people from the position of an "insider" researcher or mapmaker. And yet it is in this work, more than in many others, that Indian people are constituted as other, distant, exotic, romantic, ancient, peaceful, rich, poor, . . . as seen from within, for those outside. Directly associated with Kuper (she worked as a research assistant on Kuper's *Indian People in Natal*), she combines this training with the privileged observations of the insider. As she notes in the preface, "My knowledge of Indian life is based mainly in personal experience," but she also draws widely on the writings of anthropologists such as Kuper and others in constructing her portrait of the Indian people. Inspired by a nonracial politics, she argues that "Indians are separated from Whites legislatively, and form part of the Non-White caste, but neither the distance in the one case, nor proximity in the other, is based on culture, but on available life chances."[54] She is clearly presenting a picture of Indian people for outside consumption, for those prevented from contact with this group by apartheid. Constructing difference through religion and rituals, she argues that "they are like any other people in their faith in the supernatural, in their regard for the institutions of marriage and family, in their desire for wealth and power, in their hopes and fears, and in their anxieties and aspirations."[55] In this light, then, do we observe the ways in which Fatima Meer, the "outsider within" sociology, constructs Indian people through a lens of exotica and "sameness." Once again, we find that the markers of difference are significantly gendered. It is a woman, for example, who graces the front cover of the book – in a pose available for quite opposing readings (see Figure 9.3). The woman's pose can be interpreted as religious and respectful, or as almost seductive, as in the traditional Western vision of the beautiful Indian woman, representing the exotic nature of Eastern culture and religion. In exploring Indian ethnicity in the South African context, this important cultural role of women – as bearers of the markers of difference – needs to be explored further.

FIGURE 9.3. Front cover Illustration from F. Meer, *Portrait of Indian South Africans* (Durban, South Africa: Avon House, 1969).

Just as the constitution of the subjects of Mabel Palmer and Hilda Kuper were bound up with "otherness" and "sameness" – attempts to interpret the other in terms and value judgments familiar to the author, scripting the other in their own lives and in the concepts available within their specific disciplinary and political grid – so Meer links into this process of constructing subjects for certain readers within a particular discursive terrain. And in an important sense, this method offers a caution to all of us who come to know of places and people – even our own – through others' texts.[56]

"MAKING TALK":
IS A POSTCOLONIAL METHOD POSSIBLE?

The significance of the positionality of the researcher in constituting the subject matter of her research has been amply demonstrated in this exploration of the writings of some South African women academics about Indian people. The subjectivities of both researcher and researched, then, are strongly implicated in the constructions and representations produced in texts such as those reviewed here, and indeed in any texts resulting from academic research. Importantly, it is not only the obvious social location of the researcher – in terms of race, class, and gender – that shapes textual productions, but also the details of disciplinary location, physical location during research, political persuasion, personality, and so forth. And an important observation is that the research process involves a process of transformation of subjectivities, as they are written into texts and as they negotiate meanings during the course of investigations. None of these processes were consciously engaged in by the women researchers I have discussed in this chapter. Kuper's reflections and methodological questionings were in many ways partitioned off from her formal representations of others, and yet the interruptions of these representations by her own subjectivity could not be contained. Rather than searching for the authentic representation or representer (whether this is thought to be the "insider" researcher or the unmediated voice of the informant) – a quixotic and futile search – I wish to explore further these spaces of mediation (of subject positions and meaning), whose insistent questionings Hilda Kuper bravely acknowledged, and then excised from her representations.

While feminists have explored issues of the relationship between researcher and researched within ethnographic research to a considerable extent (and I will return to this topic shortly), it is within the postcolonial idiom that I find some of the most useful pathways through – though not solutions to – this relationship which seems to present a persistent and dis-abling stumbling block to contemporary researchers. Crucially, the ques-tion we need to address now is whether it is possible for the researcher and the "other" to find "postcolonial" ways of producing understandings and knowledge that are not simply reproducing the colonial/apartheid map-pings and placings of earlier researchers and that are not denying the presence of the researcher in the construction of such representations. And I think that the analysis I have offered here of the texts of white women researching Indian subjects points to a way forward. For in the midst of their efforts to fix static "other" subjects from an exterior, unimplicated position, I have pointed out the ineradicable presence of these researchers' subjectivities in the texts they produce, and the absolutely necessary process of engagement and mutual transformations of subjectivities that comes along with the process of naming and mapping others. Here I wish to explore the possibilities, within the context of research methodology, for responding to Bhabha's call for "a more dialogic process that attempts to track the processes of displacement and realignment that are already at work, constructing something different and hybrid from the encounter: a third space that does not simply revise or invert the dualities, but revalues the ideological bases of division and difference."[57]

The emblematic "postcolonial" position is that of the hybrid, or syn-cretic subject.[58] The closed positions of "the same" and "the other" are not easily available in a world "after" colonialism, except insofar as they may be retained by mechanisms and strategies of social closure. Apart-heid, for example, serves as a constant signifier of the binary dualisms that support(ed) all sorts of opposing dichotomous subject positions.[59] To defend unmediated positions in a world after colonialism, then, we would have to deny our global past and erect complex barriers around our sub-jectivities in order to defend our endocentricity. Colonized and excolonized people have been inextricably entwined in the subjectivities of the coloniz-ers, have inhabited the "in-between spaces" that cross-cultural contact – even of the most violent and segregating kind, such as apartheid – creates.

Not wanting to be utopian, or to neglect the power relations involved in interactions across subject positions – or to deny the power of inhabit-ing the margins[60] – I feel that the idiom of the postcolonial subject inspires what I term, following Spivak, a "speaking with" model of engagement between researcher and researched.[61] Possibly, this offers us a way of moving forward in the context of seeking modes of research and represen-tation that disrupt – but do not suspend – the effects of positionality, the "outside" perspectives, which inevitably accompany processes of enquiry and reflection about the lives of others. "Speaking with" people from other places and cultures involves an openness to their influence, to their "talk-ing back."[62] It involves consciously inhabiting and exploring the spaces of negotiated and partial meanings, which are all that our inquisitive in-vestigations into others' lives can ever produce. But, as Peckham notes in the context of white liberals and apartheid, "What dialogue is possible, what relationship to their (black South Africans) realities and the condi-tions of their lives, if we do not disenfranchise ourselves from our privileged identity, and experience the rootlessness that identity represents for them."[63] All colonial peoples have experienced the dis-placement associat-ed with colonization: South Africa's population perhaps more so than most. To dis-place (not erase or deny) our own subjectivities is essential if we are to "unlearn our privilege."[64] And it is not to a position outside of the center, an "ex-centric" or "ec-centric" positionality, that we can "retreat"[65] – for these positions are still centric in their (dis)orientation – but to the messy "spaces in between," to the multidimensionality of sub-jectivities and the partialities and tensions of the situated and yet cons-tantly changing subjects who, in Haraway's hopeful and imaginative words, "just live here and strike up non-innocent conversations."[66] Of course, we remain trapped within the binds of both "complicity and critique," as Hutch-eon reminds us,[67] but perhaps here we at least have a model for carry-ing on.

For me as a white woman researcher in Natal, the question of whether it was possible to "carry on" with research in my very complex society was not easy to answer in the context of the debates that flared up amongst feminists in 1991. The debates reviewed in the second section of this chapter seemed to suggest that in fact it was not appropriate for outsiders to do such research: privileged insider researchers were to explore these ques-tions, and I should concentrate on understanding my own subjectivity, location, and community. Aware that the "privileged insider" position was also fraught with difficulties (as the very brief consideration of Fati-ma Meer's text suggests), and afraid of being confined to such an intellec-tually and politically impoverished future, I decided to attempt to embark on such a piece of "outsider" research and to explore the issues being de-bated for myself.[68]

My methodological concerns were to find ways in which my own voice – necessarily engaged in writing and mapping subjects with whom I engage in research – could be mediated in the process. Inspired by notions such as "speaking with" rather than *for* or *to* people one is enagaged in research with, and by notions of syncretic, postcolonial subjects, always transformed by their location in a postcolonial or colonial situation, I was determined to try and find a way in which the horizons of meaning of

myself and "subjects" could intersect, negotiate interpretations, explore contradictions, and learn mutually. I recalled feminist concerns with researchers
as "friends,"[69] and was interested in the explorations of communities of
meaning and local discourses, such as that explored by Isobel Dyck in
her research in Vancouver on the ways in which women in a neighborhood negotiated and transformed their understandings of motherhood.[70]

As with all efforts to escape the predicaments of the research situation, this effort too is doomed to failure. Constructing friendships, or even
pursuing already existing friendships, within the context of a research exercise has more than a semblance of instrumentality, and necessarily coexists
with the power relations inherent in the context (both in terms of
race/class/gender positions and in terms of who initiates the research). Judith
Stacey's experiences researching Silicon Valley families are instructive here:
she warns us that a utopian solution to these problems of power and position in the research context does not exist.[71] There will always remain,
she suggests, a measure of discomfort that necessarily goes along with
the coincidence of a sensitivity to the needs and rights of others and a
desire to write about and explore other worlds. Ethnographic honesty about
such feelings is one response – as it was for Stacey. She writes, for example, of her concerns about the morality of her continued fieldwork within a working-class family experiencing a series of devastating losses, and
whose own emotional responses to this "calamity culture" led her to seek
to arbitrarily define an end to the research exercise. But while Stacey reflected at length on her fieldwork experiences, and offered the women whose
lives she was researching the opportunity to respond to her manuscript,
these mediations of understandings were secondary to her primary project,
which was to document family change in postindustrial Silicon Valley.
My proposal is to make the mediations of meaning and the interactions
of interpretations among those engaged in the research process the object
of investigation, acknowledging that the experiences of women in different cultures are always going to be accessible only in such a form – refracted
through our multiple and necessarily intersecting and mutually transforming
experiences.[72]

As a research methodology this would avoid the suggestion that the
"informant" has an authentic view of her community or her own life,
yet it would include the voice of the "researched" centrally in the discourse
constructed. It would certainly serve to displace (but not to eradicate) the
authoritative voice of the researcher; and it would capture the transformative possibilities of the postcolonial idiom, in exploring the spaces in
between the static subject positions and cultures that are constituted in
colonial vein and fixed in conventional ethnographic reporting practices,

as well as in more experimental polyvocal texts. Crucial here is the displacement of both the questioning researcher and the questioned research subject: the exploration of the intersections among subjects involves the interrogation of all subjects involved in research and the displacement of the privileged fixed position of the "same" from which the author/researcher speaks/writes and interrogates. Insofar as informants would need to be articulate, and would inhabit a different discursive universe, and perhaps not see "questioning" as an appropriate or possible mode of engaging with other subjects, the power relationship with the initiating researcher dominant in the interactions will remain.[73] But the focus of our explorations will have been dis-located, moved from the mapping of subjects to the explorations of the spaces in which mapping and interpretation occur: processes which are always mediated, always intersubjective, and always complicit with the complex power relations of modernity. At this point, then, the production of the text will have been disrupted by the questions that conventional researchers like Hilda Kuper so skillfully excluded from their mappings of others.

ACKNOWLEDGMENTS

I would like to thank the Gender Reading Group at the University of Natal, and especially Debbie Bonnin, Cathy Campbell, Roger Deacon, and Rob Morrell for lots of discussions, ideas, and support during the period I have been thinking about these issues; and I would also like to thank Raphael de Kadt for similar inspiration and editorial assistance. Gillian Rose, Jonathan Crush, and Linda McDowell were also helpful. Funding for some of this research was provided by the University of Natal Research Fund and by the Human Sciences Research Council, neither of which bodies bears any responsibility for the content of this chapter. A version of this chapter was presented at the Society for Geography Conference in Port Elizabeth, South Africa, in July 1993; I must thank participants in the session for a lively and useful discussion.

NOTES

1. A. Ashforth, *The Politics of Official Discourse in Twentieth Century South Africa* (Oxford: Clarendon Press, 1990). J. Comaroff and J. Comaroff, *Of Revelation and Revolution,* vol. 1 (Chicago: University of Chicago Press, 1991); M. L. Pratt, *Imperial Eyes: Travel Writing and Transculturation* (London: Routledge, 1992); J. Crush, "Gazing on Apartheid: Postcolonial Travel Narratives of the Golden City," in *Writing the City,* P. Simpson-Housley and P. Preston eds. (London: Routledge, forthcoming); C. Mather, "Oral Testimony as Text: Knowledge, Power and Space in Rural

South Africa (paper presented at the Society for Geography Conference, University of Port Elizabeth, Port Elizabeth, South Africa, July 1993).

2. H. Adam and K. Moodley, *The Negotiated Revolution: Society and Politics in Post-Apartheid South Africa* (Johannesburg: Jonathan Ball, 1993).

3. For reviews of this work, see B. Bozzoli, "Marxism, Feminism and South African Studies," *Journal of South African Studies 9,* (1983): 139–171, and C. Walker, ed., *Women and Gender in South Africa to 1945* (Cape Town: David Philip, 1990).

4. My reasons for arguing this have a most immediate history. My initial proposal for this chapter was to look empirically at ways in which some Indian women in the town I live in understand and "map" their social and spatial world, and to contrast these with dominant mappings of Indianness and femininity within Indian communities. The publishers and editors were not unreasonably concerned that I was simply reenacting an "othering" process, the criticism of which was at the heart of this collection. Curiously, though, my very preliminary efforts to pursue the substantive topic I have briefly outlined here were specifically designed to enable me to confront and experiment with the possibilities of "new" ways of interpreting and researching in a socially and culturally complex setting. Pleased to link into the broader concerns of the text, I have brought these more methodological questions to the fore.

5. K. Letlaka-Rennert, in "Impressions: Conference on Women and Gender in Southern Africa," *Agenda 9* (1991): 22; F. Lund, "Impressions: Conference on Women and Gender in Southern Africa," *Agenda 9* (1991): 20.

6. D. Lewis, "The Politics of Feminism in South Africa," *Staffrider 10,* no. 3 (1992): 15–21, quote from p. 16.

7. I wish to thank Debbie Bonnin for information and ideas regarding the issue of the logo.

8. Lewis, "Politics of Feminism in South Africa."

9. But see the discussion of her conference paper below – D. Lewis, "Theorizing about Gender in South Africa" (paper presented at the African Association of Political Science/Southern African Political Economy Series Conference on South Africa: Which Way Forward?, Cape Town, August 18–22, 1992).

10. Lewis, "Politics of Feminism in South Africa."

11. Bozzoli, "Marxism, Feminism, and South African Studies"; Beall, "Class, Race, and Gender: The Political Economy of Women in Colonial Natal" (MA thesis, Department of Economic History, University of Natal, Durban, South Africa, 1982).

12. Lewis, "Theorizing about Gender in South Africa."

13. Ibid., 3.

14. Ibid. Some of the more established feminists whose work was criticized by Lewis have pointed out some textual and interpretative inaccuracies in her work – although no formal written response has yet been made. In my opinion, the broad thrust of her argument will stand further investigation – and this is an important task for local feminist researchers to take up.

15. D. Haraway, "A Manifesto for Cyborgs: Science, technology, and Socialist Feminism in the 1980s," in *Feminism/Postmodernism,* L. Nicholson, ed. (London: Routledge, 1989), 190–233.

16. S. Hassim and C. Walker, "Women's Studies and the Women's Movement," *Transformation 18–19* (1992): 78–85; P. Horn, "Post-Apartheid South Africa: What about Women's Liberation?", *Transformation 15* (1991): 26–40.

17. Although this would assist in the important institutional political project of improving the position of usually junior black women academics within the academy.

18. Lewis, "Politics of Feminism in South Africa," 21.

19. Ibid., 19.

20. I too have felt angry at Western men, for example, talking about "other places" and "third world countries" and "women" as the "other", in a pious and ill-considered way.

21. And here I feel there may be a larger genealogy of the subjects questioning of the researcher to explore. When did the first subject enquire of a researcher, "What's in this for me? – an archetypically modernist question for premodern people to be asking. Of course, so many subjects of research have questioned and criticized the process of representation that there is clearly a crucial issue at stake here; for a recent example, see J. Stacey, *Brave New Families* (New York: Basic Books, 1990). I simply feel that it requires further exploration.

22. P. H. Collins, "Learning from the Outsider Within: The Sociological Significance of Black Feminist Thought" in *Beyond Methodology*, M. M. Fonow and J. A. Cook, eds. (Bloomington: Indiana University Press, 1991), 35–59.

23. M. Palmer, *The History of Indians in Natal* (Cape Town: Oxford University Press, 1957), 186.

24. I. Goldin, "Coloured Identity and Coloured Politics in the Western Cape Region of Southern Africa," *The Creation of Tribalism in Southern Africa*, L. Vail, ed. (London: James Currey, 1989), 241–254.

25. Atkinson, for example, makes some extremely important points in regard to the negotiation of meaning and legitimacy around governance in the context of township administration and Comaroff and Comaroff have a substantial contribution to make on this general issue. See D. Atkinson, *Cities and Citizenship* (Ph.D. thesis, Department of Politics, University of Natal, Durban, 1991); Comaroff and Comaroff, *Of Revelation and Revolution.*

26. I need to stress an important caveat that the analysis presented here is in many ways a very preliminary exploration in a field in which an enormous amount of work remains to be done. My analysis of the work of Hilda Kuper, for example, is based on her most well-known published work, and is interpreted textually (rather than contextually). Her contribution to anthropology locally and internationally has been somewhat overlooked, and the project of exploring the nature and meaning of her work is long overdue. Jonathan Crush, of Queen's University, Kingston, Ontario, is presently embarking on such a more substantial exploration of her work.

27. D. Chetty, "Identity and 'Indianness': Reading and Writing Ethnic Discourses" (paper presented to the Conference on Ethnicity, Society and Conflict in Natal, University of Natal, Pietermariyzburg, South Africa, September 1992).

28. Of course, the intertextual nature of such discourses makes the isolation of such an academic input into the "othering" or mapping process impossible,

but I will begin exploring this discursive net here: others will, I'm sure, build up a much more comprehensive picture than I can in this short space and within the context of this very specific project.

29. S. Marks, *Not Either an Experimental Doll: The Separate Worlds of Three South African Women* (Durban and Pietermartitzburg, South Africa: Killie Campbell Africana Library and University of Natal Press, 1987); S. Vietzen. "Fabian Transplant: The Adams College Vacation Schools and the University, 1936–1952 (paper presented to the Natal University Jubilee History Conference, July, 1985).

30. Marks, *Not Either an Experimental Doll.*

31. U. Mesthrie, "From Rose Day Shows to Social Welfare: White and Indian Women in Joint Co-operation in the 1930s." (Paper presented at the Conference on Women and Gender in Southern Africa, University of Natal, Durban, January 1991); see also P. B. Rich, *White Power and the Liberal Conscience: Racial Segregation and South African Liberalism* (Johannesburg: Ravan Press, 1984).

32. M. Palmer, *History of the Indians in Natal,* 169.

33. Ibid., 175.

34. Ibid., 181.

35. H. Kuper, *A Witch in My Heart: A Play Set in Swaziland in the 1930s* (London: Oxford University Press, 1970), x.

36. Ibid., xiv.

37. Gluckmann in Kuper, *A Witch in My Heart,* viii.

38. Kuper, *A Witch in My Heart,* xxix.

39. H. Kuper, *An African Aristocracy: Rank among the Swazi* (1947; reprint, London: Oxford University Press, 1961), 1.

40. Ibid.

41. Ibid., 4.

42. Ibid., 2.

43. Ibid., 3.

44. Ibid.

45. Ibid., 5.

46. H. Kuper, *Indian People in Natal* (Pietermaritzburg, South Africa: University of Natal Press, 1960), xvi.

46a. Ibid., 270.

47. Ibid., xix.

48. Ibid.

49. Ibid., xiii.

50. Ibid., xv.

51. Ibid., xx.

52. Ibid., 264.

53. F. Meer, *Portrait of Indian South Africans* (Durban, South Africa: Avon House, 1969).

54. Ibid., ii.

55. Ibid.

56. J. Marcus, *A World of Difference: Islam and Gender Hierarchy in Turkey* (London: Zed Press, 1992).

57. H. Bhabha, "Postcolonial Authority and Postmodern Guilt," in *Cultural Studies*, L. Grossberg et al., eds. (London: Routledge, 1992), 56–68, quote from p. 58.

58. B. Ashcroft, G. Griffiths, and H. Tiffin, *The Empire Writes Back: Theory and Practice in Post-Colonial Literatures* (London: Routledge, 1989).

59. T. Minh-ha, *Woman, Native, Other* (Bloomington: Indiana University Press, 1989).

60. B. Hooks, *Talking Back: Thinking Feminist—Thinking Black* (London: Sheba Feminist Publishers, 1989).

61. G. C. Spivak, *In Other Worlds: Essays in Cultural Politics* (London: Routledge, 1988).

62. Hooks, *Talking Back*.

63. L. Peckham, "Ons Stel Bie Belang Nie/We Are Not Interested In: Speaking Apartheid," in *Out There: Marginalisation and Contemporary Cultures*, R. Ferguson et al., eds. (Cambridge, MA: MIT Press, 1990), 367–376, quote from p. 370.

64. Spivak, *In Other Worlds*, 30.

65. Compare T. Lauretis, "Eccentric Subjects: Feminist Theory and Historical Consciousness," *Feminist Studies 16*, no. 1 (1990): 115–150; see also L. Hutcheon, *A Poetics of Postmodernism: History, Theory, Fiction* (London: Routledge, 1988).

66. D. Haraway, "Situated Knowledges: The Science Question in Feminism and the Privilege of Partial Perspective," *Feminist Studies 14* (1988): 575–599, quote from p. 594.

67. Hutcheon, *A Poetics of Postmodernism*.

68. For a variety of practical reasons (students needing employment, language and proximity, available literature, postcolonial interest in "orientalism"), I felt that it would be possible and appropriate to embark on such a study among the Indian community in Durban. Inspired by Jo Beall's account of African, Indian, and European women in colonial Natal, I decided that an important, neglected area of research was the experiences of wealthier Indian women who had not attracted the attention of radical and Marxist scholars interested in the working class and their struggles and who, in feminist terms, have been seen as accepting and reproducing archetypically oppressive patriarchal institutions; see Beall, "Race, Class, and Gender," and Mesthrie, "From Rose Day shows to Social Welfare." Isolated theoretically and physically, by virtue of the persistence of traditions of exclusion and sometimes purdah, these women have indeed been silenced, their voices unheard in the corridors of radical and feminist academic enquiry.

But if I open up my own, often subconscious, thinking about why I felt that this would be a "useful" case study (in itself highlighting the inevitable embeddedness of research in the will and intentions of the researcher) some less noble impulses emerge. For example: I was walking down the street in the Indian part of the central town one day when I passed a woman I knew. She was very pregnant, dressed in traditional clothes, and accompanied by an elderly, very traditional-looking Indian woman. I was struck by the different image she presented from the one I remembered her by, which had been that of a young, energetic, modern, enquiring woman, usually dressed in jeans. I knew that she had recently embarked on an "arranged" marriage. Because I was engrossed at the time in a literature concerned with the "other" and notions of postcolonialism, the image of my friend in Victoria Street (itself not unsymbolic) remained in my head for a long time. On another occasion I was showing a visitor around the same Indian part of town and became involved in exoticizing a familiar and relatively ordinary part of my hometown: looking for indications of Indianness, pointing out the mosques, different goods in the street, the old colonial buildings with Indian names engraved on them, and trying to link this place to the little I knew of Indian history. I was placing and clearly mapping this emerging "other" in what was usually an unexamined part of my everyday surroundings – even as Hilda Kuper had, in her imagining of the Indian community in the 1950s.

69. Reinharz, *Feminist Methods in Social Research* (Oxford: Oxford University Press, 1992).

70. I. Dyck, "Space, Time, and Renegotiating Motherhood: An Exploration of the Domestic Workplace," *Environment and Planning D: Society and Space 8* (1990): 459–483. I also have enjoyed so much the very localized negotiated meaning systems that I have built up with friends over time, in different places. Through long hours of talk and tears, women friends especially have constructed with me (and never for me) ways of understanding life, people, relationships, and often theories about the world. I felt that perhaps this type of negotiation of meaning could help capture the contrasts and similarities between women in different situations, avoiding the imposition of interpretations by myself.

71. Stacey, *Brave New Families.*

72. And indeed Stacey's narrative account is constructed in such a way that her subjects lead her, on several occasions, to review her own assessments of their situations.

73. Indeed, I am chastened here by Spivak's reminder via Derrida of "the impossibility of remaining in the in-between"; see *In Other Worlds,* 147.

10

Remapping the Body/Land: New Cartographies of Identity, Gender, and Landscape in Ireland

CATHERINE NASH

In discussing Mahasweta Devi's story "Douloti the Bountiful," Gayatri Chakravorty Spivak describes the story's ending. Douloti, the daughter of an Indian, tribal, bonded worker, is sold into prostitution in order to repay her father's debt. Devastated by venereal disease, she dies while walking to the hospital, having lain down on the comfort of the bare earth, where the local schoolmaster had drawn the map of India in order to teach his students nationalism in preparation for Independence Day. The next morning the schoolmaster and his students find the dead body of Douloti on the map.[1] This tension between the assertion of national identity in the postcolonial nation and the presence of the female subaltern can be paraphrased as a problematic relationship between the map and the body. The map in Devi's story stands as an emblem of the national territory, both constituting and symbolizing the "imagined community" of the nation.[2] This chapter will address this tension and discuss other sorts of postcolonial and feminist mapping strategies.

I am concerned with addressing the issue of feminist and postcolonial relationships to place. Through a discussion of images of the female body and maps in the work of the Irish artist Kathy Prendergast, I will explore the links between the gendered body and the national landscape. I will look at her work in relation to ideas of gender and national identity in traditional Irish landscape imagery and also in relation to other contemporary articulations of identity, especially those that deal with issues of placenames, language, and landscape. In considering contemporary Irish culture, I am concerned not only to address the subject of identity in relation to both feminism and postcolonialism, but to raise the issue of "place" and its intersection with identity. The idea of place operates at the abstract level of the nation. It also concerns the visual relationship to place associated with the concept of "landscape," and the sensual, lived experience of the local environment.[3] In contemporary critical writing, spatial metaphors – the terms "position," "place," "site," "space," "ground," "field," "territory," "terrain," "margin," "periphery," and "map" – recur.[4] The metaphor of mapping functions at a number of levels. It stands most commonly for a positioning on a theoretical and ideological plane, but it also describes a location within lived geographical space. In the relationship between the Western and Third Worlds, theoretical and spatial positions are not unconnected. Mapping can be taken to conceptualize diverse ways of representing space, in textual, visual, and multidimensional artistic media, and in conventional cartographic media. In my discussion of the relationship between identity and gender, the body and the map, through the work of the Irish artist Kathy Prendergast, I retain the reference to geographic space in my use of the mapping metaphor. This is not to distinguish between the "real" and "imagined" space of the nation, but to make clear that the concept of space mobilized here refers to more than purely theoretical positioning. A theoretical stance does, however, underlie its formulation.

The term "remapping" is used in the title of this chapter for two reasons. First, it is used to draw attention to ideas of landscape, and the ways in which they are tied to issues of gender in the negotiation of ideas concerning Irish identity. Second, it highlights the way in which forms of cultural expression that deal with national identity in this postcolonial context do so in relation to the earlier colonial construction of Irishness. The contemporary use of ideas of place in mapping Irish identity relates to its earlier construction in the colonial period. It is in this sense a remapping, dealing with notions of place and in reaction to a previous construction of Irish identity. Three processes, the colonial mapping of Ireland in the 19th century, the concurrent Anglicization of Irish placenames, and the decline of the Irish language, provide the historical background for the expression of themes of cultural loss and recovery in contemporary Irish culture. Both the act of naming and the act of mapping assert the power of representation. Attempts to rename and remap claim this power to recover an authentic identity and relationship to place. The contemporary use of the map and placenames prompts a consideration of the commonly accepted links between gender, language, landscape, and identity. Yet the shift from colony to independent nation did not entail the redundancy of the discourses of male power; rather these were transposed and translated into new forms within Irish nationalist discourse.[5]

Through a discussion of issues arising in the work of Kathy Prendergast, this chapter raises the possibility of a feminist and postcolonial identification with place; a feminist use of ideas of place and landscape that avoids the biologism and essentialism of the idea of a natural, organic, and intuitive closeness to nature; and a postcolonial relationship to landscape that distances itself from colonial notions of a native, childlike, and racial closeness to nature.[6] All this calls for a revised notion of both identity and space. This chapter discusses feminist and postcolonial approaches that appropriate the concept of landscape, despite its masculinist and colonial usage. The map is a potent metaphor for both.

GEOGRAPHY AND GENDER: LANDSCAPE AND THE BODY

Issues of gender and national identity intersect in multiple ways: in the gendering of the concept of the nation; in the idea of the national landscape as feminine; in the concern with issues of race, place, and the national population; and in the delimiting of gender roles in the idealization and representation of rural life. The symbolic representation of Ireland as female derives from the sovereignty goddess figure of early Irish tradition, the personification of this goddess in the figures of Irish medieval literature, and the allegorization of Ireland as woman in the 18th-century classical poetic genre, the *aisling*, following colonial censorship of the expression of direct political dissent.[7] It also relates to the colonial feminization of Ireland and the Irish that was adopted, adapted, and contested within nationalist discourse.[8] The continued use of the notion of Ireland as female, against which male poets assert both personal and national identity, endorses and strengthens the signifying use of women in Ireland, their erosion from Irish history, and their contemporary silencing.[9] The relationship between the female body and the idea of the nation in contemporary Ireland is central to the constitution and to the intersection of the Catholic church and the state in their control of women's reproduction. Traditional landscape representations in Ireland are imbued with conceptions of both national and gender identity, most significantly in the imagery of the West of Ireland.

These issues of geography and gender arise in the work of Kathy Prendergast, one of a younger generation of Irish artists who have adopted a critical, ironic, and sometimes humorous approach to traditional Irish landscape art. In her use of the map motif, she raises connections between landscape and the female body, between political control of landscape and territory and the control of female sexuality. Prendergast rejects the interpretation of her images as feminist statements and describes her work as a representation of a "personal geography."[10] The work can, however, be read as an instance where the tension between this "personal geography" of the body and the space of the nation is made manifest.

In 1983 Kathy Prendergast produced a series of drawings, entitled the *Body Map Series*.[11] These drawings, with the coloring and style of Victorian maps and diagrams, chart the processes of exploration, description, alteration, and control of a landscape. However, in these drawings the land explored, described, altered, and controlled is a female body, depicted from neck to upper thighs. In *Enclosed Worlds in Open Spaces* (see Figure 10.1),

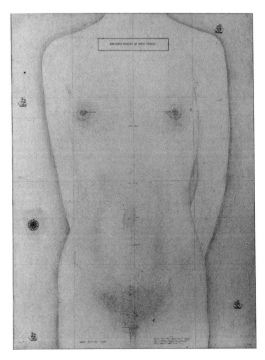

FIGURE 10.1. Kathy Prendergast, *Enclosed Worlds in Open Spaces* (1983). (Courtesy of Vincent Ferguson.)

the drawing of this truncated female body evokes cartographic conventions of grid lines, compass points and ships on the sea surrounding the body/land. The inked annotations of the diagrams and maps name this body as land in apparent innocence. The breasts are labeled as volcanic mountains, the abdomen as desert, the navel as crater. The map of this body in *Enclosed Worlds in Open Spaces* is flanked by cross sections of the volcanic mountains/breasts, the desert/abdomen, and a tableland above the pubic area marked as a mountain range. This body/land is then mapped at a larger scale in four parts, named as the North-West, North-East, South-West, and South-East Regions. Having investigated, mapped, and made

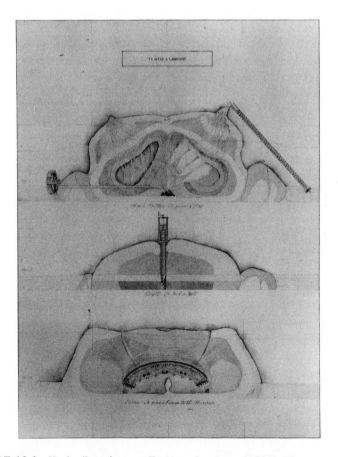

FIGURE 10.2. Kathy Prendergast, *To Alter a Landscape* (1983). (Courtesy of Vincent Ferguson.)

known this geography, Prendergast provides diagrams suggesting the means to alter this landscape: how the fires in the volcanic mountains/breasts may be quenched, how water may be found in the desert/navel, how to mine a passage to the harbor/vulva through the cavern/womb (see Figure 10.2, *To Alter a Landscape*).[12] The styles of geomorphological, surveying, or civil engineering diagrams and plans are used. These convention are conflated with the styles of anatomical and gynacological diagrams. In the drawings operations of control, manipulation, and alteration are in process on and within the passive land/body. In their dissection of the female body they evoke anatomical drawings of female organs that functioned in the medico-moral politics of the late 19th century.

The final drawings of the series indicate the eventual control that may be achieved (see Figure 10.3, *To Control a Landscape—Irrigation,* and Figure 10.4, *To Control a Landscape—Oasis*). The text of each describes the outcome. Its tone of detachment, rationality, scientism, logic, and self-confidence matches the detail and precision of the diagrams. It is the familiar tone of traditional geographic description and medical discourse, simultaneously expressing omnipotence and the erasure of the author:

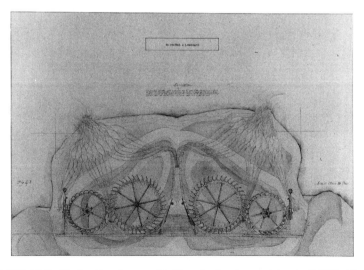

FIGURE 10.3. Kathy Prendergast, *To Control a Landscape—Irrigation* (1983). (Courtesy of Vincent Ferguson.)

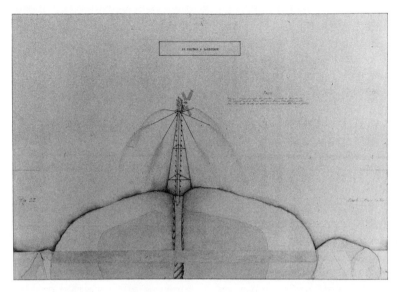

FIGURE 10.4. Kathy Prendergast, *To Control a Landscape—Oasis* (1983). (Courtesy of Vincent Furguson.)

> The fires being quenched, water is pumped into the core of the mountains and stored in tanks. The connecting tubes are attached to the tanks and as the mills turn water is pumped to the surface through volcanic ducts. Thus instead of emitting fire and smoke, the mountains will now exude water and irrigate the soil.[13]

The claims of discourse both to know and to control are based on these codes of representation. Kathy Prendergast's ironic adoption of these conventions exposes the process through which authority is established by their use. Her use of heavy parchment, embossed with the insignia of publication, the cartographic conventions she echoes, and the tone of the annotations, make ironic allusions to authenticity and truth. Only our awareness that the "landscape" is the body of a woman disrupts the drawings' neutrality. These subtle images problematize both the discourse of geography and the representation of women and their reciprocal use. Both share this process of making the unknown known, through exploration, investigation, and inscription. Though Kathy Prendergast presents a naked female body, her drawings unsettle the customary erotic potential of images of the female body by using the codes of cartography. She exposes the fear of and desire to know and control female difference in male representations of women. Her images draw us in as explorers, navigators, engineers, in search of fullness, wholeness, and simplicity of meaning, only to disrupt the process of reasoning and understanding by their ambiguity. This search, and its frustration by ambiguity, provokes a recognition of complicity in forms of knowledge acquisition and the power relations of claims to know, to speak for, to represent. The ambiguity of the series, the answers it does not supply, also has a subversive effect. What has been previously named and known does not attempt a renaming but rests in its ambiguity, in what Chris Prentice describes as "the un-naming power of ambiguity."[14]

In the *Body Map Series* the collaboration of geography in colonial projects becomes evident. Both the representation and control of female biology and the role of geography in the exploration, alteration, and control of territory is highlighted in the quiet violence of these images. The familiarity of the connection between colonial control of other lands and the control of female sexuality and the use of gender in the discourse of discovery is displaced by the powerful subtlety of these images.[15]

Kathy Prendergast draws on traditions of representation of women in order to deconstruct their supposed neutrality. It is her ironic position as a female artist in relation to these traditions that gives Prendergast's reinscriptions their counterstrategic power. The artist's use of the idea of land and landscape and its relationship to control of the feminine is understandable in the historical context of colonial efforts to control what was considered "an essentially feminine race" and postindependence attempts to employ notions of femininity, rural life, and landscape in the construction of Irishness and the subordination of Irish women.[16] Both the colonial mapping of subject lands and the representation of women within patriarchy are forms of representation that seek to reinforce the stability of the controlling viewpoint and to negate or suppress alternative views. The map can be read as a manifestation of a desire for control that operates effectively in the implementation of colonial policy. The strategies used in the production of the map – the reinscription, enclosure, and heirarchization of space – provide an analogue for the acquisition, management, and reinforcement of colonial power. In the cataloguing process the world is normalized, disciplined, appropriated, and controlled.[17] The mapping of the Irish landscape did not function merely to ease colonial administration, but fixed the "other" and neutralized the threat of difference by the apparent stability of the map's coherence.[18] In the same way, representation of women fixes their bodies as landscapes of control and signifying use. The map, which relies on a controlling viewpoint (whose stability cannot be guaranteed), is revealed as covering over alternative spatial configurations, which "indicate both the plurality of possible perspectives on, and the inadequacy of any single model of the world."[19]

Kathy Prendergast's drawings must be seen in relation to this colonial mapping project. They also reflect upon traditional Irish landscape art from the early 20th century and the complex gendering of landcape and the gender codes implicit in its depiction.

NATION, GENDER, AND THE IRISH LANDSCAPE

Representation of landscape in early 20th-century Ireland was loaded with meaning in terms of both national and gender identity. The image of the West of Ireland stood at the center of a web of discourses concerning racial and cultural identity, femininity, sexuality, and landscape that were being used in attempts to secure cultural identity and political freedom. The discourses that primitivized both women and the colony fused in the representation of the female colonial subject. Yet, as a result of nationalist antiurbanism and anti-industrialism, this primitivizing continued in nationalist accounts of the West.[20] While convergences can be noted between the colonial appropriation of the landscape of the colony and the production of the subject woman, the codes of representation of both the peasant woman and the West as landscape of desire were reemployed in nationalist writing. The idea of the primitive was appropriated but positively evaluated against the urban, industrial, colonial power. This primitivization of the West and of women, which has as a strong element the supposed unsuppressed instinctiveness, sexuality, and un-self-conscious sensuality of the primitive, had to be reconciled with the use of woman by cultural nationalists as signifier of moral purity and sexual innocence.

Images of the peasant women of the West in travel writing, photography, literature, and painting were one set of several versions of femininity being contested in the first two decades of the 20th century, as part of a set of discourses that participated in the negotiation and inscription of ideas of femininity, and through femininity, the future ideal form of Irish society. The Irish suffrage movement was at this time posing questions about the role of women in political life and within the independent state, as were the women's military nationalist organizations.[21] This threat to the male monopoly of political power by politically active women intensified the drive to fix the role, position, and very nature of womanhood. These issues overlapped with concerns about cultural purity and preservation, centered on the image of the West of Ireland as an Irish cultural region whose physical landscape provided the greatest contrast to the landscape of Englishness. Onto the body of the peasant woman were focused concerns over racial, sexual, and cultural purity and the social and moral organization of future independent Ireland.

Ideas of antiurbanism, nationalism, and concern about the body, health, and physique were projected onto the woman's body, and against England as urban, industrial, and debased. The emphasis on dress in the description of the people of the West corresponds to the importance of dress as a marker of national identity, constructed from elements of race, class, and geography.[22] Its importance was testified to in the concern over national costume associated with the Gaelic Revival movement, which amounted to a "national dress debate" in the 1910s. In that debate, the emphasis on the red skirts of peasant women was tied to the symbolism of that color as an indication of vitality, to the belief in the national love of color evident in ancient costume, and to the rejection of modern fashion, which was considered to restrict female reproductive functions. The concern over dress can be understood in the context of the cultural and biological role afforded to women within Irish nationalism.

However, in the context of the construction of femininity by cultural nationalists and, later, by church and state, which denied women an autonomous sexuality in their idealization of asexual motherhood, the visual representation of the idealized countrywomen rested uneasily with the history of eroticized images of women within Western art. Less problematic was the depiction of old peasant women who could represent the successful outcome of a life lived in accordance with the demands of motherhood, as well as be emblematic of the traditions, folklore, language, and way of life extolled by the state. Alternatively, the depiction of young women was replaced by the portrayal of Western men, who epitomized the Gaelic masculine ideal, as nationalist writers of the Irish Ireland movement, in reaction to the 19th-century construction of the Celtic as feminine, asserted masculinity as the essential characteristic of the "Gael." While the idea of "woman" remained the embodiment of national spirit and the allegorical figure for the land of Ireland, this land now became the domain of the overtly masculine. The West of Ireland was redefined as Gaelic, masculine, wholesome, pragmatic, and Catholic in contrast to the femininity and natural spirituality associated with the Celtic. This denial of the female was also linked to the control of sexuality by Catholicism. This moral code supported the economic and social system of family farming, which demanded the regulation of sexuality for the control of inheritance.[23] With the perceived threat of an autonomous female sexuality to this social order, the counterpart of the Gaelic male had to be the desexualized mother figure.

The cottage in the landscape came to carry the cultural weight of the idealization of traditional rural family life and its fixed morality and gender roles. It became a surrogate for the depiction of the Irish rural woman and the values of motherhood, tradition, and stability. The cottage as "cradle of the race" evoked the idea of women as preservers of the race, active only as nurturers and reproducers of the masculine Gael. The homosocial bonding of Irish nationalism depended upon the exclusion of women from the body politic, while the conception of landscape as female facilitated a masculinist relationship to place. The discourses that confined women within the domestic sphere simultaneously conferred on them the responsibility of maintaining the national population. Women's function was to reproduce the bodies of the "body politic" represented as masculine.[24] Concerns over the national population were closely linked to ideas of landscape. The idea of an organic link between environment and people was utilized in discourses that employed scientific conceptions of current climatology and anthrogeography to discourage emigration.[25] Fears of loss of population were made more urgent by the associated loss of Irish language speakers, cultural bearers and vigorous genetic stock from the West of Ireland. Concern over emigration fused issues of gender and race, as it was felt that loss of those who "would have made the best mothers and wives" leaves "at home the timid, the stupid, and the dull to help in the deterioration of the race and to breed sons as sluggish as themselves."[26] Both ideas of racial pride and racial fear were thus projected onto the body of the woman.

The cottage as an "Irish citadel" stood for a preservation and reproduction of the Irish language, traditions, and folklore, for which women were considered to have paramount responsibility in their capacity as childcarers.[27] Thus the isolated rural cottage represented the realization, both in the physical fabric of the landscape and in the moral and spiritual domain, of the ideal form of Irish society. Its depiction in Irish landscape painting participated in the construction of Irish identity and the gender identities upon which it relied. It is with this symbolic investment in images of Irish landscape that contemporary Irish cultural exploration of issues of landscape and gender must engage.

POSTCOLONIALISM, FEMINISM, AND LANDSCAPE

Contemporary use of landscape imagery is forced to confront its historical use in both the colonial and the early national contexts, and the issues of race and gender implicit in such use. The issue of land and landownership is central to the colonial situation, but is also important symbolically in the postcolonial context when identification with landscape and place is one of the prime sources of cultural identity. The association between national identity and landscape is thus made manifest in the postcolonial literary and symbolic reappropriation of place. In postcolonial literature the development or recovery of an effective relationship to place, after dislocation or cultural denigration by the supposedly superior cultural and racial colonial power, becomes a means to overcome the sense of displacement and crisis of identity.[28] Yet, as Annamaria Carusi writes, "A discourse which includes in an un-ironic and un-parodic way terms such as 'identity,' 'consciousness' and 'origin' appears both regressive and reactionary from a poststructuralist point of view."[29] Nevertheless, as Diana Byrdon has noted, to criticize ideas of authenticity is problematic when they have been used as recuperative weapons by colonized peoples.[30]

Feminism and postcolonialism share a problematic relationship to postmodernism, with its appropriation of the critical insights of both and the erasure of their source and political efficacy.[31] Both postcolonialism and feminism are engaged in the conflict between a politics of identity and a politics of difference.[32] The poststructuralist rejection of the humanist conception of a universal subject and a stable core of identity undermines the liberatory and consolidatory aims of both. Yet, however fraught with difficulty, the conception of identity within poststructuralist theory offers a way to consider feminist and postcolonial relationships to place that avoids the essentializing of masculinist and colonialist discourse.

The dual agenda of postcolonial texts becomes "to continue the resistance to (Neo)colonialism through a deconstructive reading of its rhetoric and to retrieve and reinscribe those post-colonial social traditions that in literature issue forth on a thematic level, and within a realist problematic, as principles of cultural identity and survival."[33] Poststructuralism, in other words, does not disallow the critical use of the concept of identity. To problematize identity allows for a cultural use of ideas of landscape that can reject its use within colonialist discourse to stereotype the native as biologically linked to the natural landscape, and therefore lower on a scale of civilization.

Similarly, a feminist use of ideas of landscape must confront the dangers of essentialism within ecofeminism and accounts that view women's relationship to place in terms of innate biological and psychological structures.[34] Issues of place and landscape are closely linked to ideas of nature. Ecofeminism celebrates a close relationship between women and nature based on the ties of body, spirituality, fertility, and female reproduction. Ecofeminist theory sees women's subordination as the result of the perception that women are closer to nature, nature which has itself been devalued in Western culture. But by valuing the previously degraded terms of the male/female, mind/body, culture/nature dualism ecofeminism risks leaving these dualisms in place. Conversely, a nonessentialist feminist employment of ideas of landscape, place, and nature in recognizing the constructed basis of both ideas of identity and landscape allows notions of place to be employed as empowering but fluid, unstable, and provisional means of liberation. It also must address the implication of masculinist position in the concept of landscape.[35] The concept of landscape has been used in the feminization of the field of vision: the landscape, the colony, the looked-upon, with its exclusion of women from knowledge production. Yet a recognition of the constructed nature of identity allows landscape to be used as a shifting strategic source of identification without implying the adoption of a masculinist position or a fixed, natural, or inherent identity, or a restrictive notion of space.

RENAMING, GENDER, AND THE POSTCOLONIAL LANDSCAPE

However important the use of landscape is in the postcolonial context, its use is problematic if it fails to address the issue of gender. In Ireland the empirical research into placenames, their reinscription on the country's maps, and their use as cultural metaphors combine two elements that are considered central to national identity: landscape and place. The attempt to recover the meaning and original form of a placename is often linked to the desire for recovery of a lost relationship to place, in Ireland expressed in a language no longer in majority use. The placename in Ireland carries cultural connotations that are being employed in a postcolonial exploration of identity, in which the placename carries the burden of a history of colonial subjugation, resultant loss of the Irish language, loss of population due to emigration, and colonial anglicization of placenames during the 19th-century British mapping project. Recently, in different mediums, this Ordnance Survey mapping of Ireland has been critically engaged with an exploration of its colonial dimensions, its cultural damage, and the complex processes of language and cultural change.[36] These maps, though part of the means through which colonial authority was asserted, provide the base upon which the Irish form of the anglicized placename, retrieved in contemporary research, is reinscribed. This current use of the placename and map prompts a consideration of the commonly accepted links between language, landscape, and identity; of the

question of attitudes to place; and of the possibility of recovery of meaning, of history, and of authenticity.

Much contemporary Irish poetry employs ideas of landscape. Places
are named. This naming is linked to ideas of language loss. This decline
of language is linked, in turn, to the idea of loss of a distinctive life-style
and of a relationship to place considered to be more intimate and authentic than that of the present. For the writer, the evocative power of the
placename provides a key to the shared social memory of a landscape whose
collective meanings were part of a unifying repository of community
knowledge, but for that writer loss of the language denies access to these
meanings. Detailed placename research in Ireland is colored by this sense
of loss and recovery. The association of language and relationship to place
depends upon the notion of a language as inherently appropriate for describing a particular landscape, and on the idea that words carry essential cultural essences. Yet the use of the Irish placename in Irish poetry in English
enables cultural difference to be inserted into the text, alerting the reader
to the cultural origins of the material.[37]

However, this use becomes problematic when linked to gendered ideas
of landscape, as in the work of Seamus Heaney, in which dualities of gender
are fused to conceptions of politics, place, and language. To a gendered
consideration of the relationship between Ireland and England, Heaney
adds a gendered view of language as symbolic also of difference. Poetic
composition, for Heaney, is an "encounter between masculine will and
intelligence and feminine clusters of image and emotion," "the feminine
element" involving "the matter of Ireland," and the masculine "drawn
from involvement with English literature."[38] This gender polarity is extended to a consideration of the way in which a place can be known.
For Heaney, the two ways, one "lived, illiterate and unconscious, the other
learned, literate and conscious," correspond, respectively, to a Gaelic feminine and to an Anglo-Saxon masculine consciousness.[39] In his poetry the
placenames that differentiate the cultural locales of the North represent
the different ways of knowing a place through the language and syntax
of the name. The Irish feminine language is soft, "guttural," sensual, and
rich in vowel sounds. The planter's demesnes are "staked out in con-
sonants."[40] Anahorish is a "soft gradient / of consonant, vowel
meadow."[41] In the name Moyola "the twaney guttural water / spells itself . . . breathing its mists / through vowels and history."[42] While the
idea of a female voice has important feminist use, Heaney's use of the
concept is problematic.[43] Heaney's poetry celebrates the home place and
mourns separation from it. But it is against this construction of this landscape of the rural home as passive, organic, and female that the poet can
assert identity, activity, and independence.[44]

The understanding of the Irish landscape as a text, coded with meaning, denigrated in the colonial period, which must be recoded through the placename, appears both in the publications of Irish geography and in literature.[45] A familiar sequence of the work of male poets is used to illustrate what is considered to be an innate literary sense of place based on the placename, for which both historical and racial explanations are offered. However critical of colonial mapping, this postcolonial renaming and remapping is exercised through the signifying function of women in Ireland and their silencing – through the dominance of those with cultural status and authority and in the employment of the idea of the land as female. As Ailbhe Smyth writes:

> In post-colonial patriarchal culture, naming strategies have an over-determined role, invested with an irresistible double force and double meaning. The long-denied power to name, to confer meaning and thus (illusion?) to control material reality, is all the more powerfully experienced and pleasurably exercised when finally acquired. It is a treacherous ambivalent power if the paradigm for its exercise remains unchanged. The liberation of the state implies male role-shift from that of Slave to Master, Margin to Centre, Other to Self. Women powerless under patriarchy, are maintained as Other of the ex-Other, colonized of the post-colonized.[46]

The asymmetry of power relations in terms of gender and class in the postcolonial state determine the nature of this remapping, which risks solidifying into fixed notions of identity and the meaning of place.

DETERRITORIALIZING IDENTITY

I suggested earlier that the postcolonial and feminist commitment to concepts of identity and their securing through relationship to place risk reproducing the dualities of masculinist and colonial discourse. Though closeness to nature is positively evaluated, it leaves the culture/nature duality intact. This final section considers another artwork by Kathy Prendergast in which I suggest the possibility of poststructuralist feminist use of ideas of place that allows for multiple perspectives without undermining the strategic, if provisional, adoption of any one position. Again the map provides a metaphor for an alternative conception of space.

In 1991 Kathy Prendergast exhibited *Land* (see Figure 10.5).[47] It consisted of a canvas tent upon which the colors, lines, and conventions of topographical mapping had been painted. The map as a flat, two-dimensional device was given volume and height. The map itself becomes the object of its representation. In this piece *Land* has become the land-

FIGURE 10.5. Kathy Prendergast, *Land* (1991). (Courtesy of the Arts Council Collection, The South Bank Centre, London.)

scape itself which the map seeks to represent. This play between representation and its object undermines the idea of a simple equation between reality and representation. The authority of the map's representation is subverted. The relations between the "natural" and the "imitated" object are exposed as neither "objective" representation nor even a "subjective" reconstruction of the "real" world, but as a "play between alternative simulacra which problematise the easy distinction between object and subject."[48] The map in *Land* becomes a shifting ground, a spatial metaphor that frees conceptions of identity and landscape from a repressive fixity and solidity. Kathy Prendergast produces works that avoid the fixing of place through the use of the name. Her works go further to deconstruct the distinction between representation and its object, between identity and its cultural construction. While she is concerned with landscape themes, in her work landscape can no longer function as a stable base upon which to secure identity. The geographical reference in her work is strong. In other works she evokes geomorphological features, built elements of the rural landscape, and Irish archaeological artifacts. She alters the conventional scales of representation, to reveal maps of familiar if previously unrecognized topographies. While revealing these, she disrupts the concept of landscape itself as something fixed, external, and distinct from its representation. Irish identity has been tied to the landscape through colonial equations between place, race, and climate, and through the political and symbolic importance of landownership. For the possibility of alternative identities, which break free from the colonial and postcolonial restrictive definitions, not only must concepts of identity be freed but so too must concepts of landscape. Kathy Prendergast's work suggests the possibility for change in rigid ideas. Her mountains move (see Figure 10.6, *Moving Mountain* [1988]).

There has been a reaction in contemporary Irish culture against ideas of Irishness based on rural life and conservative and restrictive moral and social codes. But rather than rejecting ideas of land and the imagery of place in Irish culture some artists are reworking their symbolic importance. The rejection of fixed conceptions of identity and place, and their racist and patriarchal use, does not mean that landscape is a redundant or inherently tainted symbol. It does not invalidate attachment to place. The strength of the traditional cultural symbolism of land and rural life gives alternative uses of imagery of place and land added weight. Landscape in the work of these artists is reemployed, recycled to make other statements, raise other issues, of gender, of sexuality, of ecology. Both Pauline Cummins and Alanna O'Kelly are Irish women artists who use emblems of Irish culture to make progressive statements, in mixed media installation and performance pieces. Pauline Cummins uses the image of the Aran sweater, a symbol of traditional Irish life in the West of Ireland, to draw attention to women's activity in knitting and to the nonexploitive enjoyment of the male body in her installation *Aran Dance—Inis t'Oirr* (1986).[49]

FIGURE 10.6. Kathy Prendergast, *Moving Mountain* (1988). (Courtesy of Kathy Prendergast.)

Alanna O'Kelly in her installation *The Country Blooms a Garden . . . and a Grave* (1992), combines imagery of the female body and the West of Ireland, a mass famine grave, and the sound of the keen–a traditional female mourning cry–to address the cultural memory and evidence in the landscape of the Great Famine of the 1840s.[50] It also reaches beyond this context to question the political basis of contemporary famine.

Helen Tiffin has described this shift toward ideas of multiple and fluid identities in postcolonial writing and its relation to the issues of identity and place. In postcolonial settler countries, the disjunction expressed between the experience of the new landscape and the language and culture of the settler group led to an impulse in fiction to use the theme of "indigenization," often involving a journey to establish a home, and the overcoming of cultural difference with the help of a native whose relationship with the land was presented as one of unself-conscious harmony.[51] Though offering a means of overcoming a crisis of identity, this fictional theme reinforces colonial stereotyping of the indigenous group. Tiffin notes the questioning by writers in Australia and Canada of enclosing space, of "defining a place and physical structure as the locus of personal identity" and their acceptance of fragmentation, hybridization, and the erosion of the dichotomies of Western thought.[52] In the novel *Maps,* by the African writer Nuruddin Farah, the map functions as an emblem of personal investment in ideas of place while at the same time exposing their instability. In the words of the main character,

> I identify a truth in the maps which I draw. When I identify this truth, I label it as such, pickle it as though I were to share it with you, and Salaado. I hope, as dreamers do, that the dreamt dream will match the dreamt reality– that is, the invented truth of one's imagination. My maps invent nothing. They copy a given reality, they map out the roads a dreamer has walked, they identify a notional truth.[53]

Recognition of the fluid, unstable nature of space does not prevent its strategic use by marginal groups. This use of a poststructural feminist concept of identity and place can retain the political importance of positionality.[54]

In much writing in Ireland the landscape is tied down with its cultural threads, burdened and immovable with the weight of its historical and cultural load. It is laden with a history and mythology of invasion, dispossession, plantation, famine, eviction, land wars, emigration, and rural depopulation. In *Land* the landscape and ideas of identity take flight, freed from the repressive fixity of identity. The land can symbolize the possibility of fluidity and openness, of multiple and diffuse "names" and "maps." Gilles Deleuze and Felix Guattari are notable for their use of spatial metaphors in which "territorialization" describes the repression and taming of desire by modernity and its institutions.[55] For Deleuze and Guattari, the map

> is open and connectable in all its dimensions; it is detachable, reversible, susceptible to constant modification. It can be torn, reversed, adapted to any kind of mounting, re-worked by an individual, group or social formation. It can be drawn on the wall, conceived of as a work of art, constructed as a political action or as a mediation.[56]

In this cartography, the map is conceived as a rhizomatic ("open") rather than as a homogeneous ("closed") construct, which allows the emphasis to shift from de- to reconstruction, from map breaking to mapmaking. In discussing the use of the map metaphor in postcolonial literature, Graham Huggan writes:

> The map no longer features as a visual paradigm for the ontological anxiety arising from frustrated attempts to define a national culture, but rather as a locus of productive dissimilarity where the provisional connections of cartography suggest an ongoing perceptual transformation which in turn stresses the transitional nature of post-colonial discourse. This transformation has taken place within the context of a shift from an earlier "colonial" fiction obsessed with the problems of writing in a "colonial space" to a later, "postcolonial" fiction which emphasizes the provisionality of all cultures.[57]

This use of the map allows for a culturally and historically located critique of colonial discourse and the possibility of alternative configurations of identity that are open, changeable, and reworkable. Similarly, the body can be read as a text whose socially inscribed attributes function as part of a deployment of power. As Elizabeth Grosz writes, the body, as well as being the site of knowledge-power, is "also a site of resistance, for it exerts a recalcitrance, and always entails the possibility of being self-marked, self-represented in alternative ways."[58] Both concepts of space and the body are open to multiple configuration. The recognition of the counterstrategic possibilities in the representation of the body and landscape that do not rely on fixed conceptions of gender, identity, and space allow ideas of landscape to be figured in multiple ways. The landscape can be traversed, journeyed across, entered into, intimately known, gazed upon. However tainted the concept of landscape is by colonial and masculinist discourse, a feminist poststructuralist understanding of identity allows its recuperation. In Kathy Prendergast's work there is a suggestion that the cartography of the nation, the national map, is no longer an appropriate metaphor. It no longer offers the support that the idea of a homogeneous, discrete, and socially integrated island did, prior to the realization of continued division, difference, and inequality in the postcolonial state. Her maps of "personal geography" resist defining their location against the cultural and political center, against the core–periphery model of attempts to validate Irish cultural production. Postcolonial feminist remapping and renaming replace one authoritative representation with multiple names and multiple maps.

ACKNOWLEDGMENT

This chapter is a revised version of an article that first appeared in *Feminist Review* 44 (1993).

NOTES

1. Gayatri Chakravorty Spivak, "Women in Difference: Mahasweta Devi's 'Douloti the Bountiful,' " in *Nationalisms and Sexualities,* Andrew Parker, Mary Russo, Doris Sommer, and Patricia Yeager, eds. (London: Routledge, 1992), 96–117.

2. Benedict Anderson, *Imagined Communities: Reflections on the Origin and Spread of Nationalism* (London: Verso, 1983).

3. The masculinist use of the concept of landscape in geography is discussed in Gillian Rose, *Feminism and Geography: The Limits of Geographical Knowledge* (Cambridge, U.K.: Polity Press, 1993), esp. ch. 5.

4. An example is the use of the cartographic metaphor in Rosalyn Diprose and Robyn Ferrell, eds., *Cartographies: Poststructuralism and the Mapping of Bodies and Spaces* (Sydney: Allen and Unwin, 1991), ix. The use of spatial metaphors is discussed in John Tagg, *Ground of Dispute: Art History, Cultural Politics and the Discursive Field* (London: Macmillan, 1992), 1–39.

5. Ailbhe Smyth, "The Floozie in the Jacuzzi," *Feminist Studies 17,* no. 1 (1991): 16–24.

6. Since notions of race gender and identity are being treated as culturally and historically formulated constructs throughout this chapter, they are presented without inverted commas, but used in the way implied in this textual strategy. See Judith Butler, *Gender Trouble: Feminism and the Subversion of Identity* (London: Routledge, 1990); Julia Epstein and Kristina Straub, eds., *Body Guards: The Cultural Politics of Gender Ambiguity* (London: Routledge, 1992), 1–24; Paul Julian Smith, *Representing the Other: "Race," Text and Gender in Spanish and Spanish American Narrative* (Oxford: Clarendon Press, 1992), 1–23; and Chris Weedon, *Feminist Practice and Poststructuralist Theory* (Oxford: Basil Blackwell, 1987).

7. Toni O'Brien Johnson and David Cairns, "Introduction," in *Gender in Irish Writing,* Toni O'Brien Johnson and David Cairns, eds. (Buckingham, U.K.: Open University Press, 1991), 1–12, esp. 3.

8. See Elizabeth Butler Cullingford, " 'Thinking of her . . . as . . . Ireland': Yeats, Pearse and Heaney," *Textual Practice 4,* no. 1 (1987): 443–460; David Cairns and Shaun Richards, "Woman in the Discourse of Celticism," *Canadian Journal of Irish Studies 13,* no. 1 (1987): 43–60; and David Cairns and Shaun Richards, *Writing Ireland: Colonialism, Nationalism and Culture* (Manchester, U.K.: Manchester University Press, 1988), 42–57.

9. See Maurice Riordan, "Eros and History: On Contemporary Irish Poetry," *Crane Bag 9,* no. 1 (1985): 49–55; and Eavan Boland, *A Kind of Scar: The Woman Poet in a National Tradition* (Dublin: Attic Press, 1989).

10. Quoted in Johnny Hanrahan, "Notes on a Conversation with Ellis O'Connell, Kathy Prendergast and Vivienne Roche," in *Edge to Edge—Three Sculptors from Ireland* (Dublin: Gandon Editions, 1991), 6–11, esp. 6.

11. Illustrated in *Kathy Pendergast* (Dublin: Douglas Hyde Gallery, 1990).

12. In the annotations to the diagrams, body parts are not referred to. I am using them here to draw attention to the use of the body.

13. Text appearing on *To Control a Landscape—Irrigation.*

14. Chris Prentice, "Rewriting Their Stories, Renaming Themselves: Post-Colonialism and Feminism in the Fictions of Keri Hulm and Audrey Thomas," *SPAN: Journal of the South Pacific Association for Commonwealth Literature and Language Studies 23* (1986): 68–80, esp. 70.

15. See Annette Kolodny, *The Lay of the Land: Metaphor as Experience and History in American Life and Letters* (Chapel Hill: University of North Carolina Press, 1975); and Louis Montrose, "The Work of Gender in the Discourse of Discovery," *Representations 33* (1991): 1–41.

16. Cairns and Richards, *Writing Ireland,* 42–57.

17. The issue of mapping, authority, and power is discussed in J. B. Harley, "Maps, Knowledge and Power," in *The Iconography of Landscape: Essays in the Symbolic Representation, Design and Use of Past Environments,* Stephen Daniels and Denis Cosgrove, eds. (Cambridge, U.K.: Cambridge University Press, 1988), 277–311; J. B. Harley, "Deconstructing the Map," in *Writing Worlds: Discourse, Text and Metaphor in the Representation of Landscape,* Trevov J. Barnes and James S. Duncan, eds. (London: Routledge, 1992), 231–247; and Graham Huggan, "Decolonising the Map: Post-Colonialism, Post-Structuralism and the Cartographic Connection," *Ariel: A Review of International English Literature 20,* no. 4 (1989): 115–131.

18. For the history of the colonial mapping project, see John Andrews, *A Paper Landscape: The Ordnance Survey in Nineteenth Century Ireland* (Oxford: Clarendon Press, 1975). For critical discussion of the project, see Mary Hammer, "Putting Ireland on the Map," *Textual Practice,* 3(2): (Summer, 1989): 184–201, and "The English Look of the Irish Map," *Circa 46* (July–August 1989) 23–25.

19. Huggan, "Decolonising the Map," p. 120.

20. The discourse of primitivism is discussed in Susan Hiller, ed., *The Myth of Primitivism: Perspectives on Art* (London: Routledge, 1991). For a more detailed

account of this issue on writing on the West, see Catherine Nash, "Embodying the Nation: The West of Ireland Landscape and Irish National Identity," in *Tourism in Ireland: A Critical Analysis,* Michael Cronin and Barbara O'Connor, eds. (Cork, Republic of Ireland: Cork University Press, 1993).

21. The extent of women's political activity is illustrated in Cliona Murphy, *The Women's Suffrage Movement and Irish Society in the Early Twentieth Century* (New York: Harvester Wheatsheaf, 1989); Rosemary Cullen Owens, *Smashing Times: A History of the Irish Women's Suffrage Movement, 1898–1922* (Dublin: Attic Press, 1984); and Margaret Ward, *Unmanageable Revolutionaries: Women and Irish Nationalism* (Dingle, Republic of Ireland: Brandon, 1983).

22. Andrew Parker, Mary Russo, Doris Sommer, and Patricia Yeager, "Introduction," in *Nationalisms and Sexualities,* Andrew Parker, Mary Russo, Doris Sommer, and Patricia Yeager, eds. (London: Routledge, 1992), 1–18, esp. 10.

23. Cairns and Richards, *Writing Ireland,* 59–63.

24. Moira Gatens, "Corporeal Representation in/and the Body Politic," in *Cartographies: Poststructuralism and the Mapping of Bodies and Spaces,* Rosalyn Diprose and Robyn Ferrell, eds. (Sydney, Australia: Allen and Unwin, 1991), 79–87.

25. For accounts of ideas of equations between race and place and degeneration, see David N. Livingstone, "The Moral Discourse of Climate: Historical Considerations on Race, Place and Virtue," *Journal of Historical Geogrpahy 17* (1991): 413–434, and " 'Never Shall Ye Make the Crab Walk Straight': An Inquiry into the Scientific Sources of Racial Geography," in *Nature and Science: Essays in the History of Geographical Knowledge,* Felix Driver and Gillian Rose, eds., Historical Geography Research Series, no. 28, 37–48; and N. Stepan, "Biological Degeneration: Races and Proper Places," in *Degeneration: The Dark Side of Progress,* J. E. Chamberlain and S. L. Gilman, eds. (New York: Columbia University Press, 1985), 97–120.

26. George Russell, *Co-operation and Nationality* (Dublin: Maunsel, 1912), 67–68.

27. This follows the role afforded to women in other nationalist movements, as discussed in Floya Anthias and Nira Yuval-Davis, eds., *Women–Nation–State* (New York: St. Martin's Press, 1989).

28. Bill Ashcroft, Gareth Griffiths, and Helen Tiffin, eds., *The Empire Writes Back: Theory and Practice in Post-Colonial Literatures* (London: Routledge, 1989), 9–10, 24–28; Stephen Gray, "A Sense of Place in the New Literatures in English," in *A Sense of Place in the New Literatures in English,* Peggy Nightingale. ed. (Saint Lucia, Australia: University of Queensland Press, 1986), 1–12.

29. Annamaria Carusi, "Post, Post and Post. Or, Where is South African Literature in All This?," in *Past the Last Post: Theorising Post-Colonialism and Post-Modernism,* Ian Adam and Helen Tiffin, eds., (New York: Harvester Wheatsheaf, 1991), 95–108, especially 100.

30. Diana Brydon, "The White Inuit Speak: Contamination as Literary Strategy," in *Past the Last Post,* Adam and Tiffin, eds., 191–203, esp. 195.

31. For discussion of the tensions between postcolonialism and postmodernism, see Adam and Tiffin, eds., *Past the Last Post;* Simon During, "Postmodernism or Postcolonialism," *Landfall 39,* no. 3 (1985): 366–380; and Helen Tiffin, "Post-Colonialism, Post-Modernism and the Rehabilitation of Post-Colonial History,"

Journal of Commonwealth Literature 23, no. 1 (1978): 169–181, and "Post-Colonial Literatures and Counter-Discourses," *Kunappi 9,* no. 3 (1987): 17–34. The conflicts between feminism and postmodernism within geography are discussed in Liz Bondi and Mona Domosh, "Other Figures in Other Places: On Feminism, Postmodernism and Geography," *Environment and Planning D, Society and Space 10,* no. 2 (1992): 199–213.

32. See Steven Best and Douglas Kellner, *Postmodern Theory: Critical Interrogations* (London: Macmillan, 1991), 205–214.

33. Stephen Slemon, "Modernism's Last Post," in *Past the Last Post,* Adam and Tiffin, eds. 1–11, esp. 5.

34. For accounts of ecofeminism, see Y. King, "Healing the Wounds: Feminism, Ecology and the Nature Culture Dualism," in *Reweaving the World: The Emergence of Ecofeminism,* Gloria Orenstein and Irene Diamond, eds. (San Francisco: Sierra Club, 1990), 106–121; Carolyn Merchant, "Ecofeminism and Feminist Theory," in *Reweaving the World,* Orenstein and Diamond, eds., 100–105; and Karen J. Warren, "Feminism and Ecology: Making Connections," *Environmental Ethics 9* (1987): 2–20. For a critical discussion, see Val Plumwood, "Woman, Humanity and Nature," *Radical Philosophy 48* (Spring 1988): 16–24. Accounts of women's experience of landscape are important, yet those that suggest a more intuitive, emotional, sensitive, gentle female response risk essentialism. See, for example, Vera Norwood and Janice Monk, "Introduction – Perspectives on Gender and Landscpae," and Lois Rudnick, "Re-Naming the Land: Anglo Expatriate Women in the Southwest," both in *The Desert Is No Lady; Southwestern Landscapes in Women's Writing and Art,* Vera Norwood and Janice Monk, ed. (New Haven, CN: Yale University Press, 1987), 1–9.

35. Rose, *Feminism and Geography.*

36. Mary Hammer is critical of the project; see Hammer, "Putting Ireland on the Map," and her "The English Look of the Irish Map." Its complexities have been explored in Brian Friel's play, *Translations,* first produced in 1981, published in Brian Friel, *Selected Plays* (London: Faber and Faber, 1984), which provoked much discussion and disagreement. Tim Robinson is working in the West of Ireland, is engaged in research on the placenames of the region, and produces maps on which the original Irish placename and formerly unrecorded placenames appear.

37. Ashcroft, Griffiths, and Tiffin, *The Empire Writes Back,* 64–66.

38. Seamus Heaney, *Preoccupations: Selected Prose, 1968–1978* (London: Faber and Fabe, 1980), 34.

39. Ibid., 131.

40. Seamus Heaney, *Selected Poems* (London: Faber and Faber, 1980), 27.

41. Ibid., 21.

42. Ibid., 22.

43. See Deborah Cameron, *Feminism and Linguistic Theory* (London: Macmillan, 1985), 114–133.

44. Patricia Coughlan, " 'Bog Queens': The Representation of Women in the Poetry of John Montague and Seamus Heaney," in *Gender in Irish Writing,* Toni

O'Brien Johnson and David Cairns, eds. (Buckingham, U.K.: Open University Press, 1991), 88–111.

45. Examples of which include Robert Sheenan, "Genius Fabulae – The Irish Sense of Place," *Irish University Review 18,* no. 2 (Autumn 1988): 191–206; Robbie Hannan, "An ball uaigneach seo: Attachment to Place in Gaelic Literature," *Eire-Ireland 26,* no. 2 (1991): 19–31; and Patrick J. O'Connor, *Living in a Coded Land,* Irish Landscape Series, no. 1: Oireacht na Mumhan Books, 1992).

46. Smyth, "Floozie in the Jacuzzi," 11–12.

47. Illustrated in Penelope Curtis, ed., *Strongholds: New Art from Ireland, Catalogue for the Exhibition, 20 Feb.–7 April 1991* (Liverpool, U.K.: Tate Gallery, 1991).

48. Huggan, "Decolonising the Map," p. 121.

49. Irish Exhibition of Living Art, *Inis tOirr* – slide/tape installation, Guinness Hop Store, 1985.

50. Irish Museum of Modern Art, 1992.

51. An early discussion of place and identity in a postcolonial context appears in D. E. S. Maxwell, "Landscape and Theme," in *Commonwealth Literature,* John Press, ed. (London: Heinemann, 1965), 82–89.

52. Helen Tiffin, "New Concepts of Person and Place in 'The Twyborn Affair' and 'A Bend in the River,' " in *A Sense of Place in the New Literatures in English,* Peggy Nightingale, ed. (Saint Lucia, Australia: University of Queensland Press, 1986), 22–31, esp. 23–25.

53. Quoted in Rhonda Cobham, "Misgendering the Nation: African Nationalist Fictions and Nuruddin Farah's 'Maps,' " in *Nationalisms and Sexualities,* Andrew Parker, Mary Russo, Doris Sommer, and Particia Yeager, eds. (London: Routledge, 1992), 42–59, esp. 55–56.

54. This is discussed in Linda Alcroff, "Cultural Feminism versus Poststructuralism: The Identity Crisis in Feminist Theory," *Signs: Journal of Women in Culture and Society 13,* no. 3 (1988): 405–436.

55. Gilles Delueze and Felix Guattari, *A Thousand Plateaus: Capitalism and Schizophrenia,* B. Massumi, trans. (Minneapolis: University of Minnesota Press, 1987). For an account of their work, see Best and Kellner, *Postmodern Theory,* 76–110.

56. Delueze and Guattari, *A Thousand Plateaus,* p. 12.

57. Huggan, "Decolonising the Map," p. 124.

58. Elizabeth Grosz, "Inscriptions and Body-Maps: Representations and the Corporeal," in *Feminine Masculine and Representation,* Terry Threadgold and Anne Cranny-Francis, eds. (Sydney, Australia: Allen and Unwin, 1990), 62–74, esp. 64.

Index

D

De Lauretis, Teresa, 7, 18
Deleuze, Gilles and Guattari, Felix, 245
Difference, 1, 3, 6, 7, 13, 36, 54, 144, 163, 170, 174, 175
Domosh, Mona, 9
Dyck, Isobel, 220

E

Environmentalism, Western. *See also,* Aboriginal Australians and Western environmentalism
ecocentrism/Deep Ecology, 171, 172, 175
ecofeminism, 171, 173–175, 179, 238, 239
and women, 182

F

Fabian, Johannes, 15
Farah, Nuruddin, 244
Femininity, 41, 55, 63, 236
Feminism. *See also* Gender; Woman, as category
ecofeminism. *See* environmentalism
essentialist, 5, 6, 36
and history, 3, 4, 8, 9, 33
and historiography, 33
and geography, 8, 9. *See also* Gender, geography of
and literary criticism, 39
poststructuralist, 5
universalist, 5, 6
Western, 1–3, 19
Feminist research, 217, 220, 221
in South Africa, 198–204
Foucault, Michel, 34, 53
Fox, Matthew, 180, 181

Fraser, Eliza, 101–104, 112–114
historical accounts, 108, 109, 111
identity, 110, 111
reports of story, 104–107
story as legend, 101, 102
Frye, Marilyn, 1, 2

G

Gale, Fay, 141, 142
Gender, 1–3, 13, 30, 33, 36
geography of, 1–3. *See also* Feminism and geography
Gluckman, Max, 210
Goldin, I., 205
Green, Martin, 36, 37
Griffin, Susan, 6
Grosz, Elizabeth, 245
Gunew, Sneja, 144, 145

H

Haggis, Jane, 11
Haraway, Donna, 5, 7, 219
Harley, Brian, 9
Hatem, M., 41
Hatoum, Mona, 17, 18
Heaney, Seamus, 240
Higginbotham, Evelyn Brooks, 4
Himid, Lubaina, 18, 19
Huggan, Graham, 245
Huggins, Jackie, 143
Hulme, Peter, 31, 32
Hurtado, Aida, 4

I

Identity, 238, 244. *See also* Class; Gender; Race
Imagery
sexual, 10, 74